CHARLES PÉGUY

Men and Saints

CHARLES PÉGUY

Men and Saints

PROSE AND POETRY

Rendered into English by Anne and Julian Green

PANTHEON BOOKS INC., NEW YORK

41 Washington Square, New York 12, N. Y.

Manufactured in the United States of America
American Book–Stratford Press, Inc., New York, N. Y.

FIRST EDITION

CONTENTS

POETRY

Julian Green

CHARLES PÉGUY'S POETRY

IN THIS SECOND VOLUME of translations from Charles Péguy, I am, as in the first one, responsible for the poetry and, as before, have not attempted to give anything like a metrical rendering of Péguy's lines.

It is not easy to state in a few sentences what Charles Péguy's poetry consists of or, indeed, why it is poetry. Its language is made up of every day words, words which might sometimes appear almost worn out for having been used so often; yet those are the words which Péguy seems to prefer to all others, those he handles with greatest care, one might almost say: with piety, as if age and hard work had made them more venerable than the rarer words used by the educated. In Péguy's mind, a word is all the more beautiful if it is used by his charwoman, or by the 'bus conductor, or by the man who sweeps the streets of Paris with a large broom that makes a noise like a storm as it drives the dead leaves into the gutter. Péguy himself talks like those people, and he makes God the Father talk like them too. Neither is his thought lowered by such a process. What happens is that the simple language he uses is incredibly exalted and takes on a majesty

which can only remind one of the Scriptures.

Such is the medium he uses: plain language so plain that in some unaccountable way it puts so-called literary styles to shame. With these every day words, what kind of poetry does he write? To begin with, his poetry, on the printed page, looks like poetry, blank verse, modern in its irregularity. But if we read it aloud, it will seem to us that it is really prose cut up into lines of different lengths and that if these lines were to be put together again, we should have excellent prose. However, if we read it again and listen to the sound of it, and stop ever so little at the end of each line, we will catch a rhythm, not exactly the rhythm of speech, but what might be termed the rhythm of thought. And there, I believe, lies the essence of Péguy's poetry.

When his characters are allowed to speak, they make the most of their opportunity. Their conversation is an exchange of monologues. They go into a monologue as one goes into a trance and whatever remains outside of their monologue ceases to exist. Nor do they ever speak as if they expected an interruption or wished to argue their point. They are constantly making a profession of faith, and just as some people think aloud, they believe aloud. Their real audience is the sun and the moon and the stars, earth, man in general and finally the person with whom they may happen to be at the time. However there is nothing vague about these monologues; they are not the ravings of a dreamer; on the contrary, they come from as logical a brain as France ever produced.

Here we have another element in Péguy's poetry, an element which might be called the beauty of his reasoning. Péguy's reasoning goes from the particular to the general with a magnificent sweep which carries one along as only logic can

do when it is enlivened by imagination. Its scope is apparently boundless. Like a true poet, Péguy instinctively, and logically, sees "a world in a grain of sand," but—and here your true 'Normalien' comes out—he is ever ready to patiently trace all the steps from the grain of sand to its cosmic fulfilment, and he enjoys the trip immensely. No poet ever had a keener sense of the poetry of logic. This passionate love of reasoning, which he shares with his race, is probably one of the strongest intellectual links between France and ancient Greece, which France so often resembles, and we can well imagine the pleasure a platonic philosopher would have found in listening to God the Father's monologue on leprosy and mortal sin, surely as serious a monologue as was ever spoken, yet spoken with occasional smiles and sallies and, in one place at least, with an unmistakable wink.

Another characteristic of Péguy's logic is its beautiful emotional quality. It is strong but not unbending, and it has a way of suddenly moving us almost to tears. The heart has its reasons of which reason knows nothing, wrote Pascal, and in Péguy it is not only the head but the heart that reasons, a hard head and a big, generous, human heart. When the French peasant who is hewing wood in the forest stops to think of the time when he will no longer be among the living, he thoroughly examines the question and by slow degrees comes to the conclusion that his own existence is bound to the very existence of France, that he as an individual is merged into the greater individuality of his country, and that although he may cease to exist, France must and will go on. This he sees as a peasant can see it, a French peasant of the XVth century, as Joan of Arc's father might have seen it, but he sees it in such a way that, in 1944, we are more than ever struck by the

inevitability of such a reasoning, we are listening to France herself telling us that she will not die, but live.

Turning to the contents of those mammoth poems which Péguy called *Mysteries,* it seems to me that of all the characters involved, God the Father is the most real if, for want of a better term, the word character can be applied to the first person of the Trinity. He is more real than Joan of Arc, because in a way he is more Joan of Arc than she could ever be herself, that is, all the qualities that are in her, he has to a supereminent degree. We sometimes smile when we listen to him, but we are awed. He is never pompous, he never has to remember to be majestic, being majesty itself. He makes us feel like children and somehow he makes us feel a little better, a little more hopeful. He has a way of making clear what seemed irreparably involved in our spiritual life and with one word unties many knots. At the same time he lowers us somewhat in our self-esteem, he makes us a little ashamed, he makes us look a little foolish in our own eyes, but he does so in such a way that we are happier in consequence; he is eminently "le bon Dieu," the good Lord.

When God the Father enlarges on the subject of his universe, in the Mystery of the Second Virtue and in the Mystery of the Holy Innocents, he does so with poise and tremendous authority. He is certainly not lyrical. He blends the simplicity and wisdom of an old French peasant with the knowledge and shrewdness of a Church father. There is something almost overwhelming about his simplicity, because it is the simplicity of truth and the simplicity of real wisdom. When he speaks of the stars, his stars, of the saints, his own saints, of Faith, of Charity, and of his "little Hope," he does so quietly, in fact so very quietly that our breath is taken away. It is not enough

to say that he is great; he is great beyond any conception that we may have of greatness, he is the Lord, and because he is the Lord he can speak of creation not only with the authority of the creator, but at the same time with the humor and the matter of fact tone of the farmer who talks about his crops. He is immensely good and immensely forgiving; he grieves to punish the wicked; he is for justice with a strong leaning toward mercy; he loves all his children, particularly the French, for reasons which he explains at length.

Whatever this conception of God the Father may be worth theologically, it bears the stamp of genius and has its origin in the depths of a truly religious heart. The mere attempt to make God the Father deliver long speeches shows courage, and genius is a form of intellectual courage, the courage it takes to allow inspiration to carry one as far as possible, sometimes too far in the eyes of many. In literature as in other fields, the man who is afraid of going too far will never be among the great, and Péguy, with his firm, steady tread and that logical head of his, and his obstinate common sense, Péguy obviously went too far according to the world's method of reckoning distances, that is, he walked straight into the kingdom of Heaven.

The danger of such an undertaking, in the field of literature, is that it may turn out to be simply ridiculous, and to be ridiculous is dreadful. "Le ridicule tue" is a saying which every Frenchman hears repeated from his childhood on. If around 1905 a Frenchman had said to another Frenchman: "I am going to write a dramatic poem, the principal character of which will be God the Father," the comment would probably have been a smile. But it does not seem to have occurred to Péguy that he was running such a risk. This child-

like man was of the same stock as the men who carved the portals of Chartres and Amiens, and he made God the Father speak just as he might have represented him above a doorway, six or seven centuries earlier.

"Faith is an oak rooted in the heart of France." If we wish to understand France, and to understand Péguy who spoke for France as few men have ever spoken, we must bear in mind that faith is an all-important element in the soul of that country. This gives us a clue to another aspect of Péguy's poetical world, I mean his vision of Calvary.

All ages have attempted to see Christ through the eyes of their great artists. Whether those artists followed the general trend of faith in their day, or whether they succeeded in imposing their own religious conception on the laity and clergy as well is a question which I cannot go into here, but the fact remains that they gave their world a visible reflection of what they saw with the inward eye. There is an early Italian Christ and there is a Flemish Christ of the XVth century, each of them intensely real; there is a French Christ contemporary of Joan of Arc and there is a German Christ of Dürer's time; there is also a Renaissance Christ and a XVIIth century Christ; most moving of all, perhaps, there is Rembrandt's Christ. Each one is different, each corresponds to a particular form of piety and to a particular form of religious experience.

Péguy viewed religion with the eyes of a primitive, not an Italian primitive, to be sure, nor a Flemish primitive although he seems, at times, very close to Van der Weyden, but with the eyes of a French primitive of the XVth century, because he himself was a French primitive who had lost his way in the XXth century. Now what characterizes French primitives

is, above all, a deep and obvious sincerity of feeling and at the same time an equally deep tranquillity of soul. They are contemplatives, but they never loose their heads in contemplation, they never let their nerves get the better of their reasoning powers, and they seldom suggest anything like ecstasy. If there be such a thing as an ecstasy of grief, we must look for it among the high-strung Sienese painters of the quattrocento or among sensitive and more obviously mystical artists such as the aforenamed Van der Weyden. The French are more placid. Their sorrow is sadness carried to an extreme, just as their inward happiness never causes their soul to loose its spiritual balance. When Péguy watches the Passion from the slopes of Mount Calvary, he sees it as a *donateur* might see it from the corner of a painting by the Master of Moulins or the Master of Avignon. He is moved, but he weeps in silence, neither does his weeping interfere with his prayers. Christ passes by, slowly bearing his heavy cross; Péguy neither faints nor tears his hair, he goes on telling his beads like a good Catholic, but his heart is breaking within his breast and when he tells us what he has seen, our own heart is very near breaking too, because he was so evidently *there* when those things took place.

This calm and stocky Normalien, this contemporary of Anatole France and Jaurès, knelt most assuredly on Calvary whilst the nails were being driven in our Lord's hands, and his faith, which was so admirably preserved from modern heresy, was the unsullied and undiluted faith of 1400.

Probably the only flaw we could find in his vision of Calvary, if we were so minded, is the slight suggestion of an effort back of it all. Saint Thomas teaches that faith is partly a question of will-power. The will to believe is the beginning

of faith; to a certain extent, it is faith itself, and Péguy's will was very strong. When he knelt and considered Christ on Calvary, he did not go into a trance, he rather willed himself into seeing. Indeed his vision of the Passion has a certain Ignatian quality about it. One is faintly reminded of the composition of place so strenuously advocated by that most willful of all saints, Saint Ignatius Loyola. But here the effort to see is blessed with a most moving glimpse of what must really have occurred.

The pictorial quality of Péguy's vision has never been properly stressed and one cannot help thinking that a study of the subject would bring forth much of interest to art and religion as well. To go back to the spiritual influence of artists on their times, it may live on for centuries and mould the thought of generations. We who are the heirs of many centuries cannot escape such an influence or, one might say, such an accumulation of influences. In a rather superficial way, it has made us richer. All of us who are interested in pictures and to varying degrees in the life of the soul, have gone through phases which correspond in a general way to periods in the history of art. There were times, to be sure, when nothing but Botticelli could satisfy the demands we made on religious art. A little later, perhaps, we discovered Rembrandt, and Rembrandt made Botticelli seem finicky and even a little morbid; we eschewed everything that did not possess the gravity and the unmistakable air of inner truth which make the Dutch master so compelling. Then, for some reason, we drifted away from Rembrandt and turned to the Primitives. Only the Primitives had a really mystical view of Christianity, we thought; we were even somewhat intolerant on this point, we drew a line, say about 1360, beyond which no really religious hand

ever wielded a brush, we were astonished and a little pained when people told us bluntly that they had never heard of our favorite painter, Barna.

And on we moved from phase to phase, learning a little, forgetting a great deal. There was, however, an influence which dominated all others, but this we did not care to admit because we were ashamed of it, in fact we loathed it, but loathing such an influence is like loathing the dampness, if you happen to be in equatorial Africa: no amount of loathing will cause it to go away; it is there, simply, and you breathe it in. In the same way, we breathed in Raphael. To this day, it is impossible to go into a church and not find some trace of that awful spell cast over religious sensibility by the great man whom our fathers called Sanzio. In an evil hour for Christianity, this magnificent genius stereotyped all the incidents of the life of Christ. He was the begetter of all the draped and nobly gesticulating figures we see in devotional books, of all the apostles and prophets with their faultless features and neatly brushed beards in illustrated bibles and on the walls of so many chapels. As Mr. Berenson so brilliantly pointed out, he changed a Hebrew world into a Greek one, and indeed when one comes to think of it, there is no essential difference between his scenes from the Old and New Testament and his School of Athens. But Raphael did much more, he infected and saturated the minds of millions with dull commonplaces about the Gospel. From one end of Europe to the other, he not only lowered the spiritual plane of art for generations, but made easy, and therefore suspicious, a certain approach to the realm of interior vision, he crowded the invisible with chromos. When a preacher enlarges on the Transfiguration, he unconsciously and irresistibly goes back

to Raphael's vision of that scene, because Raphael is in his blood, although he may never have seen a Raphael in his life. Raphael is probably one of the most dangerous heretics since the Church began; his heresy is a subtle one which begins with a yawn and ends with nausea. His good intentions are as plentiful as they are demoralizing. He kills devotion with an almost infallible aim. Charity turns into a lump of ice under his nefarious gaze, and great though he was, the fact that he ever touched a paint-brush is the equivalent of one of those spiritual disasters from which the world has apparently not recovered.

I doubt that Péguy bothered much about painting or about Raphael's influence on the statuary sold in the pious shops of the rue Saint Sulpice, but whether he knew it or not, he was, as I have said, a French primitive, and because he was a primitive he fought with all his might against the dark angel of religious painting, he fought him simply by drawing in beautiful stiff lines and using colors which the Church itself seemed to have mixed for him.

It may be interesting at this point to indicate one of the sources of Péguy's inspiration. As we might have guessed, it was liturgical. Like his elder and greater brother, Francis Thompson, Péguy was a careful reader of the Catholic prayer book, that compact little volume which the French call their *paroissien* and which contains much of the spiritual wealth stored up by the Church since the early days of Christianity. He read the missal with the zeal of the convert. In a way he rediscovered it and studied its many pages with an eye which had become disaccustomed to its language. This allowed him to see things which habit kept Catholics of a longer standing from seeing for themselves.

One instance of what I mean is to be found in the ceremony of Holy Saturday, when the paschal candle is blessed and lighted. This ancient rite is known in English-speaking countries as the Blessing of the New Fire. It is as beautiful as it is old and the prayers read on that occasion are permeated with a feeling of happiness and even of exultation which lend them an almost lyrical quality. We expect them at times to break into a hymn, as if the very words called for music. This impression is heightened by a very moving use of repetitions. A few words from these prayers may be quoted here: "This is the Paschal solemnity, in which the true Lamb is slain . . . This is the night in which Thou didst first cause our forefathers to pass through the Red Sea with dry feet. This therefore is the night which purged away the darkness of sinners by the light of the pillar. This is the night which restores to grace and unites in sanctity those that believe in Christ. This is the night in which Christ arose victorious from the grave . . . O wonderful condescension of Thy Mercy towards us! O inestimable affection of charity . . . ! O truly needful sin of Adam, which was blotted out by the death of Christ! O happy fault, that merited so great a Redeemer! O truly blessed night, which alone deserved to know the time and hour in which Christ rose again from the grave! This is the night of which it is written: And the night shall be enlightened as the day; and the night is my light in my enjoyments . . ."

If having listened to the beautiful music of those words, we turn to Péguy and read the last pages of his second Mystery, we can, I believe, catch an echo of the Catholic liturgy in his invocation of night, whom God the Father calls his daughter:

"You, night, are my great sombre light.* I am glad to have

* Splendor nocturna, *says the Church.*

created night . . . Night, my most beautiful invention . . . O night, o my daughter night, the most religious of my daughters, the most devout . . . Night, you are a beautiful invention of my wisdom. Night, o my daughter night, o my silent daughter at Rebecca's well, at the Samaritan woman's well, it is you who draw the deepest water from the deepest well. O night, you who rock all creation to sleep . . . O night, you who wash all wounds . . . At the Samaritan woman's well, you who draw from the deepest well the deepest prayer. O night, o my daughter night, you who know how to hold your peace, o my daughter of the beautiful mantle . . . you who put the Child Jesus to bed every evening in the arms of the very Holy and Immaculate One. O my daughter sparkling and sombre, I greet you . . ."

There probably never was a Catholic more thoroughly enamoured of the Church than Péguy, and yet he was remarkably free from any kind of bigotry. Bigotry is one of the besetting sins of converts; a bigot is a person who goes about in a sort of mental cage, but Péguy remained a free man until the moment he was killed; he never lost contact with humanity, he loved humanity, he considered himself, to a great extent, his brother's keeper (and as such assumed the right to shout at him and, if necessary, to kick him), nor did he ever lose his magnificent sense of humor. His greatest gift as a man and a poet was that of being able to speak intelligibly to all men, and to help them; his greatest gift was to give.

Julian Green.

PROSE

LA BONNE ANNÉE

SOUHAITONS-NOUS comme nos pères la bonne année; au commencement de cette année de fortune ou de fatalité, amis, souhaitons-nous une bonne année. Si nous étions des anciens, nous pourrions nous réduire à nous souhaiter que cette année, aujourd'hui commençante, soit une année heureuse. Mais puisque nous sommes des modernes, issus des quatre disciplines, hébraïque, hellénique, chrétienne, et française, ayons au moins les vertus de nos vices. N'oublions pas que l'humanité n'a point connu seulement Platon, qu'elle n'a point connu seulement ce plus grand philosophe de l'antiquité, mais qu'elle a connu aussi les grands philosophes modernes, Descartes, Kant, Bergson.

Héritiers, autant que nous le pouvons, de la culture antique, autant et même un peu plus que nous n'en sommes dignes, souhaitons-nous que cette année soit une année heureuse et qui nous réussisse, mais souhaitons-le-nous sans aucun orgueil,

These New Year's greetings were written in 1905, a crucial year in the life of Péguy and of France. It was the year of the Morocco crisis and of Germany's intervention in the domestic affairs of France, when she requested, and obtained, the resignation of Delcassé, French Minister of Foreign Affairs. From this moment on Péguy had the premonition of the war in which he was to die. In the face of this future, he sums up his cultural heritage, and the civil and military obligations of a Frenchman forced to live under the system of "armed peace."

HAPPY NEW YEAR

FOLLOWING THE CUSTOM of our fathers, let us exchange the season's greetings. Friends, let us exchange the season's greetings at the beginning of this year of good fortune or fatality. If we were ancients we might content ourselves with wishing that this year, new today, be a happy year. But as we are moderns, the inheritors of the four disciplines, Hebrew, Greek, Christian and French, let us at least have the virtues of our vices. Let us remember that humanity has not only known Plato, that it has not only known this greatest philosopher of antiquity, but that it has also known the great modern philosophers: Descartes, Kant, Bergson.

Heirs as we are of ancient culture, not only to the extent to which we are able but even a little more than we deserve, let us wish this year to be a happy year and one that will be successful. But let us wish this without any pride, without any presumption, without any anticipation, without any arroga-

sans aucune présomption, sans aucune anticipation; sans aucune usurpation; c'est-à-dire croyons que la fortune et que le bonheur considéré comme la réussite de l'événement est un élément capital de toute vie, et ne méprisons point la réussite, ni cette réussite qui se nomme la paix et le maintien de la paix, ni cette réussite qui se nomme la victoire; mais souhaitons-la-nous de telle sorte et dans un langage tel que nous n'attirions sur nos têtes ni la jalousie des dieux ni la vengeance de la fatalité; ne faisons point comme l'autre qui brave.

Héritiers autant que nous le pouvons, autant que nous le voulons, et quelquefois même un peu plus, de la discipline hébraïque, héritiers des Juifs anciens, cohéritier des Juifs anciens avec les Juifs modernes, au moins avec certains d'entre eux, ami de certains Juifs nouveaux, particulièrement qualifiés, des plus nobles, des plus dévoués, des plus dignes de leur éternité terrestre et de leur incomparable race,—commensaux des Juifs, c'est-à-dire aujourd'hui mangeant à la table de la même cité,—de la discipline hébraïque, des anciens et des nouveaux Juifs recevons cet enseignement que le salut temporel de l'humanité a un prix infini, que la survivance d'une race, que la survivance terrestre et temporelle d'une race, que la survivance infatigable et linéaire d'une race à travers toutes les vagues de tous les âges, que le maintien d'une race est une œuvre, une opération d'un prix infini, que l'immortalité terrestre et temporelle d'une race élue, quand même ce serait une race humaine simplement,—que ce maintien et que cette immortalité est un objet, une proposition d'un prix infini, qui paie tous les sacrifices.—

Héritiers autant que nous le pouvons et plus que nous ne le méritons de la discipline antique, des anciens recevons cet enseignement que nous sommes des citoyens, que la cité a une

tion. That is, let us believe that good fortune and happiness, considered as the successful issue of an event, are a capital element of all life, and let us not despise success, not that success which is called peace and the maintenance of peace, nor that success which is called victory. But let us wish it in such a fashion and in such terms that we do not call down upon our heads the jealousy of the gods, nor the vengeance of fate. Let us not be defiant, as those others are.

As much as we can, as much as we will and sometimes even a trifle more, we are the heirs of the Hebrew discipline, we are the heirs of the ancient Jews, we are, together with the modern Jews, the co-inheritors of the ancient Jews,—at least together with certain among the modern Jews,—we are friends with certain particularly qualified new Jews, those that are the most noble, the most devoted, the most worthy of their earthly eternity and of their incomparable race. We are the fellow-guests of the Jews, that is, eating today at the table of the same commonwealth. Let us receive this teaching from the Hebrew discipline, from the ancient and modern Jews: that the temporal salvation of humanity is of infinite price, that the survival of a race, that the earthly and temporal survival of a race, that the indefatigable and lineal survival of a race throughout all the waves of all the ages, that the maintenance of a race is a work, an operation of infinite worth, that the earthly and temporal immortality of a chosen race, even though this would mean simply a human race,—that this maintenance and that this immortality is an object, a proposition of infinite worth which repays all sacrifices.—

We are, as much as we can and more than we deserve, the heirs of the ancient discipline. From the ancients let us receive this teaching: that we are citizens, that the state has its

valeur propre, une valeur en elle-même, une valeur éminente, qu'elle est une institution, une proposition d'un prix parfait, que la survivance et que la conservation, que l'immortalité poussée toujours plus loin de la cité est une œuvre, une opération qui est elle-même d'un prix parfait.

Héritiers des chrétiens, nos pères, de Pascal recevons cet enseignement que le salut éternel est d'un prix infiniment infini; c'est-à-dire que dans le même temps que nous ferons tout ce qui nous sera possible humainement pour assurer la perpétuité, la survivance de cette race et la conservation de cette cité, nous nous garderons scrupuleusement de rien commettre qui soit attentatoire, nous rappelant que tout ce qui tient à la sainteté est d'un ordre infiniment supérieur; *la distance infinie des corps aux esprits figure la distance infiniment plus infinie des esprits à la charité, car elle est surnaturelle.*

Platoniciens nous saurons toute notre cité, kantiens nous saurons tout notre devoir. Platoniciens, ou héritiers des anciens platoniciens, nous saurons toute notre République et nous saurons toutes nos lois. Kantiens ou héritiers des—nouveaux—kantiens, nous saurons toutes nos obligations morales. Mais nous demanderons aux anciens que ces obligations morales demeurent belles, nous demanderons aux chrétiens que ces obligations morales demeurent saintes, demeurent charitables, aux messianiques nous demanderons qu'elles demeurent ardentes, aux cartésiens nous demanderons qu'elles demeurent distinctes et claires, aux bergsoniens nous demanderons qu'elles demeurent profondes, intérieures et vivantes, mouvantes et réelles.

Et réciproquement aux kantiens nous emprunterons que la cité soit morale, que la République demeure morale, que l'action, que l'idée, que la race, que la sainteté même et la charité,

own value, an intrinsic value, an eminent value; that it is an institution, a plan of perfect worth, that the survival and that the conservation, that the immortality of the state reaching ever further, is a work, an operation which in itself is of perfect worth.

Heirs of the Christians, our fathers, let us receive this teaching of Pascal: that eternal salvation is of an infinitely infinite worth. That is to say, that while we will do all that is humanly possible to ensure the perpetuance, the survival of this race and the preservation of this state, we will scrupulously refrain from committing whatever is aggressive, remembering that all that pertains to holiness is of an infinitely superior order. *The infinite distance between bodies and spirits measures the distance infinitely more infinite between spirits and charity. For charity is supernatural.*

As Platonists we will know everything about our state, as Kantians we will know our whole duty. As Platonists, or as the heirs of the ancient Platonists, we will know everything about our Republic and we will know all of our laws. As Kantians or as the heirs of the neo-Kantians we will know all of our moral obligations. But we will ask of the ancients that these moral obligations remain beautiful. We will ask of the Christians that these moral obligations remain holy, remain charitable. Of the Messianic we will ask that these moral obligations remain ardent. Of the Cartesians we will ask that these moral obligations remain distinct and clear. Of the Bergsonians we will ask that these moral obligations remain deep, interior and living, animated and true.

And reciprocally, we will borrow from the Kantians the proposition that the state be moral, that the Republic remain moral, that action, thought, race, holiness itself and charity,

que la vie, l'intérieur et la profondeur, que le mouvement et la réalité demeure humainement et absolument morale.

Français, héritiers de nos pères, à celui qui fit les guerres d'Allemagne, à tant de Français qui firent la guerre et qui plusieurs fois combattirent et chacun une fois moururent pour la liberté du monde nous demanderons cette forme de courage si particulière et si éminente que l'historien sera contraint de nommer le courage français, ce courage essentiellement fait de calme et de clarté, de non épatement, ce courage classique, essentiellement fait de non romantisme.—

Quand un peuple de culture est menacé d'une invasion militaire par un peuple barbare, ou par un gouvernement barbare qui a toujours fait marcher son peuple, quand un peuple libre est menacé d'une invasion militaire par un peuple de servitude, le peuple de culture, le peuple libre n'a qu'à préparer parfaitement sa mobilisation militaire nationale, et sa mobilisation une fois préparée, il n'a qu'à continuer le plus tranquillement du monde, le plus aisément et de son mieux son existence de culture et de liberté; toute altération de cette existence par l'introduction de quelque élément de peur, d'appréhension, ou même d'attente, serait déjà une réussite, un essai, un commencement de cette invasion, militaire, barbare et de servitude, littéralement une défaite, littéralement une conquête, une entrée dedans, puisque ce serait un commencement de barbarie et un commencement de servitude, la plus dangereuse des invasions, l'invasion qui entre en dedans, l'invasion de la vie intérieure, infiniment plus dangereuse pour un peuple qu'une invasion, qu'une occupation territoriale.

Pareillement un simple citoyen, quand il a mis prête et quand il tient prête sa petite mobilisation individuelle, il n'a plus qu'à continuer de son mieux son petit train-train de vie

that life in its inwardness and profundity, that movement and reality remain humanly and absolutely moral.

As Frenchmen, heirs of our fathers, we will ask of the ancestor who waged the wars in Germany, we will ask of the many Frenchmen who waged war and who fought several times and who each of them died once for the liberty of the world, this form of courage which is so particular and so eminent that historians will be obliged to call it French courage; this courage essentially made of calm and clarity, this courage without bluff, this classical, essentially non-romantic courage.—

When a cultivated people is threatened with military invasion by a barbarous people, or by a barbarous government which has always led its people by the nose,—when a free people is threatened with military invasion by a servile people,—the cultivated people, the free people needs only to perfectly prepare its national military mobilisation. And its mobilisation once prepared, needs only to continue in the greatest peace and ease, while doing its best, its life of culture and liberty. Any change in this existence caused by the introduction of some element of fear, of apprehension, or even of expectation would already mean a successful attempt, a beginning of this military, barbarous and enslaving invasion. Literally, it would mean a defeat, literally a conquest, a foothold for the invaders; because it would mean a beginning of barbarism and a beginning of servitude, the most dangerous of invasions: the invasion which crosses the threshold of inner life and which is infinitely more dangerous for a people than an invasion, than a territorial occupation.

In the same manner, when a simple citizen has prepared and holds in readiness his little individual mobilisation, he

d'honnête homme; car il n'y a rien de mieux au monde qu'une vie d'honnête homme; il n'y a rien de meilleur que le pain cuit des devoirs quotidiens.—

Surtout gardons ce trésor des humbles, cette sorte de joie entendue qui est la fleur de la vie, cette sorte de saine gaité qui est la vertu même et plus vertueuse que la vertu même.—

Il ne dépend pas de nous que l'événement se déclanche. Mais il dépend de nous de faire notre devoir.

C'est une angoisse épouvantable que de prévoir et de voir la mort collective, soit que tout un peuple s'engloutisse dans le sang du massacre, soit que tout un peuple chancelle et se couche dans les retranchements de bataille, soit que toute une classe meure accélérément du travail qui est censé lui donner la nourriture. Et comme l'humanité n'a pas des réserves indéfinies, c'est une étrange angoisse que de penser à la mort de l'humanité.

Les crises de l'enseignement ne sont pas des crises de l'enseignement; elles sont des crises de vie.

needs only to continue to do his best as he leads the humdrum life of an honest man. For there is nothing in the world better than the life of an honest man. There is nothing better than the baked bread of daily duties.—

Above all, let us cling to this treasure of the humble, to this sort of implied joy which is the flower of life, this kind of healthy gayety which is virtue itself and more virtuous than virtue itself.—

It does not rest with us to provoke the event. But it rests with us to do our duty.

It is a dreadful anguish to foresee and to see collective death, whether it be that a whole people goes under in the blood of a massacre, whether it be that a whole people reels and succumbs in the retrenchments of battle, whether it be that a whole class dies at accelerated speed under the stress of the work which is supposed to give it food. And as humanity possesses no inexhaustible reserves, it is a strange anguish to think upon the death of humanity.

The crises of teaching are not crises of teaching; they are crises of life.

L'HÉROÏSME est essentiellement une vertu, un état, l'action héroïque est essentiellement une opération de santé, de bonne humeur, de joie, même de gaieté, presque de blague, une action, une opération d'aisance, de largesse, de facilité, de commodité, de fécondité; de bien allant; de maîtrise et de possession de soi; d'habitude presque pour ainsi dire et comme d'usage, de bon usage. De fécondité intérieure; de force comme d'une belle eau de source de force puisée dans le sang de la race et dans le propre sang de l'homme, un trop plein de sève et de sang. Sans aucun raidissement, sans aucune raideur. Sans trimer. Sans suer.—

La vie d'héroïsme, pour qui n'emploie pas ce mot dans un vague sens de littérature, est infiniment, (temporellement) infiniment une opération de joie. Ne les plaignons donc pas. Envions-les plutôt. Quand ils ne se plaignaient pas, ne les plaignons pas, pour eux, ne leur faisons pas l'injure de les plaindre, pour eux. Quand ils ne geignaient pas, ne geignons pas, pour eux, sur eux. Ne leur faisons pas cet outrage.

D'autant qu'il n'échappe pas que geindre sur eux serait déjà une manière, traîtresse, de les faire geindre.

Pleurer, gémir est également lâche. Je réserve prier,— prier est d'un autre ordre que les deux autres.

Le héros, le vrai héros, doit puiser dans la force de sa race comme dans une source inépuisable. Il n'a qu'à se baisser pour en prendre. Et il y puise inépuisablement une force inépuisable de joie.

Heroism is essentially a virtue, a condition. Heroic action is essentially an operation of health, of good humor, of joy, even of gayety, almost of banter; an act, an operation of ease, of bounty, of readiness, of dexterity, of fecundity; of well-being, of mastery and self-possession; almost of habit, so to speak, and as it were, of usage, of good usage. Of inner fecundity; of strength like fine spring water drawn from the blood of the race and from the blood itself of Man; an overflow of sap and of blood. Without any tension, without any rigidity. Without drudgery. Without sweat.—

The life of heroism, for one who does not use this word in a vaguely literary sense, is infinitely, (temporally) infinitely an operation of joy. Therefore, let us not pity them (the heroes). Rather, let us envy them. Since they did not complain, let us not pity them, for their sakes, since they did not whine, let us not whine, for them, over them. Let us not insult them thus.

All the more since it is evident that to whine over them would constitute a betrayal: to make them whine against their will.

To cry, to moan, both are cowardly. I except the term to pray. Prayer is an act of another order than are the other two.

The hero, the real hero should draw strength from the strength of his race as from an inexhaustible source. He needs but stoop to draw it up. And inexhaustibly he draws from it an inexhaustible strength of joy.

L'HUMANITÉ S'EN VA

L'HOMME SE CONSOLERAIT aisément de vieillir, et de passer, et de disparaître, puisque telle est sa nature, et que telle est sa destinée, s'il avait au moins cette consolation que les générations passent et que l'humanité demeure.

Nous n'avons malheureusement plus cette consolation même; et même nous avons la certitude contraire que l'humanité ne demeure pas. Les générations passent, et l'humanité ne passe pas moins. L'humanité grecque meurt aujourd'hui sous nos yeux. Ce que n'avaient pu obtenir les invasions ni les pénétrations d'aucuns barbares, ce que n'avaient pu obtenir les persécutions d'aucuns barbares chrétiens—ce que n'avait pas obtenus le temps même, infatigable démolisseur, le passager triomphe de quelques démagogies politiciennes est en train de l'effectuer sous nos yeux.—

De grandes et de fortes humanités se sont battus pendant des siècles pour et contre la culture grecque, c'est-à-dire pour et contre une des cultures essentielles de l'humanité. Un immense effort a été donné pour l'oppression, pour l'ensevelissement, pour l'anéantissement de la culture antique. Un respectable effort de conservation, de continuation a été fait par un

HUMANITY TAKES LEAVE

MAN MIGHT EASILY be reconciled to the idea of growing old, of passing and of disappearing, since doing so is his nature and doing so his destiny, had he but the consolation that though generations pass away humanity remains.

Unfortunately we no longer possess even this consolation; and we even possess the contrary certainty that humanity does not remain. Generations pass away and humanity passes away no less. Under our very eyes today Greek humanity is dying. What the invasions and the penetrations of no barbarians could achieve, what the persecutions of no Christian barbarians could achieve, what time even, that indefatigable demolisher, could not obtain, the shortlived triumph of a few political demagogies is accomplishing under our very eyes.—

During centuries great and powerful philosophies have battled for and against Greek culture, that is, for and against one of the essential cultures of humanity. An immense effort has been made to oppress, to bury, to annihilate ancient culture. A notable effort of preservation and continuance has been made by a certain number of Christians. An admirable effort of restoration has been made by the men of the Renais-

certain nombre de chrétiens. Un admirable effort de restitution a été fait par les hommes de la Renaissance.—Les grands républicains,—je ne parle évidemment pas de ceux d'aujourd'hui,—les républicains de la première, de la deuxième, et du commencement de la troisième république avaient vu très nettement combien il importait au maintien de l'esprit public sous un gouvernement républicain que les humanités fussent premières maintenues.

C'est un phénomène très fréquent dans l'histoire de l'humanité. Pendant des siècles de grandes humanités se battent pour et contre une grande cause. Et puis tout passe. Et puis, un jour, pendant que l'humanité a le dos tourné, une petite bande de malandrins arrive, détrousseurs de cadavres, chacals et moins que chacals, et on s'aperçoit le lendemain que la dite grande cause a été étranglée dans la nuit.

C'est ce qui vient de nous arriver dans le monde moderne avec le Grec. Par une simple altération, par une simple prétendue réforme des programmes de l'enseignement secondaire —toute une culture, tout un monde, une des quatre cultures qui aient fait le monde moderne,—il est vrai que ce n'est pas ce qu'elles ont fait de mieux,—disparaît tout tranquillement et tout posément sous nos yeux de la face du monde et de la vie de l'humanité. Sous nos yeux, par nos soins disparaît la mémoire de la plus belle humanité. Et en deuxième ligne, au deuxième degré, sous nos yeux, par nos soins périt tout l'effort des humanistes et des hommes de la Renaissance. Tout cet admirable seizième siècle aura fermenté et restitué en vain.—

On nous dit en vain que le Grec s'est réfugié dans l'enseignement supérieur, qu'il demeure entier dans quelques chaires et dans quelques bibliothèques. C'est ici la plus grande

sance.—The great republicans,—naturally I do not speak of those of today,—the republicans of the first, of the second, of the beginning of the third republic had seen very clearly how important it was for the preservation of the public spirit under a republican government that the humanities first of all be maintained.

Here is a very frequent phenomenon in the history of humanity. During centuries great philosophies fight for and against some great cause. And then, all is over. And then, one day, while humanity has turned its back, a small band of scoundrels, grave-robbers, jackals and less than jackals come along. And the next day it is discovered that the said great cause has been strangled in the night.

This is what has just happened to us in the modern world with Greek. By a simple alteration, by a simple so-called reform of the secondary (or high-school) educational programs, —a whole culture, a whole world, one of the four cultures which have created the modern world—true, this last achievement is not their best—disappears quite quietly and quite calmly right beneath our eyes from off the face of the world and from the life of humanity. Beneath our eyes, thanks to our solicitude the memory of the most beautiful humanity vanishes. And in the second line, in the second degree, beneath our eyes, by our own doing, there perishes the whole effort of the humanists and of the men of the Renaissance. All that admirable sixteenth century will have fermented and made its restitutions in vain.—

Vainly we are told that Greek has taken refuge in college curricula, that it is fully preserved by a few university chairs and in a few libraries. Of all the follies uttered in modern times, in which we have been lavish in uttering follies, this is

stupidité que l'on ait dite dans les temps modernes, où pourtant on ne s'est pas privé de dire des stupidités. C'est comme si l'on disait que les anciens Égyptiens vivent et revivent dans les momies des sarcophages des salles basses du Louvre.—Il y a un abîme pour une culture, pour une histoire, pour une vie passée dans l'histoire de l'humanité, pour une humanité enfin, entre figurer à son rang linéaire dans la mémoire et dans l'enseignement de quelques savants et dans quelques catalogues de bibliothèques, et s'incorporer au contraire, par des études secondaires, par des *humanités*, dans tout le corps des artistes, des philosophes, des poètes, des écrivains, des savants, des hommes d'action, de tous les hommes cultivés, des critiques mêmes et des historiens, de tous les hommes de goût, de tous les hommes de sens, de tous les hommes de droiture et de fécondité, de tous ces hommes en un mot qui formaient un peuple cultivé dans le peuple, dans un peuple plus large. Ce sont deux existences qui ne sont pas du même ordre. L'existence dans le corps des producteurs de tout un peuple est une existence de vie. L'existence dans les rayons, sur les rayons de quelques bibliothèques est une existence de mort. Surtout étant donné ce que sont les bibliothèques modernes. Un poète qui gisait manuscrit, ignoré, incompris, non lu non lisible en quelque monastère perdu n'était lui-même ni un poète perdu ni un poète mort. Quelque moine pieux, méritant notre éternelle reconnaissance, pouvait le soigner, le conserver, le recopier, nous le transmettre enfin. Il n'était donc pas mort. Il vivait donc pour la vie à venir de l'humanité. Un poète, connu, compris, classé, catalogué, qui gît imprimé aux rayons de cette stérile Bibliothèque de l'École Normale et qui ne serait point quelque autre part, qui ne serait point couvé dans quelque coeur, est un poète mort.

the greatest. As well say that the ancient Egyptians live and come to life again in the sarcophagus-encased mummies of the basement rooms of the Louvre.—For a culture, for a history, for a life spent in the history of humanity, in short for a humanity, there lies an abyss between its figuring as part of a linear evolution in the memory and the teaching of a few professors and in a library catalogue, or, on the contrary, being incorporated by means of secondary studies, by *humanities,* in the whole body of artists, of philosophers, of poets, of writers, of savants, of men of action, of all cultured men, of critics even and historians, of all men of taste, of all sensible men, of all righteous and fruitful men, of all those men, in a word, who form a cultivated people within the people, within an ampler people. These two forms of existence are not of the same order. Existence in the body of those who produce for an entire people is a living existence. Existence on the shelves, on the shelves of a few libraries is an existence of death. Particularly in view of what modern libraries are like. A poet who lay in manuscript form, unknown, not understood, unread, unreadable in some lost monastery was in himself neither a lost nor a dead poet. It was possible for some pious monk deserving of our eternal gratitude to care for him, preserve him, copy his works, in fine hand him down to us. Therefore he was not dead. So he lived on for the future life of humanity. A poet, recognized, understood, classified, catalogued, who lies in print on the shelves of that barren library of the Ecole Normale, and who would not have life elsewhere, who was not warmed in some heart, is a dead poet.

LES SUPPLIANTS ET LES SUPPLIÉS

CHEZ LES MODERNES, une supplication est une opération d'aplatissement, une manifestation de platitude; le prosternement est une prostration, physique et morale; pour tout dire d'un mot, le suppliant est un candidat. Tel a été le retentissement de nos mœurs politiques parlementaires sur toute la vie, sur toutes nos relations sociales, et telle la déteinte. Infiniment plus profonde, et je pourrais presque dire incomparablement, infiniment plus vraie, toute autre, toute sage, toute renseignée la supplication antique. Dans Homère, dans les tragiques, le suppliant n'est point un candidat; il n'est point un demandeur; il n'est point un homme qui s'abaisse, qui s'humilie, même chrétiennement; à peine ai-je besoin de dire qu'il n'est point un moderne, qui s'aplatit. La supplication antique, la seule qui étant digne de ce nom de supplication doive nous retenir, la supplication antique n'est en aucun sens, en aucune forme, une opération de platitude. Au

THE SUPPLICANTS AND THE SUPPLICATED

WITH THE MODERNS, a supplication is an act of abasement, a manifestation of platitude; prosternation becomes physical and moral prostration. To sum up in a word, the supplicant is an applicant. Such has been the infiltration of our political morals into the whole of life, into the whole of our social relations and such has been its coloration of it. Supplication in antiquity was an infinitely deeper thing, I might almost say, incomparably, infinitely truer, wholly different, wholly wise, wholly informed. In Homer, in the tragic authors, the supplicant is not an applicant; he is not a petitioner; he is not a man who abases himself, who humbles himself, even in a Christian sense. I need hardly say that he is not a modern who cringes. The ancient supplication, alone worthy of the word supplication and as such the only one worthy of holding our attention, the ancient supplication is in no sense, under no form, an act of platitude. Quite the contrary. On

contraire. Lisez attentivement au contraire une de ces admirables supplications antiques, la supplication de tout ce peuple aux pieds d'Oedipe, ou celle qui est encore plus admirable, assurément, celle qui est peut-être la plus admirable de toutes, la supplication du vieux Priam aux pieds d'Achille. Relisez-les attentivement: Ce n'est pas le supplié, c'est le suppliant au contraire qui tient le haut de la situation, le haut du dialogue, au fond. Dans toute la supplication antique,—le supplié est un homme qui paraît avoir une belle situation; c'est même un homme qui a, comme on dit, une belle situation, qui a ce que l'on nomme une belle situation: c'est un roi; c'est un tyran; c'est quelque chef; dans la guerre c'est un vainqueur; c'est un homme qui a quelque domination, apparente; réelle? c'est un puissant de la terre; dans la paix c'est un riche, un puissant, un homme qui a beaucoup de bœufs; disons-le d'un mot: c'est un homme heureux, un homme qui paraît être, qui est heureux.—Il est un homme heureux. Donc il est, pour les Grecs, un homme à plaindre.—Le supplié ne peut parler qu'au nom de son bonheur, tout au plus au nom du bonheur en général. C'est peu. C'est rien. C'est moins que rien. C'est même le contraire de tout avantage. Le bonheur, entendu en ce sens, comme la réussite de l'événement, la réussite un peu insolente et comme injurieuse, est pour les Grecs le signe le plus infaillible de ce qu'un homme est marqué pour la Fatalité,—par la Fatalité.—D'innombrables Grecs ont désiré, convoité, poursuivi de toutes leurs forces les biens de ce monde, comme les modernes, autant que les innombrables modernes, et par toutes sortes de moyens: l'or, la puissance, les jouissances de toutes sortes; ils étaient des hommes comme nous; ils aimaient mieux le bonheur que le malheur et communément le beau temps que la pluie. Mais il n'en demeure

the contrary, read attentively one of those admirable ancient supplications, that supplication of the whole people at the feet of Oedipus, or what surely is even more admirable, what is perhaps the most admirable of all, the supplication of old Priam at the feet of Achilles. Read them over attentively: it is not the supplicated but, on the contrary, the supplicant who, at bottom, carries off the situation, the dialogue with a high hand. In all ancient supplication,—the supplicated is a man who appears to have a fine position; he is even a man who, as we say, has a fine position, who has what is called a fine position. He is a king; he is a tyrant; he is a chief of a kind. In a war, he is a victor; he is a man of some preponderance, visible preponderance. Real preponderance? He is one of the mighty of the earth. In peace he is a rich man, a mighty man, a man who owns a lot of oxen. Let us describe him in a word: he is a happy man, a man who appears to be, who is happy.—He is a happy man. So, for the Greeks he is a man to be commiserated. The supplicated can speak only in the name of his happiness, at most in the name of happiness in general. This is little. This is nothing. This is less than nothing. This is even the contrary of all advantage. Happiness, understood in this sense as the success of an event, the rather insolent and almost abusive success, is for the Greeks the most infallible sign that a man is marked out for Fate,—by Fate.—Innumerable Greeks, like the moderns, have desired, coveted, pursued with all their might the goods of this world, as much as have the innumerable moderns and by every kind of means: gold, power, the enjoyment of all pleasures. They were men such as we are. They preferred happiness to misfortune and, commonly, fine weather to rain. But nevertheless it remains, and it remains entirely true, that happiness understood technically

pas moins acquis, et il n'en demeure pas moins entier, que le bonheur, entendu techniquement comme la réussite de l'événement, est pour les Grecs le signe le plus infaillible de ce qu'un homme est marqué pour la Fatalité. De sorte que dans cette rencontre, dans ce dialogue du suppliant et du supplié, qui fait toute la supplication antique, c'est le suppliant, quel qu'il soit, qui que ce soit, que ce soit le mendiant errant au long des routes, que ce soit l'aveugle misérable, que ce soit le proscrit, l'exterminé, le citoyen chassé de la cité, coupable ou non coupable, l'enfant chassé de la famille, coupable ou non coupable, ceci dans l'ordre politique et dans l'ordre de la paix, ou, dans l'ordre de la guerre, le prisonnier, le vaincu, le vieillard impotent, que ce soit l'orphelin ou au contraire le contre-orphelin, le vieillard dépouillé de sa descendance, toujours c'est le suppliant qui en réalité tient le dessus, qui tient le haut du dialogue, le haut de la situation.

Le supplié, lui, a une grande, une haute situation humaine. Mais ce n'est jamais qu'une toute misérable situation humaine.—Et c'est tout. Ce n'est rien. Surtout en comparaison d'autres grandeurs.—Ce qui fait la faiblesse, la petitesse du supplié, c'est qu'il n'est que lui-même, et son petit morceau de situation humaine. Il ne représente pas.

Le suppliant représente. Il n'est plus seulement lui-même. Il n'est même plus lui-même. Il n'existe plus, lui. Il ne s'agit plus de lui. Et c'est pour cela qu'il faut que l'autre se méfie. Dépouillé de tout par ce même événement qui a précisément fait le dangereux bonheur du supplié, citoyen sans cité, tête sans regard, enfant sans père, père sans enfants, ventre sans pain, nuque sans lit, tête sans toit, homme sans biens, il n'existe plus comme lui-même. Et c'est à partir de cet instant qu'il devient redoutable. Il représente.

as the success of an event is for the Greeks the most infallible sign that a man is marked by Fate. So that in this encounter, in this dialogue between the supplicant and the supplicated, which makes up the whole of an ancient supplication, it is the supplicant, no matter what he be, who he be, whether he be the beggar wandering along the highways, whether he be the wretched blind man, whether he be the outlaw, the exterminated, the citizen banished from the city, guilty or not guilty, the child expelled from his family, guilty or not guilty, this in the order of politics and in the order of peace, or, in the order of war, the prisoner, the vanquished, the feeble old man, whether it be the orphan or, on the contrary, the man who has been orphaned, the old man deprived of his descendants, it is always the supplicant who really has the advantage, who carries off the dialogue, who carries off the situation with a high hand.

As to the supplicated, he occupies a great, a high human position. But it is never more than a perfectly wretched human position.—And that is all. It is nothing. Particularly in comparison with other grandeurs.—What makes the weakness, the smallness of the supplicated is that he is only himself and his small portion of the human position. He does not represent.

The supplicant represents. He is no longer himself alone. He is not even himself any longer. He no longer exists. It is no longer he who matters. And that is why the other, the supplicated, must be on his guard. Despoiled of everything by the same event which precisely has made the dangerous happiness of the supplicated: a citizen without a city, an eyeless head, a fatherless child, a childless father, a stomach without bread, a pillowless neck, a roofless head, a man without pos-

Parce qu'il a été manié, pétri, manipulé par les doigts humains surhumains des dieux, il est devenu soudainement cher au cœur humain surhumain des dieux. Parce qu'il a été une cire aux doigts divins surdivins de la fatalité, il est devenu mystérieusement cher au cœur divin surdivin de la fatalité. Parce que les puissances d'en haut ont appesanti leur main sur lui, par un singulier retour,—non point par une compensation,—par une sorte de filiation, plutôt, d'enfantement supérieur, d'adoption particulière, il est devenu leur protégé, leur fils. Les dieux et au-dessus d'eux, derrière eux, la fatalité, lui ont pris son père. Mais les dieux sont devenus son père. Les dieux, et derrière eux la fatalité, les dieux lui ont pris la cité. Mais les dieux lui ont en quelque sorte conféré leur propre cité. Les dieux, sous-ordres de la fatalité, lui ont pris ses biens. Mais ces mêmes dieux lui ont donné ce bien que nul bien ne saurait remplacer, les dieux lui ont donné ce premier des biens: qu'il est devenu un représentant des dieux.

Nulle idée de compensation, ni même de justice: une telle idée serait une idée chrétienne, au moins une idée relativement récente, en un certain sens une idée moderne.—Mais une idée beaucoup plus profonde, un sentiment beaucoup plus profond et beaucoup plus vrai, autant qu'il est permis de se reconnaître un peu dans ces sentiments mystérieux, profonds, vrais, un sentiment de vie, d'art et d'œuvre: que ces hommes ont fait leur preuve qu'ils étaient des hommes plastiques aux doigts statuaires de la fatalité.—

De là vient, nous n'en pouvons douter—que les dieux sont à ce point avec l'homme, que la fatalité est à ce point derrière l'homme qu'elle a une fois travaillé. Quand nous lisons dans les textes que *Zeus* est *hospitalier*, qu'il est le *dieu* des *hôtes*, que les hôtes viennent de Zeus, que l'étranger vient des

sessions, the supplicant no longer exists as himself. And it is from that moment that he becomes formidable. He represents.

Because he has been handled, kneaded, manipulated by the human, superhuman fingers of the gods, suddenly he has become dear to the human, superhuman heart of the gods. Because he has been wax in the divine, superdivine fingers of fate he has become mysteriously dear to the divine, superdivine heart of fate. Because the hand of the powers above has weighed heavily upon him, by a singular reversal—not by a compensation—by a sort of filiation, rather, a superior childbirth, a particular adoption, the supplicant has become their protégé, their son. The gods and above them, behind them, fate, have taken away his father. But the gods have become his father. The gods and behind them, fate, the gods have taken away from him the city. But in a way the gods have conferred upon him their own city. The gods, subordinates of fate, have taken away his worldly goods. But those same gods have given him that good which no other good could replace, the gods have given him the first among all goods: he has become a representative of the gods.

There is no idea of compensation or even of justice: such an idea would be a Christian idea, at least a relatively recent idea, in a certain sense a modern idea.—There is a much deeper idea, a sentiment much deeper and far truer, as far as it is permissible to feel one's way a little among these mysterious, deep, true sentiments—a sentiment of life, of art, of creation: that these men have proven themselves malleable men in the shaping hands of fate.—

Hence, without a doubt, comes the fact that the gods are so closely unified with man, that fate is so closely behind the man on whom she has once acted. When we read in the texts

dieux, que le mendiant, que le suppliant, que le malheureux est un envoyé des dieux, gardons-nous surtout de croire que ce sont là des métaphores et des élégances. Les modernes traitent ces graves questions par des métaphores et par des élégances. Les anciens entendaient ces expressions littéralement. Réellement. Ces misérables hommes, les suppliants, étaient comme des témoins ambulants de la fatalité, deux fois œuvres (ne disons point deux fois créatures) des dieux.

C'est pour cela que dans la supplication antique,—c'est le suppliant qui tient le haut de la supplication. L'autre est tout seul, tout nu, et ne représente rien. Il a, lui, derrière lui, tout l'Olympe, et ce qui domine l'Olympe même. Il représente tout un monde de dieux, et même il représente ce qui ensevelira les dieux mêmes.

Il représente la misère, le malheur, toute infortune, la maladie, la mort, la fatalité, qui frappera les dieux mêmes.

Dans toute supplication antique, c'est le suppliant qui est le maître, c'est le suppliant qui domine. Veuillez bien noter qu'on peut lui refuser ce qu'il demande. Si l'autre veut aggraver son cas, libre à lui. Mais c'est lui, le suppliant, l'homme *plié* aux pieds de l'autre, qui domine, la supplication, l'opération, le commerce de la supplication; c'est lui qui est le maître, qui parle un grand langage, un langage maître et venu de loin, venu de tout à fait ailleurs.—

Ils sont tous des ambassadeurs. Et les ambassadeurs d'un grand roi.—

Devant de telles promotions que devient, pour des Grecs, la contrariété pourtant si importante du juste et de l'injuste, de l'innocence et du crime. Que devient la catégorie du juste? Que devient la justice. Quel honneur ou quel déshonneur humain, ou si ceci est un mot moderne, quel avantage ou quel

that *Zeus* is *hospitable,* that he is the *god* of *guests,* that guests come from Zeus, that a stranger comes from the gods, that the beggar, that the supplicant, that the poor wretch is an emissary of the gods, let us above all things refrain from believing that these merely are metaphors and embellishments. The moderns treat these grave questions with metaphors and embellishments. The ancients took these expressions literally. Quite truly. These wretched men, the supplicants, were like the ambulant witnesses of fate, doubly the works (let us not say doubly the creatures) of the gods.

That is why in ancient supplication the supplicant has the better part of the supplication. The other, the supplicated, is quite alone, quite naked and represents nothing. He, the supplicant, has behind him all of Olympus and what dominates Olympus itself. He represents a whole world of gods and even represents that which will bury the gods.

He represents destitution, woe, all misfortune, illness, death, the fate which will strike the gods themselves.

In all ancient supplication it is the supplicant that is master, it is the supplicant who dominates. Please note that what he asks can be refused him. If the other, the supplicated, wishes to aggravate his own case he is free to do so. But it is he, the supplicant, the man *bowed* at the feet of the supplicated who dominates the supplication, the act, the business of the supplication; he it is who is the master, who speaks a grand language, a masterly language and one which has come from afar, which has come from a quite other world.—

They are all of them ambassadors. And the ambassadors of a great king.—

In the face of such an elevation, what do the Greeks make of the meanwhile most important contrast between the just

désavantage humain peut affronter l'avantage d'avoir été choisi pour devenir la matière plastique des dieux, et de celle qui domine et qui modèlera les dieux mêmes et qui les gouvernera dans le sommeil de la mort. Et c'est pour cela que le suppliant criminel, ou, pour parler exactement, ancien criminel,—car, puisqu'il est suppliant, il ne peut plus être criminel,—c'est pour cela que le suppliant prétendu criminel est chez les Grecs un homme infiniment plus sage, plus près des dieux, plus innocent que le plus sage et que le plus innocent des hommes heureux. Il peut toujours donner des leçons à l'homme heureux, des leçons de sagesse et d'innocence. L'homme heureux est toujours coupable. Au moins d'être heureux. Mais c'est le plus grand des crimes.

NOUS NE COURONS PAS après l'inédit; nous ne courons pas après l'inconnu; nous ne courons pas après l'extraordinaire: nous cherchons le juste et le convenable, et beaucoup de juste et beaucoup de convenable fut dit avant nous mieux que nous ne le saurions dire.

NOUS SOMMES AUSSI BÊTES que saint Augustin et que saint Paul, que saint Louis et que saint François, et que Jeanne d'Arc, et pourquoi ne pas le dire que Pascal et que Corneille.—

Nous autres nous ne faisons *aucun progrès*. Ce sont les modernes qui font des progrès. Nous sommes bêtes une fois pour toutes.

and the unjust, between innocence and crime? What becomes of the category of the just? What becomes of justice? What human honor or dishonor—or if this is too modern a term—what human advantage or disadvantage can compare with the advantage of having been chosen to become the plastic material of the gods and of Her who dominates and who will model the gods themselves, and govern them in the slumber of death? And that is why the criminal supplicant, or to speak exactly, the former criminal—for, since he is a supplicant he can no longer be a criminal—that is why the supplicant termed criminal is for the Greeks a man infinitely wiser, nearer the gods, more innocent than the wisest and the most innocent of happy men. To the happy man he can always give lessons, lessons in wisdom and innocence. The happy man is always guilty. At least guilty of being happy. But that is the greatest of crimes.

WE DO NOT run after the new; we do not run after the unknown; we do not run after the extraordinary; we look for the right and the fitting, and much that is right and much that is fitting was said before us, better than we ourselves would know how to say it.

WE ARE AS STUPID as Saint Augustin and as Saint Paul, as Saint Louis and as Saint Francis and as Joan of Arc, and why not say it, as stupid as Pascal and as Corneille.—

We others, we make *no progress*. It is the moderns who make progress. We are stupid once and for all.

L'ANCIENNE FRANCE

C'ÉTAIT EN 1880.—Heureuse enfance. Heureuse innocence. Bénédiction sur une bonne race. Tout nous était bon. Tout nous réussissait. Nous prenions de toutes mains et c'étaient toujours de saines nourritures. Nous allions au catéchisme, le jeudi je pense, pour ne pas déranger les heures de classe. Le catéchisme était fort loin de là, en ville, dans notre antique paroisse de Saint-Aignan. Tout le monde n'a pas une paroisse comme ça. Il fallait remonter à moitié du faubourg jusqu'à la porte Bourgogne, descendre la moitié de la rue Bourgogne, tourner cette rue à gauche qui se nommait je crois la rue de l'Oriflamme et traverser le cloître froid comme une cave sous ses marronniers lourds. Nos jeunes vicaires nous disaient exactement le contraire de ce que nous disaient nos jeunes élèves-maîtres.—Nous ne nous en apercevions pas. La République et l'Église nous distribuaient des enseignements diamétralement opposés. Qu'importait, pourvu que ce fussent

OLD FRANCE

IT WAS IN 1880.—Happy childhood. Happy innocence. Blessing on a good race. We thrived on everything. Everything succeeded with us. We received at all hands and it was always healthy food. We went to catechism, I think on Thursday, so as not to interfere with school hours. The catechism class was a long way off, in town, in our ancient parish of Saint-Aignan. Not everyone has such a parish. You had to walk up half the faubourg to the porte Bourgogne, go down half of the rue Bourgogne, turn left into that street which was called, I think, rue de l'Oriflamme and cross the cloister which was cold as a cellar under its heavy chestnut trees. Our young vicars told us exactly the opposite of what was told us by our young pupil-teachers.—We were not aware of it. The Republic and the Church dealt out to us diametrically opposite teachings. It mattered little as long as there were teachings. In instruction and in childhood there is something so

des enseignements. Il y a dans l'enseignement et dans l'enfance quelque chose de si sacré, il y a dans cette première ouverture des yeux de l'enfant sur le monde, il y a dans ce premier regard quelque chose de si religieux que ces deux enseignements se liaient dans nos cœurs et que nous savons bien qu'ils y resteront éternellement liés. Nous aimions l'Église et la République ensemble, et nous les aimions d'un même cœur, et c'était d'un cœur d'enfant, et pour nous c'était le vaste monde, et nos deux amours, la gloire et la foi, et pour nous c'était le nouveau monde. Et à présent . . . A présent évidemment nous ne les aimons pas sur le même plan, puisqu'on nous a appris qu'il y a des plans. L'Église a notre foi, et tout ce qui lui revient. Mais Dieu seul sait combien nous sommes restés engagés d'honneur et de cœur dans cette République, et combien nous sommes résolus à y rester engagés, parce qu'elle fut une des deux puretés de notre enfance.

Nous étions des petits garçons sérieux de cette ville sérieuse, innocents et au fond déjà soucieux. Nous prenions au sérieux tout ce que l'on nous disait, et ce que nous disaient nos maîtres laïques, et ce que nous disaient nos maîtres catholiques. Nous prenions tout au pied de la lettre. Nous croyions entièrement, et également, et de la même créance, à tout ce qu'il y avait dans la grammaire et à tout ce qu'il y avait dans le catéchisme.—Nous n'avons oublié ni l'un; ni l'autre. Mais il faut en venir ici à un phénomène beaucoup moins simple. Je veux parler de ce qui s'est passé en nous pour ces deux métaphysiques, puisqu'il est entendu qu'il faut bien qu'il y ait une métaphysique dessous tout.—

Tout le monde a une métaphysique. Patente, latente. Je l'ai assez dit. Ou alors on n'existe pas.—La métaphysique de nos maîtres c'était la métaphysique scolaire, d'abord. Mais

sacred, in this first opening of childish eyes on the world, in this first glance there is something so religious that these two teachings were bound together in our hearts and we know very well that they will remain there eternally linked. We loved the Church and the Republic together and we loved them with the same heart, and this heart was the heart of a child, and for us the two were the wide world, and our two loves, glory and faith, and for us the whole was the new world. And at present . . . At present obviously we do not love them on the same level since we have learned that there are levels. The Church has our faith and all that belongs to her. But God alone knows how much we have remained bound by honor and heart to this Republic, and how much we are resolved to remain bound to it because it was one of the two purities of our childhood.

We were serious little boys of this serious town, innocent and at bottom already full of worries. We took seriously all that was said to us, both what our lay teachers said to us and what our Catholic teachers said to us. We took everything literally. We believed entirely, and equally, and with the same credence, everything contained in the grammar and everything contained in the catechism.—We have forgotten neither one nor the other. But this leads to a far less simple phenomenon. I refer to what took place within us regarding those two systems of metaphysics, since it is self-evident that a system of metaphysics must underlie everything.—

Everyone has a system of metaphysics. Patent, latent. I have said so often enough. Otherwise one does not exist.—The metaphysical system of our teachers was, in the first place, a system of educational metaphysics. But it also was, and above all, the metaphysics of science, the system, or at

c'était ensuite, c'était surtout la métaphysique de la *science*, c'était la métaphysique ou du moins une métaphysique matérialiste, (ces êtres pleins d'âme avaient une métaphysique matérialiste, mais c'est toujours comme ça), (et en même temps idéaliste, profondément moraliste et si l'on veut kantienne), c'était une métaphysique positiviste, c'était la célèbre métaphysique du progrès.—

Nous croyions intégralement tout ce que l'on nous disait. Nous étions des petits bonshommes sérieux et certainement graves. J'avais entre tous et au plus haut degré cette maladie. Je ne m'en suis jamais guéri. Aujourd'hui même je crois encore tout ce qu'on me dit. Et je sens bien que je ne changerai jamais. D'abord on ne change jamais. J'ai toujours tout pris au sérieux. Cela m'a mené loin. Nous croyions donc intégralement aux enseignements de nos maîtres, et également intégralement aux enseignements de nos curés. Nous absorbions intégralement les ou la métaphysique de nos maîtres, et également intégralement la métaphysique de nos curés. Aujourd'hui je puis dire sans offenser personne que la métaphysique de nos maîtres n'a plus pour nous et pour personne aucune espèce d'existence et la métaphysique des curés a pris possession de nos êtres à une profondeur que les curés eux-mêmes se seraient bien gardés de soupçonner. Nous ne croyons plus un mot de ce qu'enseignaient, des métaphysiques qu'enseignaient nos maîtres. Et nous croyons intégralement ce qu'il y a dans le catéchisme et c'est devenu et c'est resté notre chair.—

Nos maîtres étaient essentiellement et profondément des hommes de l'ancienne France. Un homme ne se détermine point par ce qu'il fait et encore moins par ce qu'il dit. Mais

least *a* system of materialistic metaphysics, (these beings so full of soul possessed a system of materialistic metaphysics, but after all that is the rule), (and at the same time, it was idealistic, profoundly moralistic, and if one wishes, Kantian), it was a system of positivistic metaphysics, it was the famous metaphysical system of progress.—

We totally believed all that was told us. We were serious little fellows and assuredly sober. More than the rest, and to the highest degree I had this disease. I have never been cured of it. To this very day I still believe all that is told me. And I strongly feel that I shall never change. To begin with, no one ever changes. I have always taken everything seriously. This has taken me far. So we believed totally in the teachings of our masters, and equally totally in the teachings of our priests. We absorbed completely the several or single systems of metaphysics of our teachers, and equally completely the system of metaphysics of our priests. I can say today without offending anyone that the system of metaphysics of our teachers has no longer for us or for anybody else any kind of a reality and that the system of metaphysics of our priests has taken possession of our being to a depth that the priests themselves would not have let themselves suspect. We no longer believe a word of what our teachers taught us, of the metaphysics which our teachers taught us. And we believe totally what is contained in the catechism, and it has become and it has remained flesh of our flesh.—

Our teachers were essentially and profoundly men of the old France. A man is not determined by what he does and still less by what he says. But in the deepest part of himself a being is determined solely by what he is. It is of little impor-

au plus profond un être se détermine uniquement par ce qu'il est. Qu'importe pour ce que je veux dire que nos maîtres aient eu en effet une métaphysique qui visait à détruire l'ancienne France. Nos maîtres étaient nés dans cette maison qu'ils voulaient démolir. Ils étaient les droits fils de la maison. Ils étaient de la race, et tout est là. Nous savons très bien que ce n'est pas leur métaphysique qui a mis l'ancienne maison par terre. Une maison ne périt jamais que du dedans. Ce sont les défenseurs du trône et de l'autel qui ont mis le trône par terre, et, autant qu'ils ont pu, l'autel.

Nos vieux maîtres n'étaient pas seulement des hommes de l'ancienne France. Ils nous enseignaient, au fond, la morale même et l'être de l'ancienne France. Je vais bien les étonner: ils nous enseignaient la même chose que les curés. Et les curés nous enseignaient la même chose qu'eux.—

Les uns et les autres et avec eux nos parents—ils nous disaient, ils nous enseignaient cette stupide morale, qui a fait la France, qui aujourd'hui encore l'empêche de se défaire. Cette stupide morale à laquelle nous avons tant cru. À laquelle, sots que nous sommes, et peu scientifiques, malgré tous les démentis du fait, à laquelle nous nous raccrochons désespérément dans le secret de nos cœurs. Cette pensée fixe de notre solitude, c'est d'eux tous que nous la tenons. Tous les trois ils nous enseignaient cette morale, ils nous disaient que un homme qui travaille bien et qui a de la conduite est toujours sûr de ne manquer de rien. Ce qu'il y a de plus fort c'est qu'ils le croyaient. Et ce qu'il y a de plus fort, c'est que *c'était* vrai.

Les uns paternellement, et maternellement; les autres scolairement, intellectuellement, laïquement; les autres dévotement, pieusement; tous avec beaucoup de cœur ils enseign-

tance in this connection that our teachers in fact possessed a system of metaphysics which aimed to destroy the old France. Our teachers were born in this very house which they wished to demolish. They were the true sons of the house. They belonged to the race and that says all. We know very well that it is not their system of metaphysics which tore down the old house. A house never perishes but from within. It was the defenders of throne and altar that tore down the throne and, as much as they could, the altar.

Our old teachers were not only men of the France of yesterday. What they really taught us at bottom was the morality itself, and the essence, of the old France. I am about to astonish them greatly: they taught us the same thing as the priests. And the priests taught us the same thing as they did.—

Both of them and also our parents,—all told us and taught us this stupid morality, which had made France and which today still prevents it from going to pieces. This stupid morality in which we have believed so much. To which, fools that we are and so little scientific, although facts have given us the lie, to which we cling desperately in the secret of our hearts. This fixed idea of our solitude, we inherit it from them all. All three taught us this morality, they told us that a man who works well and who behaves well is always certain to lack for nothing. The strangest of all is that they believed this. And the strangest of all is that it *was* true.

Our parents paternally and maternally; our teachers academically, intellectually, as laymen; our priests devoutly, piously; all of them with a great deal of heart taught, believed and *bore witness* to this stupid morality: (our sole recourse, our secret strength): that a man who works as hard as he can and who has no great vice, who is neither a gam-

aient, ils croyaient, ils *constataient* cette morale stupide: (notre seul recours; notre secret ressort) : qu'un homme qui travaille tant qu'il peut, et qui n'a aucun grand vice, qui n'est ni joueur, ni ivrogne, est toujours sûr de ne jamais manquer de rien et comme disait ma mère qu'il aura toujours du pain pour ses vieux jours. Ils croyaient cela tous, d'une croyance antique et enracinée, d'une créance indéracinable, indéracinée, que l'homme raisonnable et plein de conduite, que le laborieux était parfaitement assuré de ne jamais mourir de faim. Et même qu'il était assuré de pouvoir toujours nourrir sa famille. Qu'il trouverait toujours du travail et qu'il gagnerait toujours sa vie.

Tout cet ancien monde était essentiellement le monde de *gagner sa vie.*

Pour parler plus précisément ils croyaient que l'homme qui se cantonne dans la pauvreté et qui a, même moyennement, les vertus de la pauvreté, y trouve une petite sécurité totale. Ou pour parler plus profondément ils croyaient que le pain quotidien est assuré, par des moyens purement temporels, par le jeu même des balancements économiques, à tout homme qui ayant les vertus de la pauvreté consent, (comme d'ailleurs on le doit), à se borner dans la pauvreté. (Ce qui d'ailleurs pour eux était en même temps et en cela même non pas seulement le plus grand bonheur, mais le seul bonheur même que l'on pût imaginer). (Bien se loger dans une petite maison de pauvreté).

On se demande où a pu naître, comment a pu naître une croyance aussi stupide.—Que l'on ne cherche pas. Cette morale n'était pas stupide. Elle était juste alors. Et même elle était la seule juste. Cette croyance n'était pas absurde. Elle était fondée en fait. Et même elle était la seule fondée en fait.

bler nor a drunkard, is always sure of wanting nothing and, as my mother used to say will always have bread in his old age. They all of them believed this with an ancient and deep-rooted belief, with an ineradicable, ineradicated conviction that a sensible and disciplined man, that a hard-working man was perfectly assured against dying of hunger. And even, that he was assured of the ability to provide for his family always. That he would always find work and that he would always earn his living.

All this old world was essentially the world of *earning one's living*.

To speak more exactly they believed that the man who confines himself to poverty and who has, even moderately, the virtues of poverty, finds in it a small, total security. Or, to speak more profoundly, they believed that daily bread was assured by purely temporal means, by the play itself of economical balance, to any man who, possessing the virtues of poverty, agrees (as in any case he ought) to confine himself to poverty. (Which in itself for them at the same time was not only the greatest happiness but even the only happiness that could be imagined). (To be well housed in the little dwelling of poverty).

One wonders where such a silly belief could have arisen, how it could have arisen.—Let us not look for a reason. This morality was not silly. It was true then. And it was even then the only true one. This belief was not absurd. It was founded on fact. And indeed it was even the sole one founded on fact. This opinion was not unreasonable, this judgment was not indefensible. On the contrary, it proceeded from the deepest reality of those times.

One often wonders where was born, and how was born, this

Cette opinion n'était point déraisonnable, ce jugement n'était point indéfendable. Il procédait au contraire de la réalité la plus profonde de ce temps-là.

On se demande souvent d'où est née, comment est née cette vieille morale classique, cette vieille morale traditionnelle, cette vieille morale du labeur et de la sécurité dans le salaire, de la sécurité dans la récompense, pourvu que l'on se bornât dans les limites de la pauvreté et par suite et enfin de la sécurité dans le bonheur. Mais c'est précisément ce qu'ils voyaient; tous les jours. Nous, c'est ce que nous ne voyons jamais, et nous le disons: Où avaient-ils inventé ça. Et nous croyons, (parce que c'étaient des maîtres d'école, et des curés, c'est-à-dire en un certain sens encore des maîtres d'écoles), nous croyons que c'était une invention, scolaire, intellectuelle. Nullement. Non. C'était cela au contraire qui était la réalité, même. Nous avons connu un temps, nous avons touché un temps où c'était cela qui était la réalité. Cette morale, cette vue sur le monde, cette vue du monde avait au contraire tous les sacrements scientifiques. C'était elle qui était d'usage, d'expérience, pratique, empirique, expérimentale, de fait constamment accompli. C'était elle qui savait. C'était elle qui avait vu. Et c'est peut-être là la différence la plus profonde, l'abîme qu'il y ait eu entre tout ce grand monde antique, païen, chrétien, français, et notre monde moderne, coupés comme je l'ai dit, à la date que j'ai dit. Et ici nous recoupons une fois de plus cette ancienne proposition de nous que le monde moderne, lui, lui seul et de son côté, se contrarie d'un seul coup à tous les autres mondes, à tous les anciens mondes ensemble en bloc et de leur côté. Nous avons connu, nous avons touché un monde (enfants nous en avons participé), où un homme qui se bornait dans la pauvreté était au moins garanti dans la

old classical morality, this old traditional teaching of labor and security in wages, of security in reward, if only one remained within the limits of poverty, and its final consequence, security in happiness. But that is precisely what they perceived; every day. As far as we are concerned, that is what we never perceive and we say: "Where on earth did they find all this." And we believe (because they were schoolteachers and priests, that is, in a certain sense, schoolteachers still), we believe that this was an academic, intellectual invention. Not at all. No. On the contrary, it was reality itself. We have known times, we have been close to times when this was reality. This morality, this idea of the world, this view of the world had, on the contrary, all the scientific sacraments. This morality was that of custom, of experience; it was practical, empirical, experimental, constantly accomplished in fact. This morality was "wise." This morality had seen the world. And here perhaps is the deepest difference, the abyss which lies between all this great ancient world, pagan, Christian, French, and our modern world, cut off, as I have said, at the date that I have said. And here once more we encounter this old proposition of ours that the modern world, by itself, and on its own side, by a single stroke, is in opposition to all the other worlds, to the men of all the old worlds blocked together, on the other side. We have known, we have been close to a world (as children we were part of it), where a man who confined himself to poverty was guaranteed in poverty at least. It was a kind of unspoken contract between man and fate; and fate never failed to fulfill its share of the contract, before the inauguration of modern times. It was understood that he who behaved whimsically, arbitrarily, that he who started gambling, that he who wished to escape from poverty,

pauvreté. C'était une sorte de contrat sourd entre l'homme et le sort, et à ce contrat le sort n'avait jamais manqué avant l'inauguration des temps modernes. Il était entendu que celui qui faisait de la fantaisie, de l'arbitraire, que celui qui introduisait un jeu, que celui qui voulait s'évader de la pauvreté risquait tout. Puisqu'il introduisait le jeu, il pouvait perdre. Mais celui qui ne jouait pas ne pouvait pas perdre. Ils ne pouvaient pas soupçonner qu'un temps venait, et qu'il était déjà là, et c'est précisément le temps moderne, où celui qui ne jouerait pas perdrait tout le temps, et encore plus sûrement que celui qui joue.—

Dans leur système, qui était le système même de la réalité, celui qui bravait risquait évidemment tout, mais celui qui ne bravait pas ne risquait absolument rien. Celui qui tentait, celui qui voulait s'évader de la pauvreté, celui qui jouait de s'évader de la pauvreté risquait évidemment de retomber dans les plus extrêmes misères. Mais celui qui ne jouait pas, celui qui se bornait dans la pauvreté, ne jouant, n'introduisant aucun risque, ne courait non plus aucun risque de tomber dans aucune misère. L'acceptation de la pauvreté décernait une sorte de brevet, instituait une sorte de contrat. L'homme qui résolument se bornait dans la pauvreté n'était jamais traqué dans la pauvreté. C'était un réduit. C'était un asile. Et il était sacré. Nos maîtres ne prévoyaient pas, et comment eussent-ils soupçonné, comment eussent-ils imaginé ce purgatoire, pour ne pas dire cet enfer du monde moderne où celui qui ne joue pas perd, et perd toujours, où celui qui se borne dans la pauvreté est incessamment poursuivi dans la retraite même de cette pauvreté.—

Il était entendu que celui qui voulait sortir de la pauvreté risquait de tomber dans la misère. C'était son affaire. Il rom-

risked all. Since he started gambling, he might lose. But he who did not gamble could not lose. No one could suspect that times were coming, and that these times already were there, and that they precisely were modern times, when the man who did not gamble would lose all the time, even more surely than he who gambled.—

In their system, which was the very system of reality, he who acted defiantly, obviously risked all, but he who did not act defiantly risked absolutely nothing. He who attempted, he who wished to escape from poverty, he who gambled to escape from poverty obviously risked falling into destitution of the most extreme sort. But he who did not gamble, he who confined himself to poverty, without gambling, without introducing the element of risk, also ran no risk of falling into destitution of any sort. The acceptance of poverty conferred a sort of diploma, constituted a sort of contract. The man who resolutely confined himself to poverty was never trapped within poverty. It was a retreat. It was an asylum. And it was sacred. Our teachers did not foresee, and how could they have suspected, how could they have imagined this purgatory, not to say this hell of the modern world where he who does not gamble loses, and always loses, where he who is confined to poverty is unceasingly pursued in the retreat of poverty itself.—

It was understood that he who wished to come out of poverty risked falling into destitution. That was his business. He broke the contract concluded with fate. But it had never been perceived that he who wished to confine himself to poverty was condemned to fall back perpetually into destitution. It had never been seen that fate would break the contract. They did not know, they could not foresee this monstrosity,

pait le contrat conclu avec le sort. Mais on n'avait jamais vu que celui qui voulait se borner dans la pauvreté fut condamné a retomber perpétuellement dans la misère. On n'avait jamais vu que ce fût le sort qui rompît le contrat. Ils ne connaissaient pas, ils ne pouvaient prévoir cette monstruosité, moderne, cette tricherie, nouvelle, cette invention, cette rupture du jeu, que celui qui ne joue pas perdît continuellement.—

À nous il nous était réservé que la pauvreté même nous fût infidèle. Pour tout dire d'un mot à nous il nous était réservé que le mariage même de la pauvreté fut un mariage adultère.—

Ils ne pouvaient prévoir, ils ne pouvaient imaginer cette monstruosité du monde moderne, (qui déjà surplombait), ils n'avaient point à concevoir ce monstre d'un Paris comme est le Paris moderne où la population est coupée en deux classes si parfaitement séparées que jamais on n'avait vu tant d'argent rouler pour le plaisir, et l'argent se refuser à ce point au travail.

Et tant d'argent rouler pour le luxe et l'argent se refuser à ce point à la pauvreté.

Ils ne pouvaient point prévoir, ils ne pouvaient point soupçonner ce règne de l'argent. Ils pouvaient d'autant moins le prévoir que leur sagesse était la sagesse antique même. Elle venait de loin. Elle datait de la plus profonde antiquité.—

Il y a toujours eu des riches et des pauvres, et *il y aura toujours des pauvres parmi vous,* et la guerre des riches et des pauvres fait la plus grosse moitié de l'histoire grecque et de beaucoup d'autres histoires et l'argent n'a jamais cessé d'exercer sa puissance et il n'a point attendu le commencement des temps modernes pour effectuer ses crimes. Il n'en est pas moins vrai que le mariage de l'homme avec la pauvreté

this modern monstrosity, this trickery, this new trickery, this invention, this break in the rules of the game: that he who did not gamble continually lost.—

To us it was reserved, it was reserved for our lot that poverty itself should be unfaithful to us. To say all in a word, to us it was reserved, it was reserved for our lot to find that the marriage itself of poverty should be an adulterous marriage.—

They could not foresee, they could not imagine this monstrosity of the modern world (which already impended), they did not have to conceive this monster of a Paris which is the modern Paris, where the population is divided into two classes so completely separated that never before has so much money been squandered on pleasure and money refused to such an extent to labor.

And so much money squandered on luxury and money refusing itself to such an extent to poverty.

They could not foresee, they could not suspect this reign of money. They could all the less foresee it as their wisdom was ancient wisdom itself. The wisdom came from afar. It went back to remotest antiquity.—

There will always be rich and poor and "*ye have the poor always with you,*" and the war between the rich and the poor takes up the greater half of Greek history and of many other histories, and money has never ceased to exert its power and it has not awaited the beginning of modern times to accomplish its crimes. But it is none the less true that the marriage of man with poverty had never hitherto been broken. And at the beginning of modern times it was not only broken, but man and poverty entered into an eternal unfaithfulness.

When one speaks of the ancients, with an eye to modern

n'avait jamais été rompu. Et au commencement des temps modernes, il ne fut pas seulement rompu, mais l'homme et la pauvreté entrèrent dans une infidélité éternelle.

Quand on dit les anciens, au regard des temps modernes, il faut entendre ensemble et les anciens anciens et les anciens chrétiens. C'était le principe même de la sagesse antique que celui qui voulait sortir de sa condition les dieux le frappaient sans faute. Mais ils frappaient beaucoup moins généralement celui qui ne cherchait pas à s'élever au-dessus de sa condition. Il nous était réservé, il était réservé au temps moderne que l'homme fût frappé dans sa condition même.

Au regard du temps moderne l'antique et le chrétien vont ensemble, sont ensemble: les deux antiques, l'hébreu, le grec. Le chrétien était autrefois un antique. Jusqu'en 1880. Il faut aujourd'hui qu'il soit un moderne. Tels sont les commandements de ces gouvernements temporels. Telles sont les prises de ces saisons du monde. Il est indéniable que les mœurs chrétiennes elles-mêmes ont subi cette rétorsion profonde. Il nous était réservé d'inaugurer ce nouvel état. En somme la chrétienté avait peu à peu étendu au temporel cette parole que *qui s'abaisse sera élevé,* et que *qui s'élève sera abaissé.* Ainsi entendue, en ce sens, temporel, ce n'est pas seulement la parole de David, *Deposuit potentes; et exaltavit;* c'est presque la parole antique même. La parole d'Hésiode et d'Homère; et de Sophocle et d'Eschyle. Il nous était réservé d'inaugurer ce régime où celui qui ne s'élève pas est abaissé tout de même.

times, the ancient ancients and the ancient Christians must be understood together. It was the principle itself of ancient wisdom that the gods would unfailingly strike at the man who wished to rise above his station in life. But they struck far less generally at the man who did not attempt to rise above his station. It was reserved for us, it was reserved for modern times to see man smitten in his very station.

Seen with the eye of modern times, the ancient and the Christian fit together, belong together: the two antiquities, the Hebrew, the Greek. The Christian used to be an ancient. Until 1880. Today he has to be a modern. Such are the commandments of these temporal governments. Such are the powers of the world. It is undeniable that Christian ethics themselves have suffered this deep retortion. It was reserved for us to inaugurate this new state. In short, Christendom had little by little extended to the temporal order this saying that *he that humbleth himself shall be exalted* and that *whosoever exalteth himself shall be abased.* Thus understood, in this temporal sense, it is not only David's saying, *Deposuit potentes; et exaltavit;* it is almost the saying of antiquity itself. The saying of Hesiod and of Homer; and of Sophocles and of Æschylus. It was reserved for us to inaugurate this regime where he who does not exalt himself is all the same abased.

Retrancher, bannir de chrétienté la pauvreté, le travail, la famille, ces trois piliers de toute vie, quelle tentative de décomposition organique, de désorganisation, de démembrement.

C'est défaire le christianisme que d'en retirer la misère, la pauvreté, la maladie. Réciproquement et ensemble c'est défaire la misère, la pauvreté, la maladie, que d'en retirer la chrétienté, intérieure, le christianisme. Le christianisme est le grand régulateur, interne, de la misère, de la pauvreté, de la maladie. La misère, la pauvreté, la maladie est certainement un ressort, un grand régulateur interne du christianisme.

Notre socialisme était un socialisme mystique et un socialisme profond, profondément apparenté au christianisme, un tronc sorti de la vieille souche, littéralement déjà, (ou encore), une religion de la pauvreté.

To RETRENCH, to banish from Christendom poverty, work, family, those three pillars of all life: what an attempt of organic decomposition, disorganisation, dismemberment!

Christianity is undone if destitution, poverty, sickness are withdrawn from it. Reciprocally and together destitution, poverty and sickness are undone if Christendom, interior Christendom, Christianity are withdrawn from them. Christianity is the great regulator, the internal regulator of destitution, poverty, sickness. Destitution, poverty, sickness are surely a spring, a great internal regulator of Christianity.

OUR SOCIALISM was a mystic socialism and a profound socialism, profoundly related to Christianity, a trunk grown from the old roots, literally then (or as ever), a religion of poverty.

LE MONDE EST CONTRE NOUS

NOUS VIVONS EN un temps si barbare que quand on voit des hommes imprimer des textes propres sur un papier propre avec une encre propre tout le monde se récrie: *Faut-il qu'ils aient du temps à perdre! Et de l'argent!* Nous n'avons pas de temps, nous n'avons plus d'argent, nous n'avons que notre vie à perdre. Nous avons failli la perdre; et nous sommes exposés à recommencer.

Nous vivons en un temps si barbare que l'on confond le luxe avec la propreté. Quand un ouvrier essaye de travailler proprement, on l'inculpe de luxe. Et comme dans le même temps et de l'autre part le luxe et la richesse travaille toujours salement, il n'y a plus littéralement aucun joint par où la culture puisse ni se maintenir, ni essayer seulement de se réintroduire, ni seulement se défendre. Par où elle puisse passer.

Ceux qui n'ont pas d'argent font de la saleté sous le nom de

THE WORLD IS AGAINST US

WE LIVE IN such barbarous times that when someone prints clean texts on clean paper with clean ink, everyone exclaims: *He must indeed have time to lose! And money!* We have no time, we have no more money, we have only our life to lose. We have been near to losing it; and we may be called upon to risk it again.

We live in such barbarous times that luxury is confused with cleanliness. When a workman tries to work properly he is accused of being luxurious. And as at the same time, and on the other hand, luxury and wealth always work sloppily, literally there no longer exists any medium through which culture either could be maintained or even through which it might seek to revive itself or merely defend itself. Through which it could return.

Those who have no money work sloppily under the name of sabotage; and those who have money work sloppily, a

sabotage; et ceux qui ont de l'argent font de la saleté, une contre et autre saleté, sous le nom de luxe. Et ainsi la culture n'a plus aucun joint; où passer. Il n'y a plus cette merveilleuse rencontre de toutes les anciennes sociétés où celui qui produisait et celui qui achetait aimaient également et connaissaient la culture.—

Nous avons créé en dix ans une firme nouvelle,* presque universellement connue, très généralement estimée, très bien cotée, universellement respectée, nous l'avons faite et nous l'avons maintenue sans jamais avoir un sou devant nous. Tout homme qui a quelque expérience des réalités économiques saura, pourra mesurer ce que représente une telle entreprise, et que c'est une véritable gageure. Mais il saura aussi ce que coûte une telle gageure, et de la tenir pendant dix ans, et où se prend ce que l'on ne prend pas à l'argent, ce que l'on ne demande pas à l'argent, car il faut toujours que cela se prenne quelque part, et que ce qui ne coûte pas à l'argent, ce qui ne coûte pas en argent, se paie par un surmenage perpétuel, un risque de mort constant, des ravages irréparables de la santé.—

Que l'on ne s'abuse pas sur ce qui nous attend. Ni sur l'avenir prochain de nos cahiers, ni sur l'avenir prochain de ce pays. Dans cette barbarie, dans cette inculture croissante, dans ce désarroi des esprits et des mœurs, dans ce désastre de la culture, plus nos cahiers seront bons, moins ils auront accès auprès du grand public, auprès de ce que nous pouvons nommer le public, tout court.—

Ne nous félicitons pas. Nous sommes des vaincus. Le monde est contre nous.—Tout ce que nous avons soutenu, tout ce que nous avons défendu, les mœurs et les lois, le

* *Les Cahiers de la Quinzaine.*

counter and different sloppiness, under the name of luxury. And thus culture no longer has any medium; through which it might infiltrate. There no longer exists that marvelous unity true of all ancient societies, where he who produced and he who bought equally loved and knew culture.—

In ten years we have created a new firm,* almost universally known, very generally esteemed, very well rated, universally respected. We have created it and we have maintained it without ever having had a cent in reserve. Any man with some experience of economic realities will know, will be able to gauge the caliber of such an enterprise, and recognize it as a wager. But he will know too what such a wager costs, to be kept going for ten years, he will know that what is not taken out of money, what is not demanded of money, must always be derived somewheres: that for which there is no money, that which is not paid with money, must be paid for in the form of perpetual overwork, at the constant risk of life, in irreparable havoc to health.—

Let none deceive himself as to what lies ahead of us. Neither on the score of the near future of our "Cahiers" nor the near future of this country. In this state of barbarism, in this growing decay of culture, in this disorder of minds and morals, in this disaster of culture, the better our "Cahiers" are going to be, the less the access they will obtain to the general public, to what we might, in short, call the public.—

There is no cause for self-congratulation. We are defeated. The world is against us.—All that we have upheld, all that we have defended, morals and laws, seriousness and severity, principles and ideas, realities and comely language, cleanliness, probity of speech, probity of thought, justice and har-

* *Les Cahiers de la Quinzaine*—literally "*The Fortnightly Notebooks.*"

sérieux et la sévérité, les principes et les idées, les réalités et le beau langage, la propreté, la probité de langage, la probité de pensée, la justice et l'harmonie, la justesse, une certaine tenue, l'intelligence et le bon français, la révolution et notre ancien socialisme, la vérité, le droit, la simple entente, le bon travail, le bel ouvrage, tout ce que nous avons soutenu, tout ce que nous avons défendu recule de jour en jour devant une barbarie, devant une inculture croissantes, devant l'envahissement de la corruption politique et sociale.

Ne nous le dissimulons pas: nous sommes des vaincus. Depuis dix ans, depuis quinze ans nous n'avons jamais fait que perdre du terrain. Aujourd'hui, dans la décroissance, dans la déchéance des mœurs politiques et privées, nous sommes littéralement des assiégés. Nous sommes dans une place en état de siège et plus que de blocus et tout le plat pays est aux mains de l'ennemi.—

Nul aujourd'hui, nul homme vivant ne nie, nul ne conteste, nul ne songe même à se dissimuler qu'il y a un désordre; un désordre croissant et extrêmement inquiétant; non point en effet un désordre apparent, un trouble de fécondité, qui recouvre un ordre à venir, mais un réel désordre d'impuissance et de stérilité; nul ne nie plus ce désordre, le désarroi des esprits et des cœurs, la détresse qui vient, le désastre menaçant. Une débâcle.

C'est peut-être cette situation de désarroi et de détresse qui nous crée, plus impérieusement que jamais, le devoir de ne pas capituler. Il ne faut jamais capituler. Il le faut peut-être moins encore d'autant que la place est plus importante et plus isolée, et qu'elle est plus menacée et que justement le pays est au pouvoir de l'ennemi.

mony, accuracy, a certain dignity of demeanor, intelligence and good French, the revolution and our former socialism, truth, right, simple faith, good work, fine work, all that we have upheld, all that we have defended, falls back day by day before an increasing barbarism and decay of culture, before the invasion of political and social corruption.

No need to conceal this from ourselves: we are defeated. For ten years, for fifteen years, we have done nothing but lose ground. Today, in the decline, in the decay of political and private morals, literally we are beleaguered. We are in a place which is in a state of siege and more than blocaded and all the flat country is in the hands of the enemy.—

Today no one, no living man denies, no one contests, no one even dreams of concealing from himself that there is a disorder; a growing and extremely disquieting disorder; not indeed an apparent disorder, a state of fermentation which antecedes a coming order, but a real disorder of impotence and sterility; no one denies this disorder any longer, this confusion of minds and hearts, this coming distress, this menacing disaster. A debacle.

It is perhaps this condition of confusion and distress which, more imperiously than ever, makes it our duty not to surrender. One must never surrender. All the less since the position is so important and so isolated and so menaced and that precisely the country is in the hands of the enemy.

LA PROBITÉ

SUR LES ARRIVISMES temporels, de part et d'autre les jeux sont faits. Les âmes turpides vont aux turpitudes; les âmes serviles vont aux servitudes.

Les imbéciles vont à l'honnêteté.

Et ce qu'il y a de plus fort, c'est qu'ils en ont tellement le goût, les imbéciles, de l'honnêteté, de la vieille probité, qu'ils y restent.

Il est quelquefois difficile à l'arriviste d'arriver, parce qu'ils sont trop. Mais rien n'est aussi facile que de n'arriver pas, pourvu qu'on y mette un peu du sien. Parce qu'on n'est pas trop. Il y a ainsi de par le monde un certain nombre de jeunes gens, pas très nombreux,—des malins, alors, des gars particulièrement astucieux, des bonshommes à qui on n'en conte point; des vieux roublards, qui ont choisi la carrière de ne point réussir, la procession de ne point arriver. Ils entreront dans la carrière quand leurs aînés n'y seront plus. Ils n'auront pas besoin d'attendre aussi longtemps. Car leurs aînés et eux ils tiennent parfaitement dans la même carrière. On dit même qu'ils n'y sont point trop serrés, qu'ils s'y meuvent à l'aise, bonnement, sans haines et sans beaucoup de compétitions. Car, du moins après les récits des voyageurs, ce serait une carrière où on ne se bouscule pas.—

PROBITY

IN THE MATTER of the chase for worldly success, we have all picked our horses: The base souls have turned to baseness; the servile souls to servitude.

Idiots have turned to honesty.

And what is more wonderful, they have a taste for it, the idiots, such a taste for honesty, for old-fashioned probity, that they cleave to it.

It is sometimes difficult for the "climber" to climb to the top because there is so much competition. But nothing is as easy as not to climb to the top if only one takes a little trouble. For in this case one crowds no one. Thus throughout the world one finds a certain number of young men, not very numerous,—well, wily ones, particularly crafty lads, fellows who can't be taken in; old foxes who have chosen the career of non-success, the procession towards non-arrival. "*They will enter the career when their elders are no longer there.*" * Nor will they have to wait that long. For their elders and they themselves will find plenty of room in this same career. According to rumor they are not at all cramped there, in fact they move at ease there, quite comfortably, without hate and without very much competition. At least, according to the reports of travellers, it seems to be a career in which elbows are not required.—

** Quotation from one of the last verses of the Marseillaise.*

Quand un pauvre homme a la probité dans la peau, il est perdu. J'entends perdu pour les grandeurs. De toutes les tares qui s'attaquent aux os mêmes et aux moelles, celle-ci est peut-être encore la plus irrémissible et celle qui pardonne le moins. L'homme qui n'arrive pas, qui ne sait pas, comment s'y prendre, qui ne veut pas savoir, le type dans nos genres, l'imbécile enfin, le pur niais, *nidax vere simplex*, le bon homme sait très bien, sent très bien, depuis qu'il est venu au monde, et même avant, parce que son père et sa mère étaient d'honnêtes gens, que toute sa vie on lui fourrera les sales besognes. Ou du moins ces admirables petits métiers, tenus et tenants, pieux et modestes, que les grands de ce monde cotent comme de sales métiers. Il sait pertinemment que toute sa vie on lui fera éreinter les yeux à corriger des copies et des épreuves d'imprimerie.—

Mais il aime cela, cet homme. Il est si bête qu'il ne pense même pas à nommer cela probité, honnêteté, goût et passion de la liberté. Il exècre le mot même de pureté. Parce que de tous les sépulcres les sépulcres blanchis sont encore ceux qui lui paraissent les plus cimetières. C'est nous, les cuistres, qui nous amusons à donner à tout cela des noms de vertus. Avec notre manie de faire des catalogues et des index. Il n'a besoin ni de nos classements, ni de nos encouragements, ni de nos conseils. Tout ce qu'il sait, cet ignorant, c'est qu'il y a des démarches que les autres font tout le temps et qu'il ne fera jamais, pas même une fois, pas même un seul quart d'heure. Parce que ce quart d'heure lui resterait sur l'estomac, lui serait impossible à digérer.

Tout ce qu'il sait aussi, tout ce qu'il sait enfin, car il voit de loin, et au loin, il voit jusqu'au bout, c'est que sa vie sera telle, tout entière, et que telle sera sa mort.

When a poor man has probity in his blood, he is lost. I mean lost for grandeurs. Of all the blemishes which attack the bones themselves and the marrow, this one is perhaps of all the most irremissible and that most stubborn. The man who does not succeed, who does not know how to go about it, who does not want to know how, fellows of our kind, in short the idiot, the plain simpleton, *nidax vere simplex,* this good man knows very well, feels very keenly, since he came into the world, and even before it, because his father and mother were honest folk, that all his life he will get all the dirty jobs. Or at least, those admirable little jobs which are taken hold of and which themselves take hold, pious and modest jobs, which the great of this world rate as dirty jobs. He knows full well that all his life he will be obliged to ruin his eyes correcting manuscripts and proofs.—

But this man likes it. He is so stupid that he does not even think of calling this probity, honesty, taste and passion for liberty. He execrates the very word of purity. Because of all sepulchers, whited sepulchers are those which remind him most of cemeteries. It is we, filthy pedants, who love to play at giving all this the names of virtues. With our mania for catalogues and indexes. That man needs neither our classifications, our encouragements, or our advice. All that he knows, this ignorant fellow, is that there are strings to be pulled which others pull all the time and that he will never pull, not even once, not even for a short quarter of an hour. Because this quarter of an hour would weigh on his stomach, would be impossible for him to digest.

All that he knows too, all that he finally knows, for he sees into the distance and far away, he sees to the end, is, that so his life will be, now and always, and that so will be his death.

SAVOIR ET CROIRE

UN PHILOSOPHE sur son lit de mort disait récemment au plus fidèle de ses disciples, qui a recueilli pour nous ce propos; parvenu à un âge avancé, quelques instants avant l'instant de sa mort ce philosophe disait sensiblement: *Je sais que je vais mourir, mais je ne le crois pas.* Il entendait sans doute par ces mots, autant que l'on peut expliquer, par l'analyse, des paroles aussi profondes et aussi justes, il entendait sans doute par ces mots qu'il connaissait, qu'il prévoyait, qu'il préconnaissait sa prochaine mort d'une pleine connaissance intellectuelle, historique et scientifique, impliquant une certitude historique et scientifique indiscutable, mais qu'il ne la préconnaissait pas, qu'il ne pressentait pas sa propre prochaine mort d'une connaissance organique intérieure. On sait sa mort, on ne la croit pas, ou on n'y croit pas. C'est je crois l'un des mots les plus profonds que l'on ait prononcé depuis qu'il y a la mort. Et il y a longtemps qu'il y a la mort. C'est

TO KNOW AND TO BELIEVE

A PHILOSOPHER on his deathbed recently said to the most faithful of his disciples, who made a note of his words for us. Having arrived at an advanced age this philosopher, a few moments before the moment of his death said approximately this: *"I know that I am going to die, but I do not believe it."* No doubt he meant by these words, as far as one can explain through analysis words so profound and so true, he meant no doubt by these words that he knew, that he foresaw, that he foreknew his approaching death with a full intellectual, historical and scientific knowledge, implying an unquestionable historical and scientific certainty, but that he did not foreknow, that he did not foresee his own approaching death with an interior organic knowledge. One knows one's death, one does not believe it, or one does not believe in it. This, I think, is one of the most profound remarks that has ever been pronounced since death came into the world. And death has

un mot si profond, et qui atteint si profondément aux plus profondes et plus essentielles sources sentimentales qu'il ne s'applique pas seulement à la mort, qu'il n'est pas vrai seulement de la mort, mais qu'il est vrai de tout ce qui est du même degré de profondeur que la mort, du même ordre de grandeur que la vie et la mort; il n'est pas vrai seulement de la probité, qui est une vertu de race, et dont les improbes ne peuvent avoir même aucune idée organique; il est vrai surtout de la misère, qui est si profondément apparentée à la mort, étant très exactement ce que dit la formule très rare de l'Antigone grecque: une mort vivante.

Celui qui n'a pas été tenté, dans la misère, ne sait pas ce que c'est que la misère et que la tentation, et par suite il ne sait pas ce que c'est que la probité, ce que c'est que d'être honnête. Ou pour parler tout à fait exactement et nous en tenir en toute rigueur au mot que nous avons rapporté, il peut le savoir, mais il ne fait que de le savoir: il ne le croit pas et il n'y croit pas.

Le génie exige la patience à travailler—et plus je vais, citoyen, moins je crois à l'efficacité des soudaines illuminations qui ne seraient pas accompagnées ou soutenues par un travail sérieux, moins je crois à l'efficacité des conversions extraordinaires soudaines et merveilleuses, à l'efficacité des passions, soudaines,—et plus je crois à l'efficacité du travail modeste, lent, moléculaire, définitif.

Plus je vais—moins je crois à l'efficacité d'une révolution sociale et extraordinaire soudaine, improvisée merveilleuse, avec ou sans fusils et dictature impersonnelle,—et plus je crois à l'efficacité d'un travail social modeste, lent, moléculaire, définitif.

been in the world for a long while. This is a remark so profound, and one which reaches so profoundly to the most profound and the most essential sentimental springs, that it does not apply to death alone, that it is not true of death alone, but is true of all things which are of the same degree of profundity as death, of the same order of greatness as life and death. It is not true of probity only, which is a virtue of race and of which the dishonest cannot have the least organic idea. It is true above all of destitution which is so closely related to death, being very exactly what the very rare expression of the Greek Antigone has indicated: a living death.

He who has not been tempted, in destitution, does not know what destitution and temptation are; and consequently he does not know what probity is, what it is to be honest. Or to speak quite exactly and to adhere strictly to the remark that we have reported, he can know it, but he does nothing but know it: he does not believe it and he does not believe in it.

GENIUS EXACTS the patience to work—and the longer I live, citizen, the less I believe in the efficiency of sudden illuminations that are not accompanied or supported by serious work, the less I believe in the efficiency of conversions, extraordinary, sudden and marvelous, in the efficiency of sudden passions,—and the more I believe in the efficiency of modest, slow, molecular, definitive work.

The longer I live—the less I believe in the efficiency of an extraordinary sudden social revolution, improvised, marvelous, with or without guns and impersonal dictatorship—and the more I believe in the efficiency of modest, slow, molecular, definitive social work.

LA RÉPUBLIQUE

JE SUIS ÉPOUVANTÉ quand je vois combien nos jeunes gens sont devenus étrangers à tout ce qui fut la pensée même et la mystique républicaine. Cela se voit surtout à ce que des pensées qui étaient pour nous des pensées sont devenues pour eux des idées, à ce qui était pour nous organique est devenu pour eux logique.—Quand un régime d'organique est devenu logique, et de vivant historique, c'est un régime qui est par terre.

On prouve, on démontre aujourd'hui la République. Quand elle était vivante on ne la prouvait pas.

On la vivait. Quand un régime se démontre, aisément, commodément, victorieusement, c'est qu'il est creux, c'est qu'il est par terre.

—Qu'importe, nous disent les politiciens, professionnels. Qu'est-ce que ça nous fait, répondent les politiciens, qu'est-ce que ça peut nous faire. Nous avons de très bons préfets. Alors qu'est-ce que ça peut nous faire. Ça marche très bien. Nous ne sommes plus républicains, c'est vrai, mais nous savons gouverner. Nous savons même mieux gouverner, beaucoup mieux que quand nous étions républicains. Nous avons désappris la République, mais nous avons appris de gouverner. Voyez les élections. Elles sont bonnes. Elles sont toujours bonnes. Elles

THE REPUBLIC

I AM APPALLED when I see how estranged our young men have become from all that was republican thought and its mysticism. This is made plain above all by the fact that the thoughts which for us were thoughts have become ideas for them, that what was organic for us has become logic for them. —When a regime which was organic becomes logical, and after being alive has become historical, it is a regime that has caved in.

Today, the Republic is a matter of proof, of demonstration. While it was alive one did not have to prove it.

One lived it. When a regime can be demonstrated easily, commodiously, victoriously, one knows that it is hollow, that it has caved in.

"What does it matter," professional politicians tell us. "What does it matter to us," answer the politicians, "what can it matter to us. We have very good prefects. So what can it matter to us. It all works admirably. We are no longer republicans, true, but we know how to govern. We even know how to govern better, far better than we did when we were republicans. We have unlearnt the Republic but we have learnt how to govern. See the elections. They are admirable. They are always admirable. They will improve. They will become

seront meilleures. Elles seront d'autant meilleures que c'est nous qui les faisons. Et que nous commençons à savoir les faire. —Le gouvernement fait les élections, les élections font le gouvernement. C'est un prêté rendu. Le gouvernement fait les électeurs. Les électeurs font le gouvernement. Le gouvernement fait les députés. Les députés font le gouvernement. On est gentil. Les populations regardent. Le pays est prié de payer. Le gouvernement fait la Chambre. La Chambre fait le gouvernement. Ce n'est point un cercle vicieux, comme vous pourriez le croire. Il n'est point du tout vicieux. C'est un cercle, tout court, un circuit fermé, un cercle fermé. Tous les cercles sont fermés. Autrement ça ne serait pas des cercles. Ce n'est pas tout à fait ce que nos fondateurs avaient prévu. Mais nos fondateurs ne s'en tiraient pas déjà si bien. Et puis enfin on ne peut pas fonder toujours. Ça fatiguerait. La preuve que ça dure, la preuve que ça tient, c'est que ça dure déjà depuis quarante ans. Il y en a pour quarante siècles. C'est les premiers quarante ans qui sont les plus durs. C'est le premier quarante ans qui coûte. Après on est habitué. Un pays, un régime n'a pas besoin de vous, il n'a pas besoin de mystiques, de mystique, de sa mystique. Ce serait plutôt embarrassant. Pour un aussi grand voyage, il a besoin d'une bonne politique, c'est-à-dire d'une politique bien gouvernementale.

Ils se trompent. Ces politiciens se trompent. Du haut de cette République quarante siècles (d'avenir) ne les contemplent pas. Si la République marche depuis quarante ans, c'est parce que tout marche depuis quarante ans. Si la République est solide en France, ce n'est pas parce que la République est solide en France, c'est parce que tout est solide partout. Il y a dans l'histoire moderne,—il y a pour les peuples modernes

all the better, since it is we who make them. And since we are beginning to know how to make them.—The government makes the elections, the elections make the government. It is give and take. The government makes the electors. The electors make the government. The government makes the deputies. The deputies make the government. All oblige. The populations look on. The country is requested to pay. The government makes the Chamber. The Chamber makes the government. This is not a vicious circle, as you might believe. It is not in the least vicious. It is a circle, just that, a closed circuit, a closed circle. All circles are closed. Otherwise they would not be circles. This is not quite what our founders had foreseen. But our founders did not manage so magnificently at that. And then after all one cannot go on founding for ever. It would be tiring. The proof that the Republic lasts, the proof that it endures is that it has already lasted forty years. It can go on for forty centuries. The first forty years are the most difficult ones. It is the first forty years that are hard. After that, one becomes inured. A country, a regime does not need you, it does not need mystics, a mystical doctrine, a mystical doctrine of its own. Such would be rather encumbering. For so great a journey, a good policy is required, that is to say a decidedly governmental policy.

They are mistaken. These politicians are mistaken. From the heights of the Republic forty centuries (of future) do not look down on them.* If the Republic has functioned for the last forty years, it is because everything has functioned dur-

* *Quotation from one of Napoleon's proclamations to his army during the Egyptian campaign: "Soldiers, from the heights of the Pyramids, forty centuries look down on you."*

de grandes vagues de crises, généralement parties de France, (1789–1815, 1830, 1848) qui font tout trembler d'un bout du monde à l'autre bout. Et il y a des paliers, plus ou moins longs, des calmes, des bonaces qui apaisent tout pour un temps plus ou moins long. Il y a les *époques* et il y a les *périodes*. Nous sommes dans une période. Si la République est assise, ce n'est point parce qu'elle est la République, ce n'est point par sa vertu propre, c'est parce qu'elle est, parce que nous sommes dans une période, d'assiette. La durée de la République ne prouve pas plus la durée de la République que la durée des monarchies voisines ne prouve la durée de la Monarchie. Cette durée ne signifie point qu'elles sont durables, mais qu'elles ont commencé, qu'elles sont dans une période, durable. Elles sont contemporaines, elles trempent dans le même temps, dans le même bain de durée. Elles baignent dans la même période. Elles sont du même âge. Voilà tout ce que ça prouve.

Dans la République, qui dure, ce n'est point la République, qui dure. C'est la durée. Ce n'est point le régime qui dure en elle. Mais en elle c'est le temps qui dure. C'est la tranquillité d'une certaine période de l'humanité.—

Ils croient aux régimes, et qu'un régime fait ou ne fait pas la paix et la guerre, la force et la vertu, la santé et la maladie, l'assiette, la durée, la tranquillité d'un peuple. La force d'une race. C'est comme si l'on croyait que les châteaux de la Loire font ou ne font pas les tremblements de terre.

Nous croyons au contraire qu'il y a des forces et des réalités infiniment plus profondes, et que ce sont les peuples au contraire qui font la force et la faiblesse des régimes; et beaucoup moins les régimes, des peuples.—Nous croyons au contraire que ce sont les peuples qui font les régimes, la paix et

ing the last forty years. If the Republic is well-established in France, it is not because the Republic is well-established in France, it is because everything is well-established everywhere. There is in modern history,—there are for modern peoples great waves of crisis, generally originating in France, (1789–1815, 1830, 1848) which cause everything to quake from one end of the world to the other. And there are stages, more or less long, periods of dead calm, lulls which pacify all things for more or less long stretches of time. There are *epochs* and there are *periods*. We are in a period. If the Republic is solidly seated, it is not because it is the Republic, it is not because of its own virtue, it is because it exists, it is because we exist in a period, of safe seatings. The duration of the Republic no more proves the durability of the Republic than the duration of neighboring monarchies proves the durability of Monarchy. This duration does not signify that they are durable, but that they have begun, that they are in a period, in a durable period. They are contemporaneous, they are steeped in the same kind of time, in the same bath of duration. They bathe in the same period. They are coeval. That is all that this proves.

In the Republic that lasts, it is not the Republic that lasts. It is duration. It is not the regime that lasts in it. But it is time that lasts in it. It is the tranquillity of a certain period of humanity.—

They believe in regimes and that a regime makes or does not make peace and war, strength and virtue, health and illness, the safe establishment, the duration, the tranquillity of a people. The strength of a race. It is as though one believed that the châteaux of the Loire cause or do not cause earthquakes.

la guerre, la force et la faiblesse, la maladie et la santé des régimes.

La seule valeur, la seule force du royalisme, la seule force d'une monarchie traditionnelle, c'est que le roi est plus ou moins aimé. La seule force de la République, c'est que la République est plus ou moins aimée. La seule force, la seule valeur, la seule dignité de tout, c'est d'être aimé. Que tant d'hommes aient tant vécu et tant souffert pour la République, qu'ils aient tant crû en elle, qu'ils soient tant morts pour elle, que pour elle ils aient supporté tant d'épreuves, souvent extrêmes, voilà ce qui compte, voilà ce qui m'intéresse, voilà ce qui existe. Voilà ce qui fonde, voilà ce qui fait la légitimité d'un régime.

ON NOUS PARLE TOUJOURS de la dégradation républicaine. Quand on voit ce que la politique cléricale a fait de la mystique chrétienne, comment s'étonner de ce que la politique radicale a fait de la mystique républicaine. Quand on voit ce que les clercs ont fait généralement des saints, comment s'étonner de ce que nos parlementaires ont fait des héros. Quand on voit ce que les réactionnaires ont fait de la sainteté, comment s'étonner de ce que les révolutionnaires ont fait de l'héroïsme.

LES FONDATEURS viennent d'abord. Les profiteurs viennent ensuite.

We believe on the contrary that there are forces and realities infinitely more profound, and that it is the peoples, on the contrary, that make the strength and the weakness of regimes; and far less the regimes who make those of the peoples.—We believe, on the contrary, that it is the peoples that make the regimes, peace and war, strength and weakness, the illness and the health of regimes.

The sole value, the sole strength of royalism, the sole strength of a traditional monarchy is that the king is more or less loved. The sole strength of the Republic is that the Republic is more or less loved. The sole value, the sole strength, the sole dignity of everything is to be loved. That so many men should have lived so much and suffered so much for the Republic, that they should have believed in it so much, that so many should have died for it, that they should have endured so many trials, often extreme, that is what interests me, that is what is real. That is what founds, that is what creates the legitimacy of a regime.

WE ARE ALWAYS being told of the republican degradation. When one sees what clerical policy has made of the Christian mystical doctrine, how can one be surprised by what radical policy has made of republican mystical doctrine. When one sees what the clerics have generally made of saints, how can one be surprised by what our parliamentaries have made of heroes. When one sees what reactionaries have made of holiness, how can one be surprised by what revolutionaries have made of heroism.

FOUNDERS come first. Profiteers come after.

NOUS SOMMES DES VAINCUS

NOUS SOMMES DES VAINCUS. Nous le sommes même tellement, si complètement, que je ne sais pas si l'histoire aura jamais enregistré un exemple comme celui que nous fournissons. Je ne sais pas si la même histoire—aura jamais connu des vaincus comme nous, battus comme nous, non pas honteux certes, mais honteusement battus; non pas d'une défaite qui apporte la gloire, à qui vont les suprêmes honneurs, —mais d'une défaite la plus mal venue que l'on puisse imaginer; la plus disgracieuse, et disgraciée, la plus petites gens que l'on ait jamais pu faire et que l'on ait jamais faite et réussi à faire. Être vaincus, ce n'est rien. Ce ne serait rien. Ça peut même être beaucoup au contraire. Ça peut être tout; le suprême. Être vaincu n'est rien: (mais) nous avons été battus. Nous avons même été rossés. En quelques années la société, cette société moderne, avant que nous ayons même eu le temps d'en esquisser la critique, est tombée à un état de décomposition tel, à une dissolution telle que je crois, que je suis assuré que jamais l'histoire n'avait rien vu de comparable. Je ne crois pas que l'égoïsme notamment et les préoccupations de l'intérêt soient jamais tombés à ce degré de

WE ARE DEFEATED

WE ARE DEFEATED. We are defeated to such an extent, so completely, that I doubt whether history will ever have to record an instance of defeat such as the one we furnish. I do not know whether history will have ever known men as defeated as we are, beaten as we are, not shamed indeed, but shamefully beaten. Not by a defeat which brings glory, to which supreme honors go,—but by the most stunted, ill-grown defeat than can be imagined; the most uncouth and ill-favored, the most vulgar which one has ever been able to achieve and which has ever been achieved and successfully achieved. To be defeated, that is nothing. It would be nothing. On the contrary it can be a great thing. It can be all: the final consummation. To be defeated is nothing: (but) we have been beaten. We have even been given a drubbing. In a few years, society, this modern society, before we have even had the time to sketch the critique of it, has fallen into a state of decomposition, such, into a dissolution, such, that I believe, that I am assured that history had never seen anything comparable. I do not believe that selfishness in particular and the preoccupations of self-interest have ever fallen to a like de-

bassesse. Cette grande décomposition historique, cette grande dissolution, ce grand précédent que nous nommons littérairement la pourriture de la décadence romaine, la dissolution de l'empire romain, et qu'il suffit de nommer avec Sorel, *la ruine du monde antique,* n'était rien en comparaison de la dissolution de la société présente, en comparaison de la dissolution et de la déchéance de cette société, de la présente société moderne. Il y avait sans doute alors beaucoup plus de crimes et encore un peu plus de vice(s). Mais il y avait aussi infiniment plus de ressources. Cette pourriture était pleine de germes. Ils n'avaient pas cette sorte de promesses de stérilités que nous avons aujourd'hui, si l'on peut dire, si ces deux mots peuvent aller ensemble.

Nous sommes des vaincus. Je crois, je suis assuré que jamais l'histoire n'a enregistré, n'a eu à enregistrer des vaincus comme nous, des vaincus autant que nous. En moins de cent vingt ans l'œuvre non pas de la Révolution française, mais le résultat de l'avortement de la Révolution française et de l'œuvre de la Révolution française sous les coups, sous la pesée, sous la poussée de la réaction, de la barbarie universelle est littéralement anéantie. Complètement. Et non seulement il n'en reste plus rien. Ni traces de rien. Mais nulles traces de promesses même, ni d'aucune fécondité ultérieure.

TOUT N'EST POINT PERDU, il s'en faut, avec un athéisme révolutionnaire. Des charités malentendues, des flambées de charité peuvent y brûler détournées, qui quelque jour seront reconduites. Mais il n'y a rien à faire avec un athéisme réactionnaire, avec un athéisme bourgeois. Il n'y a rien à attendre, il ne faut rien espérer d'un athéisme réactionnaire, d'un athéisme bourgeois. C'est un athéisme sans étincelle, qui ne

gree of baseness. That great historical decomposition, that great dissolution, that great precedent which in a literary manner we call the decay of the Roman decadence, the dissolution of the Roman Empire and which it suffices to call, with Sorel, *the ruin of the ancient world,* was nothing by comparison with the dissolution of present society, by comparison with the dissolution and degradation of this society, of the present modern society. Doubtless, at that time there were far more crimes and still more vice(s). But there were also infinitely more resources. This putrefaction was full of seeds. People at that time did not have this sort of promise of sterility, which we have today, if one may say so, if these two words can be used together.

We are defeated. I believe, I am assured, that history has never recorded, has never had to record such defeated men as we, men defeated as much as we are. In less than a hundred and twenty years, the work not of the French Revolution, but the result of the abortion of the French Revolution and the work of the French Revolution is literally annihilated under the blows, under the weight, under the thrusts forward of the reaction, of universal barbarism. Completely. And not only nothing remains of it. No traces of anything. But no traces of promises even, nor of any fruitfulness to come.

ALL IS NOT LOST, far from it, in the case of revolutionary atheism. Mistaken charities, flames of charity can burn deflected there, which some day will be led back to the right place. But there is nothing to be done with a reactionary atheism, with a bourgeois atheism. There is nothing to be expected, nothing must be hoped from, a reactionary atheism, from a bourgeois atheism. It is atheism without a spark, which

s'allumera, qui ne flambera jamais. C'est un athéisme sans charité, et même sans imitation ni contrefaçon de charité. C'est donc un athéisme sans espérance. L'espérance ne peut jouer que dans un certain minimum de charité. L'espérance, la lueur d'espérance ne peut s'allumer que d'un certain feu. De l'athéisme réactionnaire, de l'athéisme bourgeois on ne peut rien attendre que cendre et que poussière, parce que tout n'y est que mort et que cendre.

LE MONDE MODERNE AVILIT. D'autres mondes avaient d'autres occupations. D'autres mondes avaient d'autres arrière-pensées, d'autres arrières-intentions. D'autres mondes avaient d'autres emplois du temps temporel, entre les repas. Le monde moderne avilit. D'autres mondes idéalisaient ou matérialisaient, bâtissaient ou démolissaient, faisaient de la justice ou faisaient de la force, d'autres mondes faisaient des cités, des communautés, des hommes ou des dieux. Le monde moderne avilit. C'est sa spécialité. Je dirais presque que c'est son métier, s'il ne fallait point respecter au-dessus de tout ce beau nom de métier. Quand le monde moderne avilit, mettons que c'est alors qu'il travaille de sa partie.

Le monde moderne avilit. Il avilit la cité; il avilit l'homme. Il avilit l'amour; il avilit la femme. Il avilit la race; il avilit l'enfant. Il avilit la nation; il avilit la famille. Il avilit même, (toujours nos limites) il a réussi à avilir ce qu'il y a peut-être de plus difficile à avilir au monde, parce que c'est quelque chose qui a en soi, comme dans sa texture, une sorte particulière de dignité, comme une incapacité singulière d'être avili: il avilit la mort.

will never be kindled, which will never blaze. It is atheism without charity and without even an imitation or counterfeit of charity. It is therefore hopeless atheism. Hope can move freely only with a certain minimal amount of charity. Hope, the gleam of hope, can be lighted only with a certain fire. From reactionary atheism, from bourgeois atheism, one can expect nothing but ashes and dust, because there all is death and ashes.

THE MODERN WORLD DEBASES. Other worlds had other occupations. Other worlds had other ulterior motives and other ulterior intentions. Other worlds had other temporal pastimes, between meals. The modern world debases. Other worlds idealized or materialized, built or demolished, meted out justice or exercised force, other worlds created cities, communities, men or gods . . . The modern world debases. This is its specialty. I would almost say that this is its calling if the beautiful word calling were not above all to be respected. When the modern world debases, let us admit that then it is at its own work.

The modern world debases. It debases the state; it debases man. It debases love; it debases woman. It debases the race; it debases the child. It debases the nation; it debases the family. It even debases (always our limitations), it has succeeded in debasing what is perhaps most difficult in the world to debase, because this is something which has in itself, as in its texture, a particular kind of dignity, like a singular incapacity for degradation: it debases death.

L'AFFAIRE DREYFUS

J'ESSAIERAI DE DONNER une représentation de ce que fut dans la réalité cette immortelle affaire Dreyfus. Elle fut, comme toute affaire qui se respecte, une affaire essentiellement mystique. Elle vivait de sa mystique. Elle est morte de sa politique. C'est la loi, c'est la règle. *C'est le niveau des vies*. Tout parti vit de sa mystique et meurt de sa politique.—

Notre dreyfusisme était une religion, je prends le mot dans son sens le plus littéralement exact, une poussée religieuse, une crise religieuse, et je conseillerais même vivement à quiconque voudrait étudier, connaître un mouvement religieux dans les temps modernes—de saisir cet exemple unique. J'ajoute que pour nous, chez nous, en nous ce mouvement religieux était d'essence chrétienne, d'origine chrétienne, qu'il

The Dreyfus case, originally fought by the left against the right as a battle for justice against tyranny and prejudice, led to the victory of the socialist party, carried to political power on the crest of popular sentiment stirred up by the case. Péguy had been one of the most ardent and active "Dreyfusists." When, however, the socialist party, under the leadership of Emile Combes, used its triumph for the establishment of its own system of intolerance and injustice, inaugurated police supervision, denunciation (the famous fiches), and a violent battle against the Catholic Church, Péguy was deeply disillusioned. Jaurès, leader of the French socialist party and his former friend, he now bitterly reproached with having succumbed to Combes' political demagogy.

THE DREYFUS CASE

I SHALL ATTEMPT an exposition of what this immortal Dreyfus case in reality was. It was, like every self-respecting affair, essentially a mystical affair. It lived by its mystical doctrine. It died of its politics. That is the law, that is the rule. *That is the level of lives.* Every party lives by its mystical doctrine and dies of its politics.—

Our Dreyfusism was a religion. I use the word in its most literally exact meaning. It was a religious urge, a religious crisis—and I should even strongly advise anyone who would wish to study, to understand a religious movement in modern times—to take hold of this unique example. I add that for us, in our hearts, in us this religious movement was of Christian essence, of Christian origin, that it grew from the Christian

poussait de souche chrétienne, qu'il coulait de l'antique source.—La Justice et la Vérité que nous avons tant aimées, à qui nous avons donné tout, notre jeunesse, tout, à qui nous nous sommes donnés tout entiers pendant tout le temps de notre jeunesse n'étaient point des justices et des vérités mortes, elles n'étaient point des justices et des vérités de livres et de bibliothèques, elles n'étaient point des justices et des vérités conceptuelles, intellectuelles—mais elles étaient organiques, elles étaient chrétiennes, elles n'étaient nullement modernes, elles étaient éternelles et non point temporelles seulement.—Et de tous les sentiments qui ensemble nous poussèrent, dans un tremblement, dans cette crise unique, aujourd'hui nous pouvons avouer que de toutes les passions qui nous poussèrent dans cette ardeur et dans ce bouillonnement, dans ce gonflement et dans ce tumulte, une vertu était au cœur, et que c'était la vertu de charité.—

Nous fûmes des héros. Il faut le dire très simplement, car je crois bien qu'on ne le dira pas pour nous. Voici très exactement en quoi et pourquoi nous fûmes des héros. Dans tout le monde où nous circulions, où nous opérions, où nous croissions encore et où nous achevions de nous former, la question qui se posait, pendant ces deux ou trois années de cette courbe montante, n'était nullement de savoir si *en réalité* Dreyfus était innocent (ou coupable). C'était de savoir si on aurait le courage de le reconnaître, de le déclarer innocent. De le manifester innocent. C'était de savoir si on aurait le double courage. Premièrement le premier courage, le courage extérieur, le grossier courage, déjà difficile, le courage social, public de le manifester innocent dans le monde, aux yeux du public, de témoigner pour lui publiquement. De risquer là-dessus, de *mettre* sur lui tout ce que l'on avait, tout un argent

root, that it flowed from the ancient spring.—The Justice and the Truth that we have so much loved, to which we have given everything, our youth, everything, to which we have given ourselves utterly during the whole time of our youth were not lifeless justices and truths, they were not the justices and truths of books and of libraries, they were not conceptual, intellectual justices and truths—but they were organic, they were Christian, they were not at all modern, they were eternal and not temporal merely.—And of all the sentiments which together urged us, in a state of trepidation, in this unique crisis, today we can own that of all the passions which urged us into this ardor and into this effervescence, into this dilatation and into this tumult, one virtue was at the heart of them, and that was the virtue of charity.—

We were heroes. It must be stated very simply for I do believe that no one will say it for us. Very exactly this is why and in what respect we were heroes. Everywhere in the world around us, everywhere we moved, everywhere we acted, where we still grew and where we were completing our formation, the question during the two or three years of that ascending curve was not at all to know whether *in reality* Dreyfus was innocent (or guilty). It was to know whether one would have the courage to recognize him, to declare him innocent. To proclaim him innocent. It was to know whether one would have the two-fold courage. Firstly the first courage, the exterior courage, the already difficult gross courage, the social courage, the public courage to proclaim him innocent to the world, before the eyes of the public, publicly to testify in his favor. To wager on him, to risk on him everything that one had, the whole of painfully, poorly earned money, all the money of the poor and the wretched, all the money of small people, of

misérablement gagné, tout un argent de pauvre et de misérable, tout un argent de petites gens, de misère et de pauvreté; tout le temps, toute la vie, toute la carrière; toute la santé, tout le corps et toute l'âme; la ruine du corps, toutes les ruines, la rupture du cœur, la dislocation des familles, le reniement des proches, le détournement (des regards) des yeux, la réprobation muette ou forcenée, muette et forcenée, l'isolement, toutes les quarantaines; la rupture d'amitiés de vingt ans, c'est-à-dire, pour nous d'amitiés commencées depuis toujours. Toute la vie sociale. Toute la vie du cœur, enfin tout. Deuxièmement le deuxième courage, plus difficile, le courage intérieur, le courage secret, s'avouer à soi-même en soi-même qu'il était innocent. Renoncer pour cet homme à la paix du cœur.

Non plus seulement à la paix de la cité, à la paix du foyer. À la paix de la famille, à la paix du ménage. Mais à la paix du cœur.

Au premier des biens, au seul bien.

Le courage d'entrer pour cet homme dans le royaume d'une incurable inquiétude.

Et d'une amertume qui ne se guérira jamais.

Nos adversaires ne sauront jamais, nos ennemis ne pouvaient pas savoir ce que nous avons sacrifié à cet homme, et de quel cœur nous l'avons sacrifié. Nous lui avons sacrifié notre vie entière, puisque cette affaire nous a marqués pour la vie. Nos ennemis ne sauront jamais, nous qui avons bouleversé, retourné ce pays nos ennemis ne sauront jamais combien peu nous étions, et dans quelles conditions nous nous battions, dans quelles conditions ingrates, précaires, dans quelles conditions de misère et de précarité.—Nous étions, une fois de plus nous fûmes cette poignée de Français qui

misery and of poverty. One's whole time, one's whole life, one's whole career; one's whole health, one's whole body, one's whole soul; the ruin of the body, all the ruins, heart-break, the dislocation of families, the disavowal of intimates, the turning-away (of glances) of eyes, the mute or furious reprobation, mute and furious, isolation, quarantines of every kind. The breaking of friendships of twenty years standing, that is, for us, of immemorial friendships. The whole of social life. The whole life of the heart, in short, everything. Secondly the more difficult second courage, the inner courage, the secret courage of owning to oneself within oneself that he was innocent. To renounce for the sake of this man the peace of the heart.

Not only the peace of the city, the peace of the hearth. The peace of the family, the peace of wedlock. But the peace of heart.

The first of treasures, the only treasure.

The courage to enter for the sake of this man into the kingdom of incurable unrest.

And of a bitterness which never will be cured.

Our opponents will never know, our enemies could not know all that we have sacrificed for the sake of this man, and with what a heart we have sacrificed it. For him we have sacrificed our entire life, since this case has marked us for life. Our enemies will never know, we who have upset, turned this country upside down, our enemies will never know how few we were and under what circumstances we fought, under what thankless, precarious circumstances, under what circumstances of misery and precariousness.—We were, once more we were that handful of Frenchmen, who, under a withering

sous un feu écrasant enfoncent des masses, conduisent un assaut, enlèvent une position.—

Non seulement nous fûmes des héros, mais l'affaire Dreyfus au fond ne peut s'expliquer que par ce besoin d'héroïsme qui saisit périodiquement ce peuple, cette race, par un besoin d'héroïsme qui alors nous saisit nous toute une génération. Il en est de ces grands mouvements, de ces grandes épreuves de tout un peuple comme de ces autres grandes épreuves les guerres. Ou plutôt il n'y a pour les peuples qu'une sorte de grandes épreuves temporelles, qui sont les guerres, et ces grandes épreuves-ci sont elles-mêmes des guerres. Dans toutes ces grandes épreuves, dans toutes ces grandes histoires c'est beaucoup plutôt la force intérieure, la violence d'éruption qui fait la matière, historique, que ce n'est la matière qui fait et qui impose l'épreuve. Quand une grande guerre éclate, une grande révolution, cette sorte de guerre, c'est qu'un grand peuple, une grande race a besoin de sortir; qu'elle en a assez; notamment qu'elle en a assez de la paix. C'est toujours qu'une grande masse éprouve un violent besoin, un grand, un profond besoin, un besoin mystérieux d'un grand mouvement.—Un mystérieux besoin d'une inscription. Historique. Un mystérieux besoin d'une sorte de fécondité historique. Un mystérieux besoin d'inscrire une grande histoire dans l'histoire éternelle. Toute autre explication est vaine, raisonnable, rationnelle, inféconde, irréelle. De même notre affaire Dreyfus ne peut s'expliquer que par un besoin, le même, par un besoin d'héroïsme qui saisit toute une génération, la nôtre, par un besoin de guerre, de guerre *militaire*, et de gloire militaire, par un besoin de sacrifice et jusque de martyre, peut-être (sans doute), par un besoin de sainteté.—

fire, effect a breach in the line, lead an attack, capture a position.—

Not only we were heroes but, at bottom, the Dreyfus case can only be explained by that need of heroism which periodically seizes this people, this race, by a need of heroism which seized us then, us, an entire generation. These great movements, these great trials of an entire people are of one stuff with those other great trials: wars. Or rather, there exists for peoples only one kind of great temporal trial, which is war, and these great trials in themselves are wars. In all these great trials, in all these great emergencies, it is far more the inner strength, the violence of eruption which make the substance of history than it is the substance which creates and imposes the trial. When a great war breaks out, a great revolution, that other kind of war, the reason is that a great people, a great race has an impulse to break out; that it is fed up; namely that it has had enough of peace. It always means that a great mass feels a violent need, a great, profound need, a mysterious need for a great movement.—A mysterious need of making history. A mysterious need of a kind of historical fertility. A mysterious need to inscribe a great story in eternal history. All other explanation is vain, reasonable, rational, unfruitful, unreal. In the same way our Dreyfus case can be explained only by a need, the same, by a need for heroism which takes hold of a whole generation, ours, by a need for war, for *military* war and for military glory, by a need of sacrifice and even martyrdom, perhaps, (no doubt), by a need of sanctity.—If we were, once more, an army of lions led by asses, then it is that we remained very precisely in the purest French tradition.

Si nous avons été, une fois de plus, une armée de lions conduite par des ânes, c'est alors que nous sommes demeurés, très exactement, dans la plus pure tradition française.

En réalité la véritable situation des gens que nous avions devant nous était pendant longtemps non pas de dire et de croire Dreyfus coupable, mais de croire et de dire qu'innocent ou coupable on ne troublait pas, on ne bouleversait pas, on ne *compromettait* pas, on ne risquait pas pour un homme, pour un seul homme, la vie et le salut d'un peuple, l'énorme salut de tout un peuple. On sous-entendait: le salut *temporel.* Et précisément notre mystique chrétienne culminait si parfaitement, si exactement avec notre mystique française, avec notre mystique patriotique dans notre mystique dreyfusiste que ce qu'il faut bien voir, *c'est que nous ne nous placions pas moins qu'au point de vue* du salut éternel de la France. Que disions-nous en effet? Tout était contre nous, la sagesse et la loi, j'entends la sagesse humaine, la loi humaine. Ce que nous faisions était de l'ordre de la folie ou de l'ordre de la sainteté, qui ont tant de ressemblances, tant de secrets accords, pour la sagesse humaine, pour un regard humain. Nous allions, nous étions contre la sagesse, contre la loi. Contre la sagesse humaine, contre la loi humaine.—Les autres disaient: Un peuple, tout un peuple est un énorme assemblage des intérêts, des droits les plus légitimes. Les plus sacrés. Des milliers, des millions de vies en dépendent, dans le présent, dans le passé, (dans le futur), des milliers, des millions, des centaines de millions de vies le constituent, dans le présent, dans le passé, (dans le futur) et par le jeu de l'histoire, par le dépôt de l'histoire la garde d'intérêts incalculables. De droits légitimes, sacrés, incalculables. Tout un peuple d'hommes, tout un peu-

In reality the true position of the people who opposed us was, for a long time, not to say and to believe Dreyfus guilty, but to believe and to say that innocent or guilty, the life and salvation of a people, the enormous salvation of a people could not be troubled, could not be upset, could not be *compromised,* could not be risked for one man, for a single man. Tacitly they meant: the *temporal* salvation. And precisely our Christian mysticism culminated so perfectly, so exactly with our French mysticism, with our patriotic mysticism in our Dreyfusist mysticism that what must clearly be recognized is *that our point of view focussed nothing less than* the eternal salvation of France. What indeed was it that we said? Everything was against us, wisdom and law, I mean human wisdom, human law. What we did was in the order of folly or in the order of holiness, which are alike in so many ways, which have so many secret correspondences, in the eyes of human wisdom, underneath the human scrutiny. We moved, we went at odds with wisdom, with law; at odds with human wisdom, with human law.—The others said: "A people, a whole people is an enormous combination of interests, of the most legitimate rights. The most sacred. Thousands, millions of lives depend on it, in the present, in the past, (in the future); thousands, millions, hundreds of millions of lives constitute it, in the present, in the past, (in the future) and by the action of history, by the deposit of history it safeguards incalculable interests. Legitimate, sacred, incalculable rights. A whole people of men, a whole people of families; a whole people of rights, a whole people of interests, legitimate ones; a whole people of lives; a whole race; a whole people of memories; all history, all the ascent, all the urge forward, all the past, all the future, all the promise of a people and of a race; all that

ple de familles; tout un peuple de droits, tout un peuple d'intérêts, légitimes; tout un peuple de vies; toute une race; tout un peuple de mémoires; toute l'histoire, toute la montée, toute la poussée, tout le passé, tout le futur, toute la promesse d'un peuple et d'une race; tout ce qui est inestimable, incalculable, d'un prix infini, parce que ça ne se fait qu'une fois, parce que ça ne s'obtient qu'une fois, parce que ça ne se recommencera jamais; parce que c'est une réussite, unique; un peuple, et notamment, nommément ce peuple-ci, qui est d'un prix unique; ce vieux peuple; un peuple n'a pas le droit, et le premier devoir, le devoir étroit d'un peuple est de ne pas exposer tout cela, de ne pas s'exposer pour un homme, quel qu'il soit, quelque légitimes que soient ses intérêts ou ses droits. Quelque sacré même. Un peuple n'a jamais le droit. On ne perd point une cité, une cité ne se perd point pour un (seul) citoyen. C'était le langage même et du véritable civisme et de la sagesse, c'était la sagesse même, la sagesse antique. C'était le langage de la raison. À ce point de vue il était évident que Dreyfus devait se dévouer pour la France; non pas seulement pour le repos de la France mais pour le salut même de la France, qu'il exposait. Et s'il ne voulait pas se dévouer lui-même, dans le besoin on devait le dévouer. Et nous que disions nous. Nous disions une seule injustice, un seul crime, une seule illégalité, surtout si elle est officiellement enregistrée, confirmée, une seule injure à l'humanité, une seule injure à la justice et au droit, surtout si elle est universellement, légalement, nationalement, commodément acceptée, un seul crime rompt et suffit à rompre tout le pacte social, tout le contrat social, une seule forfaiture, un seul déshonneur suffit à perdre, d'honneur, à déshonorer tout un peuple. C'est un point de gangrène, qui corrompt tout le

is inestimable, incalculable, of infinite price, because it can be achieved once only, because it can be obtained once only, because it can never be achieved again; because it is a unique achievement; a people and particularly, namely this people that is of a unique worth; this old people. A people has not the right, and the first duty, the strict duty of a people is not to expose all that, not to expose itself for one man, no matter who he may be, no matter how legitimate his interests or his rights. No matter how sacred, even. A people has never this right. One does not lose a city, a city is not lost for the sake of a (single) citizen." It was the very language not only of true civism and of wisdom, it was wisdom itself, antique wisdom. It was the language of reason. From this point of view it was evident that Dreyfus should sacrifice himself for France; not only for the peace of France but for the salvation itself of France, which he imperilled. And if he did not wish to sacrifice himself, of his own free will, if the need arose, he should be sacrificed. And we, what did we say? We said that a single injustice, a single crime, a single illegality, particularly if it is officially recorded, confirmed, a single wrong to humanity, a single wrong to justice and to right, particularly if it is universally, legally, nationally, commodiously accepted, that a single crime shatters and is sufficient to shatter the whole social pact, the whole social contract, that a single legal crime, a single dishonorable act will bring about the loss of one's honor, the dishonor of a whole people. It is a touch of gangrene that corrupts the entire body. What we defend is not our honor alone. It is not only the honor of our whole people, in the present, it is the historical honor of our people, all the historical honor of our whole race, the honor of our ancestors, the honor of our children. And the more we have of a past,

corps. Ce que nous défendons, ce n'est pas seulement notre honneur. Ce n'est pas seulement l'honneur de tout notre peuple, dans le présent, c'est l'honneur historique de notre peuple, tout l'honneur historique de toute notre race, l'honneur de nos aïeux, l'honneur de nos enfants. Et plus nous avons de passé, plus nous avons de mémoire, (plus ainsi, comme vous le dites, nous avons de responsabilité), plus ainsi aussi ici nous devons la défendre ainsi. Plus nous avons de passé derrière nous, plus (justement) il nous faut le défendre ainsi, le garder pur. *Je rendrai mon sang pur comme je l'ai reçu.* C'était la règle et l'honneur et la poussée chrétienne. Une seule tache entache toute une famille. Elle entache aussi tout un peuple. Un seul point marque l'honneur de toute une famille. Un seul point marque aussi l'honneur de tout un peuple. Un peuple ne peut pas rester sur une injure, subie, exercée, sur un crime, aussi solennellement, aussi définitivement endossé. L'honneur d'un peuple est d'un seul tenant.

Qu'est-ce à dire, à moins de ne pas savoir un mot de français, sinon que nos adversaires parlaient le langage de la raison d'État, qui n'est pas seulement le langage de la raison politique et parlementaire, du méprisable intérêt politique et parlementaire, mais beaucoup plus exactement, beaucoup plus haut qui est le langage, le très respectable langage de la continuité, de la continuation temporelle du peuple et de la race, *du salut temporel du peuple et de la race.* Ils n'allaient pas à moins. Et nous par un mouvement chrétien profond, par une poussée très profonde révolutionnaire et ensemble traditionnelle de christianisme, suivant en ceci une tradition chrétienne des plus profondes, des plus vivaces, des plus dans la ligne, dans l'axe et au cœur du christianisme, nous nous n'allions pas à moins qu'à nous elever je ne dis pas jusqu'à la concep-

the more we have of a memory (the more thus, as you say, we have of a responsibility) the more thus also we are obliged to defend it. The more we have of a past behind us, the more, (precisely) we must defend it thus, keep it pure. *I will give back my blood pure as I received it.* That is the rule and the honor and the Christian urge. A single spot defiles a whole family. It also defiles a whole people. A single spot equally blemishes the honor of a whole family. A single spot equally blemishes the honor of a whole people. A people cannot remain passive before a wrong endured, imposed, before a crime so solemnly, so definitively countersigned. The honor of a people is a seamless coat.

What would this mean, unless one did not know a word of French, except that our opponents spoke the language of the interests of the State, which is not only the language of political and parliamentary reason, of the contemptible political and parliamentary interests, but far more exactly, far more loudly, is the language, the very respectable language of continuity, of the temporal continuation of the people and of the race, *of the temporal salvation of the people and of the race.* They meant no less. And we by a deep Christian reaction, by a very deep urge, simultaneously revolutionary and in the Christian tradition, following in this a Christian tradition in the deepest, the liveliest, the most orthodox sense, situated in the center and in the heart of Christianity, we meant no less than to rise, I don't say to the conception, but to the passion, to the anxiety for eternal salvation, the eternal salvation of this people; we aimed at nothing less than life in constant anxiety, in preoccupation, in mortal, eternal anguish, in a constant anxious care for the eternal salvation of our people, for the eternal salvation of our race. Quite at bottom we were

tion mais à la passion, mais au souci d'un salut éternel, du salut éternel de ce peuple, nous n'atteignions pas à moins qu'à vivre dans un souci constant, dans une préoccupation, dans une angoisse mortelle, éternelle, dans une anxiété constante du salut éternel de notre peuple, du salut éternel de notre race. Tout au fond nous étions les hommes du salut éternel et nos adversaires étaient les hommes du salut temporel. Voilà la vraie, la réelle division de l'affaire Dreyfus. Tout au fond nous ne voulions pas que la France fut constituée en état de péché mortel. Il n'y a que la doctrine chrétienne au monde, dans le monde moderne, dans aucun monde, qui mette à ce point, aussi délibérément, aussi totalement, aussi absolument la mort temporelle comme rien, comme une insignifiance, comme un zéro au prix de la mort éternelle, et le risque de la mort temporelle comme rien au prix du péché, mortel.

C'EST PAS FACILE d'être Juif. Quand ils demeurent insensibles aux appels de leurs frères, aux cris des persécutés, aux plaintes, aux lamentations de leurs frères meurtris dans tout le monde vous dites: *C'est des mauvais Juifs.* Et s'ils ouvrent seulement l'oreille aux lamentations qui montent du Danube et du Dnièpr vous dites: *Ils nous trahissent. C'est des mauvais Français.*

Ainsi vous les poursuivez, vous les accablez sans cesse de reproches contradictoires. Vous dites: *Leur finance est juive, elle n'est pas française.*—Et la finance française, mon ami, est-ce qu'elle est française.

the men of eternal salvation and our opponents were the men of temporal salvation. Such was the true, the real division in the Dreyfus case. Quite at bottom, we did not wish France to be constituted in a state of mortal sin. In this world, in this modern world, in any world, it is the Christian doctrine alone which to this extent, so deliberately, so totally, so absolutely insists upon holding temporal death as nothing, as an insignificant matter, as a zero in comparison with the cost of eternal death, and the risk of temporal death as nothing in comparison with the cost of sin, of mortal sin.

IT IS NOT EASY to be a Jew. When they remain insensible to the appeals of their brothers, to the cries of the persecuted, to the wails, to the lamentations of their bruised brothers throughout the world, one says: "*They are bad Jews.*" And if they merely open an ear to the lamentations which arise from the Danube and the Dnieper, one says: "*They betray us. They are bad Frenchmen.*"

Thus you pursue them, you continually overwhelm them with contradictory reproaches. You say: "*Their finances are Jewish, they are not French finances.*" And French finances, my friend, are they French?

Ils (les Juifs) sont victimes d'une illusion d'optique très fréquente, très connue dans les autres ordres, dans l'ordre de l'optique même. Comme on pense toujours à eux, à présent, comme on ne pense qu'à eux, comme l'attention est toujours portée sur eux, depuis que la question de l'antisémitisme est soulevée, comme ils sont toujours dans le blanc du regard ils sont très exactement victimes de cette illusion d'optique bien connue qui nous fait voir un carré *blanc sur noir* beaucoup plus grand que le même carré *noir sur blanc*, qui paraît tout petit. Tout carré blanc sur noir paraît *beaucoup* plus grand que le même carré *noir sur blanc*. Tout ainsi tout acte, toute opération, tout carré *juif sur chrétien* nous paraît, nous le voyons beaucoup plus grand que le même carré *chrétien sur juif*.

Pour mesurer toute la valeur, toute la grandeur, toute l'amplitude, tout l'angle de cette illusion, pour corriger cet angle d'erreur, pour nous redonner, pour retrouver la justice et la justesse, il est un exercice salubre, excellent pour la bonne santé intellectuelle et morale, excellent pour l'hygiène intellectuelle et mentale.—Il consiste à faire la meilleure des preuves, qui est la preuve par le contraire. Il consiste à retenir certains faits, nombreux, à mesure qu'ils passent, et à dire, à se demander, de l'auteur: *Qu'est-ce qu'on dirait s'il était Juif*. Non seulement cet exercice rend toujours, mais on est surpris de voir comme il rend, comme il rectifie. On voit vite alors, on compte aisément que les plus grands scandales et les plus nombreux ne sont point des scandales juifs. Et il s'en faut.

They (the Jews) are the victims of an optical delusion very frequent, very well-known in the other orders, in the order of optics itself. As one thinks about them always, at present, as one thinks of nothing besides them, as attention is always focussed on them since the question of antisemitism has been raised, as they are always in the public eye, they are very exactly the victims of this well-known optical delusion which causes us to see a square *white on black* as much larger than the same square *black on white,* that appears quite small. Any white square on black appears *much* larger than the same square *black on white.* Exactly thus any act, any operation, any square *Jew on Christian* appears to us, seems to us much larger than the same square *Christian on Jew.*

To measure all the value, all the greatness, all the amplitude, the whole angle of this delusion, to correct this angle of error, to give back to us, to find once again justice and accuracy, there is a healthy exercise, excellent for intellectual and moral health, excellent for intellectual and mental hygiene.—It consists in applying the best of proofs, which is the proof by the contrary. It consists in retaining certain facts, numerous facts, as they happen all along, and to say, to ask of oneself, to ask of their author: "*What would one say if he were a Jew.*" Not only does this exercise always give results but one is surprised to see how much result it gives, how it rectifies. Then one sees quickly, one reckons easily that the greatest scandals and the most numerous are not Jewish ones. Not by a long shot.

BERNARD-LAZARE

LE PROPHÈTE, en cette grande crise d'Israël et du monde, fut Bernard-Lazare. Saluons ici l'un des plus grands noms des temps modernes,—l'un des plus grands parmi les prophètes d'Israël.—

Je ferai le portrait de Bernard-Lazare. Il avait, indéniablement, des parties de saint, de sainteté. Et quand je parle de saint, je ne suis pas suspect de parler par métaphore. Il avait une douceur, une bonté, une tendresse mystique, une égalité d'humeur, une expérience de l'amertume et de l'ingratitude, une digestion parfaite de l'amertume et de l'ingratitude, une sorte de bonté à qui on n'en remontrait point, une sorte de bonté parfaitement renseignée et parfaitement apprise, d'une profondeur incroyable. Comme une bonté à revendre. Il vécut et mourut pour eux comme un martyr. Il fut un prophète. Il était donc juste qu'on l'ensevelît prématurément dans le silence et dans l'oubli. Dans un silence fait. Dans un oubli concerté.—

Bernard-Lazare, journalist, was one of the first to set in motion the press campaign for the revision of the sentence which had sent Dreyfus to Devil's Island in 1894.

BERNARD-LAZARE

THE PROPHET, in this great crisis of Israel and all the world was Bernard-Lazare. Let us salute here one of the greatest names of modern times,—one of the greatest among the prophets of Israel.—

I will paint the portrait of Bernard-Lazare. Unquestionably he possessed elements of holiness, of sanctity. And when I use the word saint, let no one suspect me of speaking metaphorically. He had a gentleness, a kindness of heart, a mystical tenderness, an evenness of temper, an experience of bitterness and of ingratitude, a perfect digestion of bitterness and of ingratitude, a sort of goodness in the full face of reality, a sort of goodness perfectly awake and perfectly aware and incredibly deep. He had goodness in superabundance. He lived and died for them (the Jews) as a martyr. He was a prophet. So it was natural that he should be buried prematurely in silence and oblivion. In a deliberate silence. In an organized oblivion.—

Les Juifs lui en voulaient surtout, le méprisaient surtout parce qu'il n'était pas riche. Je crois même qu'on disait qu'il était dépensier. Cela voulait dire qu'on n'avait plus besoin de lui. Peut-être en effet leur coûtait-il un peu; leur avait-il coûté un peu plus. C'était un homme qui avait la main ouverte.

Seulement il faudrait peut-être considérer qu'il était sans prix.—

Il avait cette fidélité à soi-même qui est tout de même l'essentiel. Beaucoup peuvent vous trahir. Mais c'est beaucoup, c'est déjà beaucoup que de ne pas se trahir soi-même. Beaucoup de politiques peuvent trahir, peuvent dévorer, peuvent absorber beaucoup de mystiques. C'est beaucoup que les mystiques ne se trahissent point elles-mêmes.—

L'honneur d'avoir fait l'affaire Dreyfus lui collait aux épaules comme une chape inexpiable.—On s'organisait fort proprement de toutes part pour qu'il mourût tout tranquillement de faim.—Tout le monde le taisait. Ceux qu'il avait sauvés le taisaient plus obstinément, plus silencieusement que tous, l'enfonçaient dans un silence plus sourd, plus obstiné.— Ceux qu'il avait sauvés étaient les plus pressés. Lui-même le savait très bien. On a beau savoir que c'est la règle. A chaque fois c'est toujours nouveau. Et c'est toujours dur à avaler.

Lui-même il ne se faisait aucune illusion sur les hommes qu'il avait défendus. Il voyait partout les politiques, les hommes politiques arriver, dévorer tout, dévorer, déshonorer son œuvre.—

Une petite minorité, un petit groupe, une immense majorité de juifs pauvres (il y en a, beaucoup), de misérables (il y en a, beaucoup), lui demeuraient fidèles, lui étaient attachés d'un attachement, d'un amour fanatique, qu'exaspéraient de

The Jews especially bore him a grudge, especially despised him because he was not wealthy. I even believe it was said that he was extravagant. That meant that they no longer had need of him. Perhaps indeed he did cost them a little; had cost them a little too much. He was open-handed.

Only, it might perhaps be taken into consideration that he himself was priceless.—

He had that truth toward himself which after all is paramount. Many persons can betray us. But it is a great deal, it is already a great deal not to betray oneself. Many policies can betray, can devour, can absorb many mystical doctrines. It is a great deal that mystical doctrines remain true to themselves.—

The honor of having given life to the Dreyfus case clung to his shoulders like an irremissible cope.—Everywhere precautions very decently were taken that perfectly quietly he die of hunger.—Nobody spoke about him. Those whom he had saved passed him over even more obstinately, more silently than all the others, thrust him into a more secret, more obstinate silence.—Those whom he had saved were the most prompt. He himself was perfectly aware of this. No matter how much one knows ingratitude to be the rule, each time it occurs it comes as a surprise. And it is always hard to swallow.

He himself was under no illusion respecting the men whom he had defended. Everywhere he saw policies, political men emerge, devour all, devour, dishonor his work.—

A small minority, a small group, an immense majority of poor Jews (there are a great many), of poor wretches (there are a great many), remained faithful to him, were attached to him with an attachment, a fanatical love, exasperated day by

jour en jour les approches de la mort. Ceux-là l'aimaient. Nous l'aimions. Les riches ne l'aimaient déjà plus.

Je dirai donc quel fut son enterrement.
Je dirai quelle fut toute sa fin.
Je dirai combien il souffrit.
Je dirai combien il se tut.

Je vois encore sur moi son regard de myope, si intelligent et ensemble si bon, d'une si invincible, si intelligente, si éclairée, si éclairante, si lumineuse douceur, d'une si inlassable, si renseignée, si éclairée, si désabusée, si incurable bonté. Parce qu'un homme porte un binocle bien planté sur un nez gras barrant, vitrant deux bons gros yeux de myope, le moderne ne sait pas reconnaître, il ne sait pas voir le regard, le feu allumé il y a cinquante siècles. Mais moi je l'ai approché. Seul j'ai vécu dans son intimité et dans sa confidence. Il fallait écouter, il fallait voir cet homme qui naturellement se croyait un moderne. Il fallait regarder ce regard, il fallait entendre cette voix. Naturellement il était très sincèrement athée. Ce n'était pas alors la métaphysique dominante seulement, c'était la métaphysique ambiante, celle que l'on respirait, une sorte de métaphysique climatérique, atmosphérique; qui allait de soi, comme d'être bien élevé; et en outre il était entendu, positivement, scientifiquement, victorieusement, que ce n'était pas, qu'elle n'était pas une métaphysique; il était positiviste, scientifique, intellectuel, moderne, enfin tout ce qu'il faut; surtout il ne voulait pas entendre parler de métaphysique(s). Un de ses arguments favoris, celui qu'il me servait toujours, était qu'Israël étant de tous les peuples celui qui croyait le moins en Dieu, c'était évidemment celui qu'il serait le plus facile de débarrasser des

day by the approaches of death. Those loved him. We loved him. Already the rich no longer loved him.

Therefore I shall relate the story of his funeral.

I shall relate the story of his end.

I shall say how much he suffered.

I shall say how much he remained silent.

I still seem to see his short-sighted glance falling upon me, so intelligent and simultaneously so good, of such an invincible, such an intelligent, such an enlightened, such an enlightening, such a luminous gentleness, of such an untiring, such an informed, such an enlightened, such a disabused, such an incurable goodness. Because a man wears a pince-nez well settled on a thick nose, barring and setting glass before two kind, big, near-sighted eyes, modern man is not able to recognize, is not able to see the glance, the fire lighted fifty centuries ago. But I have been close to him. I alone have lived in his intimacy and in his confidence. One should have heard, one should have seen this man who naturally believed himself to be a modern! One should have seen that look, one should have heard that voice! Of course he was very sincerely an atheist. At that time it was not only the dominant metaphysical system, it was the encompassing metaphysical system, that which one drew in with each breath, a kind of climatic, atmospheric metaphysical system; which was self-understood, as good breeding is self-understood; and moreover it was understood, positively, scientifically, victoriously, that this system was not a *metaphysical* system; he was positivistic, scientific, intellectual, modern, in a word all that was proper; above all he would hear no talk about metaphysics. One of his favorite arguments, the one which he always served

anciennes superstitions; et ainsi ce serait celui qui montrerait la route aux autres. L'excellence des Juifs était selon lui, venait de ce qu'ils étaient comme d'avance les plus libres penseurs. Et là dessous, et là dedans un cœur qui battait à tous les échos du monde, un homme qui sautait sur un journal et qui sur les quatre pages, sur les six, huit, sur les douze pages d'un seul regard comme la foudre saisissait une ligne et dans cette ligne il y avait le mot Juif, un être qui rougissait, pâlissait, un vieux journaliste, un routier du journal(isme), qui blêmissait sur un écho, qu'il trouvait dans ce journal, sur un morceau d'article, sur un filet, sur une dépêche, et dans cet écho, dans ce journal, dans ce morceau d'article, dans ce filet, dans cette dépêche il y avait le mot Juif; un cœur qui saignait dans tous les ghettos du monde, et peut-être encore plus dans les ghettos rompus, dans les ghettos diffus, comme Paris, que dans les ghettos conclus, dans les ghettos forclus; un cœur qui saignait en Roumanie et en Turquie, en Russie et en Algérie, en Amérique et en Hongrie, partout où le Juif est persécuté, c'est-à-dire, en un certain sens, partout; un cœur qui saignait en Orient et en Occident, dans l'Islam et en Chrétienté; un cœur qui saignait en Judée même, et un homme en même temps qui plaisantait les Sionistes; ainsi est le juif; un tremblement de colère, et c'était pour quelque injure subie dans la vallée du Dnièpr. Aussi ce que nos Puissances ne voulaient pas voir, qu'il fût le prophète, le juif, le chef,—le dernier colporteur juif le savait, le voyait, le plus misérable juif de Roumanie. Un tremblement, une vibration perpétuelle. Tout ce qu'il faut pour mourir à quarante ans. Pas un muscle, pas un nerf qui ne fût tendu pour une mission secrète, perpétuellement vibré pour la mission. Jamais homme ne se tint à ce point chef de sa race et de son peuple, responsable pour sa

up to me, was that Israel—since among all the peoples it was the one which believed the least in God—obviously was the people most easy to rid of ancient superstitions; and therefore this would be the people that would show the way to the others. The excellence of the Jews came, according to him, from the fact that they were by anticipation the most freethinking of peoples. And underneath this and inside this, a heart that beat to all the echoes of the world, a man who pounced upon a newspaper and who, over four pages, over six, eight, over twelve pages, with a single lightning glance fastened on a line, and in this line there occurred the word Jew. A creature who blushed, turned pale, an old journalist, an old stager of journalism who blanched at a small news item that he found in this paper, at a fragment of an article, at a short article, at a cable, and in this news item, in this paper, in this fragment of an article, in this short article, in this cable there occurred the word Jew. A heart that bled in all the ghettos of the world, and perhaps more in the disrupted ghettos and scattered ghettos, like that of Paris, than in the closed ghettos, in the excluded ghettos. A heart that bled in Rumania and in Turkey, in Russia and in Algeria, in America and in Hungary, in all places where the Jew is persecuted, which is to say, in a certain sense, everywhere. A heart that bled in the East and in the West, in Islam and in Christendom. A heart that bled in Judea itself, and a man who made fun of Zionists. Such is the Jew. A tremor of anger and that was for some wrong suffered in the valley of the Dnieper. Also what our Powers did not wish to see—that he was the prophet, the Jew, the leader,—that, the least of Jewish peddlers knew, saw, the most wretched Rumanian Jew. A tremor, a perpetual vibration. All that is needed for death at forty.

race et pour son peuple. Un être perpétuellement tendu. Pas un sentiment, pas une pensée, pas l'ombre d'une passion qui ne fût tendue, qui ne fût commandée par un commandement vieux de cinquante siècles, par le commandement tombé il y a cinquante siècles; toute une race, tout un monde sur les épaules, une race, un monde de cinquante siècles sur les épaules voûtées; sur les épaules rondes, sur les épaules lourdes; un cœur dévoré de feu, du feu de sa race, consumé du feu de son peuple; le feu au cœur, une tête ardente, *et le charbon ardent sur la lèvre prophète.*—

Il faut penser que c'était un homme, j'ai dit très précisément un prophète, pour qui tout l'appareil des puissances, la raison d'État, les puissances temporelles, les puissances politiques, les autorités de tout ordre, politiques, intellectuelles, mentales même ne pesaient pas une once devant une révolte, devant un mouvement de la conscience propre.—Pour lui ils n'existaient pas. Il ne les méprisait même pas. Il les ignorait, et même plus. Il ne les voyait pas, il ne les considérait pas. Il était myope.—Elles n'étaient pas de son grade, de son ordre de grandeur, de sa grandeur.—Jamais je n'ai vu un homme croire, savoir à ce point que les plus grandes puissances temporelles, que les plus grands corps de l'État ne tiennent, ne sont que par des puissances spirituelles intérieures.—Donc il avait une affection secrète, une amitié, une affinité profonde avec les *autres* puissances spirituelles, même avec les catholiques, qu'il combattait délibérément. Mais il ne voulait les combattre que par des armes spirituelles dans des batailles spirituelles. Il ne voulait pas qu'on fit aux autres ce que les autres vous avaient fait, mais qu'on ne voulait pas qu'ils vous fissent. *Les cléricaux nous ont embêtés pendant des années,* disait-il, et plus énergiquement encore, *il ne s'agit pas à pré-*

Not a muscle, not a nerve but was held taut for a secret mission, perpetually quivering for the mission. Never did a man consider himself to this extent the leader of his race and of his people, responsible for his race and for his people. A being perpetually taut. Not a feeling, not a thought, not the shadow of a passion that was not taut, that was not commanded by a commandment fifty centuries old, by a commandment delivered fifty centuries ago. An entire race, an entire world on his shoulders, a race, a world of fifty centuries on bowed shoulders, on rounded shoulders, on sagging shoulders. A heart devoured by fire, by the fire of his race, consumed by the fire of his race. Fire at heart, a flaming head, *and the burning coal on the prophetic lip.*—

It must be considered that this was a man—as I have very precisely said a prophet, for whom all the mechanism of power, the interests of State, the temporal powers, the political powers, the authorities of all orders, political, intellectual, even rational did not weigh an ounce set against a revolt, against a movement of the conscience itself.—For him they did not exist. He did not even despise them. He ignored them, and even more. He did not see them, he did not take cognizance of them. He was near-sighted.—They were not of his rank, of his degree, of his degree of greatness, of his greatness.—Never have I seen a man believe, know to such an extent that the greatest temporal powers, that the greatest bodies of State stand, exist only by grace of interior spiritual powers.—Thus he had a secret affection, a friendship, a deep affinity with the *other* spiritual powers, even with the Catholics whom he deliberately fought. But he wished only to fight them with spiritual weapons, in spiritual battles. He did not wish that there should be done to others what others had done

sent d'embêter les catholiques. On n'a jamais vu un Juif aussi peu partisan, aussi peu pensant, aussi peu concevant du talion. Il ne voulait pas rendre précisément le bien pour le mal, mais très certainement le juste pour l'injuste.—

D'une manière générale il n'aimait pas, il ne pouvait pas supporter que le temporel se mêlât du spirituel.—Que des organes aussi grossiers que le gouvernement, la Chambre, l'État, le Sénat, aussi étrangers à tout ce qui est spirituel, missent les doigts de la main dans le spirituel, c'était pour lui non pas seulement une profanation grossière, mais plus encore, un exercice de mauvais goût, un abus, l'exercice, l'abus d'une singulière incompétence. Il se sentait au contraire une secrète, une singulière complicité de compétence spirituelle au besoin avec le pape.—

Je n'ai jamais vu un homme croire, à ce point, avoir conscience à ce point qu'une conscience d'homme était un absolu, un invincible, un éternel, un libre, qu'elle s'opposait victorieuse, éternellement triomphant, à toutes les grandeurs de la terre.—

Je dirai sa mort, et sa longue et sa cruelle maladie, et tout le lent et si prompt acheminement de sa mort. Cette sorte de maladie féroce. Comme acharnée. Comme fanatique. Comme elle-même forcenée. Comme lui. Comme nous. Je ne sais rien de si poignant, de si saisissant, je ne connais rien d'aussi tragique que cet homme qui se roidissant de tout ce qui lui restait de force, se mettait en travers de son parti victorieux. Qui dans un effort désespéré, où il se brisait lui-même, essayait, entreprenait de remonter cet élan de la victoire et des abus, de l'abus de la victoire.—Je le revois encore dans son lit. Cet athée, ce professionnellement athée, cet officiellement

to you, but which one did not wish them to do to you. "*The clericals have been pestering us for years,*" he said and more energetically still, "*but pestering the Catholics at present is not to the point.*" Never has there been seen a Jew so little partisan, thinking so little about, contemplating so little the law of retaliation. He did not exactly wish to return good for evil, but most certainly justice for injustice.—

Fundamentally he did not like, he could not bear to have the temporal interfere with the spiritual.—That organs as coarse as the government, the Chamber, the State, the Senate, so foreign to all that is spiritual, should lay the fingers of their hand upon the spiritual, that for him was not only a gross profanation but even more, an exertion of bad taste, an abuse, the activation, the abuse of a most singular incompetence. On the contrary he felt in himself a secret, a singular complicity of spiritual competence, if needs be, with the pope.—

I have never seen a man believe so deeply, have so deep a conviction, that a man's conscience was an absolute, an invincibility, an eternity, a freedom, that it was opposed, victoriously, eternally triumphant, to all the grandeurs of the earth.—

I shall relate his death and his long and cruel illness and all his slow and yet so rapid journey towards his death. That sort of ferocious illness. So relentless. As though it were fanatical. As though it itself were frantic. Just like himself. Just like ourselves. I know of nothing so poignant, so startling, I know of nothing so tragic as this man who, bracing himself with all that remained to him of strength, barred the road to his victorious party. Who in a desperate effort which

athée en qui retentissait, avec une force, une douceur incroyable, la parole éternelle; avec une force éternelle; avec une douceur éternelle; que je n'ai jamais retrouvée égale nulle part ailleurs. J'ai encore sur moi, dans mes yeux, l'éternelle bonté de ce regard infiniment doux, cette bonté non pas lancée, mais posée, renseignée. Infiniment désabusée; infiniment renseignée, infiniment insurmontable elle-même. Je le vois encore dans son lit, cet athée ruisselant de la parole de Dieu. Dans la mort même tout le poids de son peuple lui pesait aux épaules. Il ne fallait point lui dire qu'il n'en était point responsable. Je n'ai jamais vu un homme ainsi chargé, aussi chargé d'une charge, d'une responsabilité éternelle. Comme nous sommes, comme nous nous sentons chargés de nos enfants, de nos propres enfants dans notre propre famille, tout autant, exactement autant, exactement ainsi il se sentait chargé de son peuple. Dans les souffrances les plus atroces il n'avait qu'un souci: que *ses* Juifs de Roumanie ne fussent point omis *artificieusement* dans ce mouvement de réprobation que quelques publicistes européens entreprenaient alors contre les excès des persécutions orientales.—

On lui avait conté des histoires sur sa maladie, des histoires et des histoires. Qu'en croyait-il? Il faisait, comme tout le monde, semblant de les croire. Qu'en croyait-il, c'est le secret des morts. *Morientium ac mortuorum.* Dans cette incurable lâcheté du monde moderne, où nous osons tout dire à l'homme, excepté ce qui l'intéresse, où nous n'osons pas dire à l'homme la plus grande nouvelle, la nouvelle de la seule grande échéance, nous avons menti nous-mêmes tant de fois, nous avons tant menti à tant de mourants et à tant de morts qu'il faut bien espérer que quand c'est notre tour nous ne croyons pas nous-mêmes tout-à-fait aux mensonges que l'on

broke his own body attempted, undertook to stem the tide of victory and its abuses, the abuses of victory.—I still see him in his bed. This atheist, this professional atheist, this official atheist in whom reverberated with a strength and an incredible gentleness, the eternal Word; with an eternal strength; with an eternal gentleness; which I have never found anywhere equalled. I still have upon me, in my eyes, the eternal goodness of his infinitely gentle gaze, this goodness which was not impulsive but poised, aware. Infinitely disabused; infinitely aware; infinitely insurmountable. I still see him in his bed, this atheist overflowing with the word of God. In death itself the whole weight of his people still weighed upon his shoulders. One could not tell him that he was no longer responsible for it. I have never seen a man thus burdened, so much burdened with a burden, with an eternal responsibility. Precisely as we are, as we feel ourselves responsible for our children, for our own children in our own families, quite so much, exactly so much, he felt himself responsible for his people. In the most atrocious suffering he had but one anxiety: that *his* Jews of Rumania be not *craftily* overlooked in that movement of condemnation that a few European publicists then undertook against the excesses of Oriental persecutions.—

He had been told falsehoods about his illness, falsehoods upon falsehoods. How much did he believe? He, like everybody else, pretended to believe. How much he believed—that is the secret of the dead. *Morientium ac mortuorum.* In this incurable cowardice of the modern world where we dare tell a man everything save what interests him, where we do not dare tell a man the greatest piece of news, the news of the arrival of the only important pay-day, we have lied our-

nous fait. Il faisait donc semblant d'y croire. Mais dans ses beaux yeux doux, dans ses grands et gros yeux clairs il était impossible de lire. Ils étaient trop bons. Ils étaient trop doux. Ils étaient trop beaux. *Ils étaient trop clairs.* Il était impossible de savoir si c'était par un miracle d'espérance (temporelle) qu'il espérait encore ou si c'était par un miracle de charité, pour nous, qu'il faisait semblant d'espérer.—

Je dirai quel fut son enterrement. Qui nous étions, combien peu dans ce cortège, dans ce convoi, dans cet accompagnement fidèle gris descendant et passant dans Paris. En pleines vacances.—Quelques-uns, les mêmes forcenés, les mêmes fanatiques, Juifs et chrétiens, quelques Juifs riches, très rares, quelques chrétiens riches, très rares, des Juifs et des chrétiens pauvres et misérables, eux-mêmes en assez petit nombre. Une petite troupe en somme, une très petite troupe. Comme une espèce de compagnie réduite qui traversait Paris. De misérables juifs étrangers, je veux dire étrangers à la nationalité française, car il n'était pas un Juif de Roumanie qui ne le sût prophète, qui ne le tînt pour un véritable prophète. Il était pour tous ces misérables, pour tous ces persécutés, un éclair encore, un rallumage du flambeau qui éternellement ne s'éteindra point.

Je n'éprouve aucun besoin d'unifier le monde. Plus je vais, plus je découvre que les hommes libres et que les événements libres sont variés.

selves so often, we have lied so much to so many of the dying and to so many of the dead that it is to be hoped that when our turn comes we will not believe entirely in the lies which are told us. So he pretended to believe in them. But it was impossible to read in his beautiful, gentle eyes, in his great, big, clear eyes. They were too kind. They were too gentle. They were too beautiful. *They were too clear*. It was impossible to know whether by a miracle of (temporal) hope, he still hoped for himself, or if it was through a miracle of charity for us that he pretended to hope.—

I shall tell the story of his funeral. Who we were, how few there were in this procession, in this funeral procession, in this faithful grey cortege descending and passing through Paris. Right in the middle of the holiday season.—A few, the same frantic, the same fanatical Jews and Christians, a few rich Jews, very rare, a few rich Christians, very rare, poor and wretched Jews and Christians, themselves in rather small number. In short a small troop, a very small troop. Like a sort of decimated company that crossed Paris. Wretched foreign Jews, I mean foreign to the French nationality, for there was not a Jew from Rumania who did not know him for a prophet, who did not hold him a true prophet. For all these poor wretches, for all these persecuted he was still a flash of lightning, a re-kindling of the torch which eternally does not go out.

I FEEL NO NEED of unifying the world. The more I see of the world, the more I discover that free men and free events are varied.

DREYFUS

IL N'EST PAS MORT, pour lui; mais plusieurs sont morts pour lui. D'autres sont morts pour lui.—

Il ne s'est pas ruiné pour lui-même. Il ne se ruinera pour nul autre. Mais beaucoup se sont ruinés pour lui.—

La plus grande fatalité, c'est précisément que cet homme ait été cette affaire, qu'il ait été jeté irrévocablement dans l'action publique, et même la plus publique. Il avait peut-être toutes les vertus privées. Il aurait fait sans doute un si bon homme d'affaires. Qu'est-ce qu'il est allé faire capitaine. Qu'est-ce qu'il est allé faire dans les bureaux de l'État-Major. Qu'est-ce qu'il est allé faire dans une réputation, dans une célébrité, dans une gloire mondiale. Victime malgré lui, héros malgré lui, martyr malgré lui. Glorieux malgré lui il a trahi sa gloire.—Mystérieuse destination du peuple d'Israël. Tant d'autres, qui voudraient la gloire, sont forcés de se tenir tranquilles. Et lui, qui voudrait bien se tenir tranquille, il est forcé à la vocation, il est forcé à la charge, il est forcé à la gloire.—Voilà un homme qui était capitaine. Il pensait monter colonel ou peut-être général. Il est monté Dreyfus. Comment voulez-vous qu'il s'y reconnaisse. Il fallait pourtant qu'il

DREYFUS

He has not died, for himself; but several died for him. Others died for him.—

He never ruined himself, for his own sake. He would never have ruined himself for the sake of another. But many went to their ruin for his sake.—

It was the greatest of fatalities that precisely this man should have constituted this affaire, that he should have been irrevocably thrust into a public event, and precisely the most public event. He had perhaps all the private virtues. Doubtless he would have made a very good businessman. Why did he have to go and become a captain. What business did he have in the offices of the General Staff. What business had he to have a reputation, to acquire a celebrity, a universal fame. Victim in spite of himself, hero in spite of himself, martyr in spite of himself. Celebrated in spite of himself, he betrayed his fame.—Mysterious destination of the people of Israel. So many others who desire fame are obliged to stay quiet. And he, who would have liked to stay quiet, was forced to the vocation, was forced to the attack, forced into fame. Here is a man who was a captain. He thought to be promoted to a colonel or

s'y reconnût, il devait pourtant s'y reconnaître. On l'a improvisé pilote, gouverneur, d'un énorme bateau qu'il n'a pas su conduire, qu'il n'a pas su gouverner. Et pourtant il en est responsable.—Brusquement revêtu, revêtu malgré lui d'une énorme magistrature, d'une magistature capitale, de la magistrature de victime, de la magistrature de héros, de la magistrature de martyr il s'en est lamentablement tiré. Et ce qu'il y a de fatal, ce qu'il y a de douloureux, ce qu'il y a de tragique, c'est que nous ne pouvons pas ne pas lui en demander compte.

Celui qui est désigné doit marcher. Celui qui est appelé doit répondre. C'est la loi, c'est la règle, c'est le niveau des vies héroïques, c'est le niveau des vies de sainteté.—Quiconque a eu le monde en main, est responsable du monde. Nous *devons* lui demander compte. Compte de cette immense bataille qu'il a perdue. Il s'est trouvé engagé sans le vouloir général en chef, plus que cela, drapeau d'une immense armée dans une immense bataille contre une immense armée. Et il a perdu cette immense bataille.—Celui qui perd une bataille, en est responsable. Nous ne pouvons que lui demander compte des mœurs publiques, de la France, *d'Israël même,* de l'humanité dont il fut un moment.

Singulière destinée. Il fut investi, institué malgré lui homme public. Tant d'autres ont voulu devenir hommes publics, et y ont mis le prix, et en ont été implacablement refoulés par l'événement. Il fut investi, institué malgré lui homme de gloire. Il a eu tout ce qu'il ne voulait pas. Mais il faut que celui qui est investi marche.

Tant d'hommes, des milliers et des milliers d'hommes, soldats, poètes, écrivains, artistes, hommes d'action, (victimes), héros, martyrs, tant d'hommes, des milliers et des milliers

perhaps a general. He was promoted to Dreyfus. How do you expect him to get his bearings. Yet he needs had to get his bearings, yet it was his duty to get his bearings. He was improvised a pilot, helmsman of an enormous ship that he did not know how to steer, that he did not know how to direct. Nevertheless he was responsible for it.—Suddenly apparelled, apparelled in spite of himself in an enormous dignity, in a martyr's dignity, he acquitted himself lamentably. And what is most fatal, most painful, most tragic is the fact that we cannot help having to call him to account for it.

He who is chosen must move forward. He who is called must answer. This is the law, this is the rule, this is the level of heroic lives, this is the level of lives of holiness.—Whoever has had the world in hand is responsible for the world. We *must* call him to account. To account for this immense battle that he has lost. Against his will he found himself engaged commander-in-chief, more than that, the banner of an immense army in an immense battle against an immense army. And he lost this immense battle.—He who loses a battle is responsible for losing it. We cannot but call him to account for the public morals, of France, of *Israel itself*, of the humanity to which he belonged for a moment.

Singular destiny. He was invested, constituted in spite of himself a public figure. So many others have wished to become public figures, and have paid the price, and have been inexorably thrust back by the reality of history. He was invested, constituted in spite of himself a man of fame. He had everything that he did not wish. But he that is invested must advance.

So many men, thousands and thousands of men, soldiers, poets, writers, artists, men of action, (victims), heroes, mar-

d'hommes ont voulu entrer dans l'action publique, devenir, se faire des hommes publics. Et ils y ont mis le prix. Ils y ont mis le génie, l'héroïsme, des efforts sans nombre, des efforts incroyables, des efforts effrayants; des souffrances effrayantes; des vies entières, et quelles vies, de véritables martyres. Et rien, jamais rien. Et lui, sans rien faire, malgré lui en quelques semaines il est devenu l'homme dont l'humanité entière a le plus retenti, son nom est devenu le nom, il est devenu l'homme dont tout le monde a le plus répété, a le plus célébré le nom depuis la mort de Napoléon. Ce que cent batailles avaient donné à l'autre, il l'a eu malgré lui. Et il n'en était pas plus fier.—

Cette situation tragique me rappelle un mot de Bernard-Lazare. Il faut toujours en revenir, on en revient toujours à un mot de Bernard-Lazare. Ce mot-ci sera le mot décisif de l'affaire. Puisqu'il vient, puisqu'il porte de son plus grand prophète sur la victime même.

Dreyfus venait de revenir. Dreyfus était rentré et presque instantanément, aux premières démarches, aux premiers pourparlers, au premier contact tout le monde avait eu brusquement l'impression qu'il y avait une paille, que ce n'était pas cela, qu'il était comme il était, et non point comme nous l'avions rêvé. Quelques-uns déjà se plaignaient. Quelques-uns, sourdement, bientôt publiquement, l'accusaient. Sourdement, publiquement Bernard-Lazare le défendait. Âprement, obstinément. Tenacement. Avec cet admirable aveuglement volontaire de ceux qui aiment vraiment, avec cet acharnement obstiné invincible avec lequel l'amour défend un être qui a tort, évidemment tort, publiquement tort.—*Je ne sais pas ce qu'ils veulent*, disait-il, riant mais ne riant pas, riant dessus mais dedans ne riant pas, *je ne sais pas ce qu'ils demandent.*

tyrs, so many men, thousands and thousands of men have wished to enter into public action, have wished to become, to make themselves public figures. And they have paid the price. They have put into it genius, heroism, efforts without number, incredible efforts, terrific efforts; terrific sufferings; whole lives and such lives, of genuine martyrdom. And nothing, never anything. And he, without doing anything, in spite of himself in a few weeks, he became the man of whom the whole of humanity has heard the most, his name has become the name, he has become the man whose name everybody has oftenest repeated, has oftenest celebrated since Napoleon died. What a hundred battles gave to the latter, he received in spite of himself. And he was none the prouder for it.—

This tragic situation reminds me of a remark made by Bernard-Lazare. One must always go back, one always goes back to a remark made by Bernard-Lazare. This remark will be the decisive pronouncement on the case. Because it came from, because coming from its greatest prophet it has a bearing on the victim himself.

Dreyfus had just returned. Dreyfus had come back and almost instantly, with the first happenings, the first negotiations, the first contact, everyone suddenly had the impression that there was a flaw somewhere, that all was not quite right, that he was as he was but not as we had dreamed him to be. Already then a few grumbled. A few, secretly, then publicly, accused him. Secretly, publicly, Bernard-Lazare defended him. Sharply, obstinately. Tenaciously. With that admirable voluntary blindness of those who really love, with that invincible obstinate blind fury with which love defends a being who is wrong, obviously wrong, publicly wrong. *"I don't know what they want,"* said he, laughing but not laughing,

Je ne sais pas ce qu'ils lui veulent. Parce qu'il a été condamné injustement, on lui demande tout, il faudrait qu'il ait toutes les vertus. Il est innocent, c'est déjà beaucoup.

La méconnaissance des prophètes par Israël et pourtant la conduite d'Israël par les prophètes, c'est toute l'histoire d'Israël.

La méconnaissance des saints par les pécheurs et pourtant le salut des pécheurs par les saints, c'est toute l'histoire chrétienne.

La méconnaissance des prophètes par Israël n'a d'égale, n'a de comparable, bien que fort différente, que la méconnaissance des saints par les pécheurs.

On peut même dire que la méconnaissance des prophètes par Israël est une *figure* de la méconnaissance des saints par les pécheurs.

laughing outwardly but inwardly not laughing, "*I don't know what they ask. I don't know what they want of him. Because he has been unjustly condemned, everything is asked of him, that he have all the virtues. He is innocent, that already means a great deal.*"

THE DISREGARD of Israel for prophets, and despite this the guidance of Israel by the prophets: this is the whole history of Israel.

The disregard of sinners for saints and despite this the salvation of sinners by saints, this is the whole of Christian history.

The disregard of Israel for the prophets is only to be equalled, is only to be compared, although most different, with the disregard of sinners for saints.

One can even say that the disregard of Israel for the prophets is a *symbol* of the disregard of sinners for saints.

JAURÈS

LA DERNIÈRE FOIS que je vis Jaurès, en effet, c'était pendant les mois où justement il préparait la publication de cette même *Humanité.*—Je ne trahirai aucun secret en rapportant que Jaurès alors venait de loin en loin me voir à l'imprimerie. De Passy à Suresnes, par le bois, la route est belle. Jaurès qui en ce temps-là travaillait beaucoup, beaucoup trop, à ses articles de la *Petite République* et surtout à son énorme *Histoire socialiste de la Révolution française,* Constituante, Législative, Convention, quatre énormes volumes au moins, si j'ai bon souvenir, *in quarto,* sang de bœuf, ne portait pas toujours très bien tant de travail. Qui l'eût porté, à sa place? Il éprouvait le besoin, par excès de travail, lourdeur de tête, afflux sanguin,—il est sanguin—congestion aux yeux,—toutes les misères de celui qui lit, qui écrit, et qui corrige des épreuves, il éprouvait le besoin de faire l'après-midi régulièrement une promenade, une marche, un peu solide, à pied. Le Bois est une des beautés monumentales de Paris. Et les routes un peu fermes sont belles sous le pied. De Passy à Suresnes il y a trente-cinq minutes, sans se presser. Jaurès venait de loin en loin me trouver à l'imprimerie. J'y étais presque toujours.

Jean Jaurès, French socialist leader, founder of L'Humanité, *the daily organ of the socialist party. Led the socialist party in its campaign for the rehabilitation of Dreyfus.*

JAURÈS

THE LAST TIME that I saw Jaurès was during precisely those months when he was preparing the publication of *L'Humanité.*—I am betraying no secret in recounting that Jaurès came to see me, at great intervals, at the printing-office, in those days. From Passy to Suresnes through the wood, the road is beautiful. Jaurès, who at that time worked a great deal, far too much, at his articles for the Petite République * and above all at his enormous Socialistic History of the French Revolution,—Constituent Assembly, Legislative Assembly, National Convention—four enormous volumes at least, if I remember rightly, *in quarto,* color of ox-blood, could not always very well stand so much work. Who else could have stood it, in his place? He felt the need, because of excessive work, heaviness in the head and a congested condition—he is full-blooded—congested eyesight—all the ailments of those who read, who write and who correct proofs, he felt the need of taking a regular walk in the afternoon, a

* *Daily newspaper.*

Ensemble nous partions par les routes bien courbes et par les droites avenues, soit que je dusse revenir ensuite à l'imprimerie pour y finir ma journée, soit que cette reconduite me fût un chemin de retourner vers Paris.

Les personnes qui m'ont quelquefois reproché de garder pour Jaurès des ménagements excessifs n'ont évidemment point connu le Jaurès que je connaissais pendant ces promenades retentissantes. Nous pouvions nous voir et causer et marcher ensemble honnêtement. Sans aucune compromission d'aucune sorte. Sans faiblesse de l'un ni de l'autre. Il avait été, dans les meilleures conditions du monde, un de nos collaborateurs. Et puis enfin, en ce temps-là, il était Jaurès. Et je n'étais point en reste avec lui. A titre de collaborateur il nous avait fourni de la très bonne copie. A titre de gérant je lui en avais fait des éditions comme il n'en avait jamais eu depuis, comme il n'en aura jamais d'autres. Au demeurant, par je ne sais quel obscur pressentiment des développements ultérieurs, ou par quelle obscure pénétration des présentes réalités profondes, par une sage administration de ce commerce oratoire, je m'étais toujours scrupuleusement conduit de telle sorte que je ne redusse rien à mon illustre partenaire. Non seulement je ne lui ai jamais demandé un de ces services d'amitié, un de ces bons offices qui lient un honnête homme. Eternellement. Mais j'avais toujours conduit nos relations de librairie, et toutes autres, j'avais toujours administré mes sentiments même de telle sorte que mon compte créditeur débordât toujours mon compte débiteur d'une assez large marge. Il y a, dans la vie, de ces profonds pressentiments.

Comme alors les pressentiments me venaient, anticipant les tristesses ultérieures, ainsi aujourd'hui, et réciproquement— les souvenirs m'assaillent, rappelant les illusions publiques à

rather substantial walk afoot. The Bois is one of the monumental beauties of Paris. And the rather firm roads are good under foot. It takes thirty-five minutes to walk from Passy to Suresnes without hurrying. At great intervals Jaurès used to come and fetch me at the printing-office. I was almost always to be found there. Together we used to set forth along well-curved roads and along straight avenues, I sometimes having to return to the printing-office to finish my day's work, while on other occasions seeing him home for me was a way of returning towards Paris.

Those persons who sometimes have reproached me for having treated Jaurès with excessive indulgence obviously did not know the Jaurès whom I knew during these vociferous walks. We could meet and talk and walk honestly together. Without any compromise of any kind. Without cession on the part of one or the other. He had been, under the best possible conditions, one of our collaborators. And finally, at that time, he was Jaurès. And I was under no obligations to him. In the capacity of a contributor he had provided us with very good copy. In the capacity of chief editor I had printed editions of his copy such as he has never had since, such as he will never have again. Besides I do not know through what obscure premonition of later developments, or through what obscure penetration of deep actual realities, through a wise management of this oratorical intercourse, I had always scrupulously conducted myself so that I owed nothing to my illustrious partner. Not only had I never asked of him one of those friendly services, one of those good offices which commit an honest man. Eternally. But I had always managed our literary business relations, and all others, I had always governed even my own sentiments in such a manner that my credit ac-

jamais perdues. Qui alors ne se fût attaché à lui? Et qui, d'avance attaché, ne se fût maintenu attaché? Son ancienne et authentique gloire de l'ancienne affaire Dreyfus, renforçant, doublant sa plus ancienne et sa non moins authentique gloire socialiste, l'entourait encore d'un resplendissement de bonté. C'était le temps où il était de notoriété que Jaurès était bon. D'autres pouvaient lui contester d'autres valeurs, mais tout finissait ainsi toujours: Il est bon. Pour ça, il est bon. Et ce fut la période aussi, les quatre ans où n'étant pas député,* sorti du monde parlementaire, presque de tout le monde politique, il eut vraiment dans ce pays une situation qu'il n'a jamais retrouvée.

Un assez grand nombre de personnes me reprochent d'avoir gardé pour Jaurès une tendresse secrète, qui transparaît même, qui transparaît surtout dans mes sévérités les plus justifiées. C'est qu'elles ne connaissent point un Jaurès que j'ai parfaitement connu, alors, un Jaurès bon marcheur et bon causeur, non pas le Jaurès ruisselant et rouge des meetings enfumés, ni le Jaurès, hélas, rouge et devenu lourdement mondain des salons de défense républicaine; mais un Jaurès de plein air et de bois d'automne, un Jaurès comme il eût été s'il ne lui fût jamais arrivé malheur, et dont le pied sonnait sur le sol dur des routes. Un Jaurès des brumes claires et dorées des commencements de l'automne.

Un Jaurès qui, bien que venu vers nous des versants des Cévennes et remonté des rives de la Garonne, goûtait parfaitement la parfaite beauté des paysages français. Un Jaurès qui admirait et qui savait regarder et voir ces merveilleux arbres de l'Ile-de-France, tout dorés par les automnes de ce temps-là. Un Jaurès qui, debout aux grêles parapets de fonte

* *1898–1902.*

count always overlapped my debit account by a rather wide margin. There are, in life, such deep presentiments.

Exactly as at that time presentiments overcame me, anticipating later sadness, so today and reciprocally—memories assail me, recalling universal illusions for ever lost. Who at that time would not have been attached to him? And who, once attached, would not have remained so? His ancient and authentic fame of the incipient Dreyfus case, strengthening, doubling his more ancient and no less authentic socialistic fame, still bathed him in a splendor of kindness. It was the time when it was public knowledge that Jaurès was kind. Others could deny his possession of other qualities, but all argument invariably ended thus: "He is kind. Undeniably, he is kind." And this was also the period, those four years, when, not being a deputy, having left the parliamentary world, almost completely the political world, he really occupied in this country a position which he has never regained.

A rather great number of persons reproach me with having retained a secret tenderness for Jaurès which even transpires, which is to be detected above all in my most justifiable severities. That is because they never knew a Jaurès that I knew perfectly in those days, a Jaurès who was a good walker and a good talker, not the perspiring and red-faced Jaurès of smoky public meetings, nor the Jaurès alas, red-faced and become clumsily elegant, of the drawing-rooms of the republican defence; but a Jaurès of the open air and of autumnal woods, a Jaurès such as he would have been, had he never experienced ill-luck, and whose footsteps rang on the hard soil of the roads. A Jaurès of the clear and golden hazes of the commencements of autumn.

A Jaurès who, although he had come to us from the foot-

ou de quelque métal du pont de Suresnes, regardant vers Puteaux, admirait, savait admirer en spectateur moderne toute la beauté industrielle de cette partie de la Seine; ou regardant de l'autre côté, planté debout face au fleuve, il regardait, il admirait, il enregistrait, il voyait comme un Français, le fleuve courbe et noble descendant aux pieds des admirables lignes des coteaux. Il m'expliquait tout cela. Il expliquait toujours tout. Il savait admirablement expliquer, par des raisons discursives, éloquentes, concluantes. Démonstratives. C'est ce qui l'a perdu. Un homme qui est si bien doué pour expliquer tout, est mûr pour toutes les capitulations. Une capitulation est essentiellement une opération par laquelle on se met à expliquer, au lieu d'agir. Et les lâches sont des gens qui regorgent d'explications.

J'ai connu un Jaurès poétique. Une admiration commune et ancienne, en partie venue de nos études universitaires, nous unissait dans un même culte pour les classiques et pour les grands poètes. Il savait du latin. Il savait du grec. Il savait énormément par cœur. J'ai eu cette bonne fortune,—et cela n'a pas été donné à tout le monde,—j'ai eu cette bonne fortune de marcher aux côtés de Jaurès récitant, déclamant. Combien d'hommes ont connu les poètes par la retentissante voix de Jaurès? Racine et Corneille, Hugo et Vigny, Lamartine et jusqu'à Villon, il savait tout ce que l'on sait. Et il savait énormément de ce que l'on ne sait pas. Tout *Phèdre,* à ce qu'il me semblait, tout *Polyeucte.* Et *Athalie.* Et *Le Cid.* Il eût fait un Mounet admirable, si la fortune adverse ne s'était pas acharnée à faire de lui un politicien. Il était venu au classique peut-être plus par un goût toulousain de l'éloquence romaine. Et je devais y être venu un peu plus peut-être par un goût français de la pureté grecque. Mais en ce temps-là on

hills of the Cévennes and from the banks of the Garonne, perfectly appreciated the perfect beauty of French landscapes. A Jaurès who admired and who knew how to look at and how to see those marvelous trees of the Ile-de-France turned golden by the autumns of those times. A Jaurès who, standing by the frail railings, made of cast-iron or some such metal, of the Suresnes bridge, looking towards Puteaux, admired, knew how to admire, all of the industrial beauty of this part of the Seine. Or, looking in the opposite direction, planted upright to face the river, looked at, admired, registered, saw as a Frenchman the curved and noble river flowing at the foot of the admirable lines of hills. He explained all this to me. He always explained everything. He knew admirably how to explain by discursive, eloquent, conclusive reasons. Demonstrative reasons. That is what ruined him. A man who is so gifted for the explanation of everything is ripe for all surrenders. A surrender is essentially an operation by which one settles down to explain instead of to act. And cowards are people crammed with explanations.

I have known a poetical Jaurès. A common and long-standing admiration, derived in part from our university studies, united us in the same veneration of the classics and of the great poets. He knew some Latin. He knew some Greek. He knew an enormous amount by heart. I have had this good fortune and this has not been given to everyone—I have had this good fortune to walk by the side of Jaurès while he recited, declaimed. How many men have known the poets through the resounding voice of Jaurès? Racine and Corneille, Hugo and Vigny, Lamartine and even Villon, he knew all that everyone knows. And he knew a lot of what everyone does not know. All of *Phèdre,* it seems to me, all of *Polyeucte.* And *Athalie.*

n'envenimait point ces légers dissentiments. Les esprits étaient à l'unité. On n'y regardait point d'aussi près. Tout Toulousain qu'il fût d'origine, il s'élevait aisément, parfaitement, naturellement, à l'intelligence et au goût de ces parfaits poètes de la vallée de la Loire, et des environs, qui sont la moelle du génie français, du Bellay, l'immortel Ronsard. Il savait les sonnets. Quand vous serez bien vieille, au soir à la chandelle. Dieu veuille que ces révélations compromettantes ne lui fassent point trop de tort dans sa circonscription.

Il n'y avait d'accidents que quand se rappelant qu'il avait commencé, normalien, par être un brillant agrégé de philosophie, il entreprenait de faire le philosophe. Alors ces entretiens devenaient désastreux. Un jour j'eus le malheur de lui dire que nous suivions très régulièrement les cours de M. Bergson au Collège de France, au moins le cours du vendredi. J'eus l'imprudence de lui laisser entendre qu'il faut le suivre pour savoir un peu ce qui se passe. Immédiatement, en moins de treize minutes, il m'eut fait tout un discours de la philosophie de Bergson, dont il ne savait pas, et dont il n'eût pas compris le premier mot. Rien n'y manquait. Mais il avait été le camarade de promotion de M. Bergson dans l'ancienne Ecole Normale, celle qui était supérieure. Cela lui suffisait. Ce fut une des fois qu'il commença de m'inquiéter.

Il était si éloquent que souvent il s'arrêtait, malgré lui, machinalement, pour être éloquent encore davantage; et qu'il marchât ou qu'il fût arrêté, les gens, dans la rue, souvent, s'arrêtaient pour le regarder parler. Tous ne le connaissaient point, bien qu'il fût l'homme le plus célèbre de France et alors dans tout l'éclat de sa gloire. Mais qu'on le connût, ou qu'on ne le connût pas,—et puisqu'aussi bien nous en sommes

And *Le Cid.* He would have made an admirable Mounet,* if adverse fortune had not insisted in making a politician of him. He had been attracted to classic style perhaps chiefly by a Toulousan taste for Roman eloquence. And I must have been attracted to it a little more perhaps by a French taste for Greek purity. But in those times one did not infuse bitterness into these slight differences. Minds were united. One was not so critical. Although he was originally from Toulouse, he rose easily, perfectly, naturally to the intelligence and the taste of those perfect poets of the Loire valley and its environs, that are the marrow of French genius: du Bellay, the immortal Ronsard. He knew the sonnets. When you are old, at evening, candle-lit.† God grant that these compromising revelations harm him little in his constituency.

Mishaps occurred only when, remembering that as a *normalien* ‡ he had begun by being a brilliant Ph.D., he undertook to play the philosopher. Then these conversations became disastrous. One day I had the misfortune to tell him that we very regularly attended M. Bergson's course of lectures at the Collège de France, at least the Friday course. I was sufficiently imprudent to give him to understand that this course must be followed if one wished to be in the know. Immediately, in less than thirteen minutes, he delivered himself of a discourse on Bergson's philosophy, of which he did not know and of which he would not have understood the very first word. It was all there. But he had graduated in the same class with M. Bergson from the former Ecole Normale, the one

* *Mounet was a well-known tragedian of the Comédie Française.*

† *The first line of one of Ronsard's "Sonnets to Helen."*

‡ *Normalien, a boy who has studied at the Ecole Normale.*

au chapitre des confessions,—dans ma sotte vanité de jeune homme, de jeune socialiste, de jeune dreyfusiste, j'étais secrètement flatté d'être publiquement le public, l'homme-public d'un homme aussi célèbre et d'un aussi grand orateur.—

La dernière fois, donc, la dernière fois que je vis Jaurès, dans ces conditions, et je ne l'ai jamais revu non plus dans aucunes autres conditions, ce fut précisément pendant les mois qu'il préparait ce journal qui est devenu l'*Humanité.* Les vieilles gens se rappellent encore tout ce que l'on attendait de ce journal en formation. Le journal de Jaurès! on en avait plein les années à venir. Depuis des années on savait bien, on avait bien dit que Jaurès finirait par faire son journal. Enfin on aurait, on verrait, on allait voir le journal de Jaurès. On attendait. Il ne fallait rien dire. Ce serait un journal comme on n'en avait jamais vu. Le journal de Jaurès, enfin! Ce mot disait tout. Ce mot valait tout. On verrait ce que ce serait que le journal de Jaurès. Les titres couraient.

Ce fut sur ces entrefaites qu'arrivant un jour à l'imprimerie un peu de temps après le déjeuner, les imprimeurs me dirent: Vous savez que Jaurès est venu vous demander. Ils n'étaient pas peu fiers, les imprimeurs, de me faire cette commission, parce que la vénération que les anciens sujets avaient pour le roi de France n'était rien auprès des sentiments que nos modernes citoyens nourrissent pour les grands chefs de leur démocratie.

Il y avait dès lors fort longtemps que je n'avais pas revu Jaurès, depuis qu'il était redevenu député.* Sa capitulation devant la démagogie combiste et bientôt sa complicité dans la démagogie combiste avait achevé de consommer une sépara-

* *Aux élections de 1902.*

called superior. That sufficed him. This was one of the moments in which he began to alarm me.

He was so eloquent that often he stopped, in spite of himself, mechanically, in order to be still more eloquent; and whether he walked or whether he stopped, people in the street often stopped to watch him talk. Not everybody did know him although he was the most famous man in France, and then in all the radiance of his glory. But whether one knew him or whether one did not,—and since we are on the subject of confessions,—in my foolish vanity as a young man, as a young socialist, as a young Dreyfusist, I was secretly flattered to be publicly the public, the public-man of a man so famous and so great an orator.—

So the last time, the last time that I saw Jaurès under these conditions, and I have never again seen him under any other conditions, was precisely during the months when he was preparing that newspaper which has become *L'Humanité*. There are old people who still remember all that was expected of this newspaper while it was in preparation. Jaurès' newspaper! Then the years to come would be filled. For years, everyone had very well known, everyone indeed had said that Jaurès would end by founding his own newspaper. At last one would have, at last one would see Jaurès' newspaper. One waited. One held one's breath. It would be a newspaper such as never had been seen. In short, Jaurès' newspaper! This term meant everything. One would see what Jaurès' newspaper would be like! There were rumors concerning the title.

It was at that time when, reaching the printing-office a short while after lunch, the printers said to me: "Do you know, Jaurès came here to look for you." Those printers were not a

tion dont le point d'origine se perdait dans les établissements de nos plus anciennes relations. Pourtant quand les imprimeurs m'eurent ainsi rapporté que Jaurès était venu me demander, je me dis que somme toute j'était le plus jeune, un tout jeune homme en comparaison de lui, que par conséquent je lui devais le respect, que je devais lui céder le pas, que nos anciennes relations n'avaient jamais rien eu que d'honnête et de hautement honorable, que le souvenir m'en serait toujours précieux, que je pouvais donc, que je devais faire la deuxième démarche. Je me présentai chez lui peut-être le lendemain matin. Il n'est pas une des maisons où je suis allé une fois où je ne puisse honorablement retourner. Peu d'hommes publics pourraient en dire autant.

Je me présentai chez lui. Je croyais qu'il avait quelque chose à me dire. Il n'avait rien. Il était un tout autre homme. Vieilli, changé, on ne sait combien. Cette dernière entrevue fut sinistre. C'est une grande pitié quand deux hommes, qui ont vécu ensemble d'une certaine vie, après une longue et définitive interruption d'eux-mêmes se remettent ou par les événements sont remis dans les conditions extérieures de cette ancienne vie. Nulle conjoncture, autant que ce rapprochement, n'imprime en creux dans le cœur la trace poussiéreuse et creuse de la vanité des destinées manquées. Il sortit. Je l'accompagnai pourtant. Nous allâmes à pied. Il mit des lettres à la poste, ou des télégrammes. Nous allâmes, nous allâmes, par ces froides avenues du seizième arrondissement. Arrivés à la statue de La Fayette, ou à peu près, il arrêta une voiture, pour faire une course. Au moment de le quitter, je sentis bien que ce serait pour la dernière fois. Un mouvement profond, presque un remords, fit que je ne pouvais pas le quitter ainsi. Au moment de lui serrer la main

little proud to give me this message for the reason that the veneration which former subjects had for the king of France was nothing in comparison with the sentiments entertained by our modern citizens for the great leaders of their democracy.

At that period it had been a very long time since I had seen Jaurès, that is, since he had been re-elected deputy.* His surrender to the Combist demagogy and shortly after, his complicity in the Combist demagogy had put the finishing touch to a separation of which the starting point could be traced to the very beginning of our relations. However when the printers gave me the message that Jaurès had called to ask for me, I said to myself that, after all, I was the younger, quite a young man in comparison with him, that in consequence I owed him respect and that I should give him precedence, that our former relations had never been anything but decent and highly honorable, that their memory would always be precious to me, that I could therefore, that I should make the next step myself. I put in an appearance at his house if I remember correctly next morning. There is not a single house at which I have visited once, where it is impossible for me honorably to return. Few public men can say as much.

I went to his house. At the time I thought that he had something to communicate to me. He had not. He was an entirely different man. Grown older, changed, one cannot say how much. This final meeting was sinister. It is a great pity when two men who have shared a certain kind of life, after a long and definitive interruption of their intercourse meet again or are brought back by circumstances into the external conditions of this old life. No juncture as much as this sort of *rapprochement* leaves on the heart the dusty and hollow im-

* *At the elections of 1902.*

pour cette dernière fois, revenant sur ce qui était ma pensée depuis la veille, et depuis le commencement de ma visite, je lui dis: Je croyais que vous étiez venu me voir hier à l'imprimerie pour me parler de votre journal.—Un peu précipitamment: non.—Quelques instants auparavant il m'avait dit d'un ton épuisé: Je fais des courses, des démarches.—Il était et paraissait fatigué.—Les gens ne marchent pas. Les gens sont fatigués. Les gens ne valent pas cher. Il était lassé, voûté, ravagé. Je n'ai jamais vu rien ni personne d'aussi triste, d'aussi désolant, d'aussi désolé, que cet optimiste professionnel.

Avait-il dès lors, et depuis quelque temps, par ces démarches mêmes, un pressentiment de la vie atroce où il allait entrer. Ce jour, ce temps avait dans sa vie une importance capitale. Pour la dernière fois il quittait la vie libre, la vie honnête, la vie de plein air du simple citoyen; pour la dernière fois, et irrévocablement, il allait plonger, faire le plongeon dans la politique. Il était frappé d'une grande tristesse. Il assistait à sa propre déchéance. Et comme il est naturellement éloquent, dans son cœur il se plaignait fort éloquemment.—Je lui dis: Ecoutez. Vous savez bien que je ne vous demande pas d'entrer dans votre journal. Ma vie appartient tout entière aux cahiers. Mais j'ai autour de moi, ou enfin il y a aux cahiers un certain nombre de jeunes gens que vous pourriez faire entrer. Ils ne sont point célèbres. Ils ne courent point après la gloire. Mais ils sont sérieux. Et ils ont la vertu qui est devenue la plus rare dans les temps modernes: la fidélité. Ce n'est point par la fidélité que brillent ceux qui vous entourent. Et moi, vous savez par quelles crises, par quelles misères les cahiers ont passé depuis cinq ans: pas un de mes collaborateurs ne m'a lâché. Cela vaut encore mieux

print of the vanity of miscarried destinies. He went out. I nevertheless accompanied him. We walked. He took letters to the post-office, or telegrams. We walked and walked through the cold avenues of the sixteenth *arrondissement*. When we reached the statue of Lafayette, or thereabouts, he stopped a cab to do an errand. At the moment of leave-taking I felt keenly that it was for the last time. A movement of feeling, almost of remorse, made me feel that I could not thus leave him. At the moment I shook his hand for the last time, returning to what had been in my mind since the day before and since the beginning of my visit, I said to him: "I thought that you had come to see me yesterday at the printing-office to talk to me about your newspaper." A little hastily he said: "No." A few moments before he had said to me in an exhausted tone of voice: "I run about, try to see people." He was weary and appeared so: "You can't get people going. They are played out. People aren't worth much." He was tired, bowed, wasted. I have never seen anything or anyone so sad, so distressing, so distressed as this professional optimist.

Did he at that moment have, and had he for some time already had, as the result of these efforts, a premonition of the atrocious life into which he was about to step. This day, this period were of prime importance in his life. Forever he quit the free life, the honest life, the open air life of the simple citizen; forever and irrevocably he was to plunge, to take the plunge into politics. He was overwhelmed with a great sadness. He was the spectator of his own decay. And as he was naturally eloquent, in his heart he complained most eloquently.—I said to him: "Listen. You know well that I am not asking you to let me collaborate on your newspaper. My whole life belongs to the "Cahiers." But I have around me, or

que tout ce que j'ai publié. C'est sans doute la première fois que ce fait se produit depuis le commencement de la troisième République.

Il était embarrassé. J'insistai.—Alors, il commença d'élever un peu les bras au ciel d'un air désolé: Vous savez bien ce que c'est. J'avais mon personnel plein avant de commencer. Il est plus facile d'avoir des collaborateurs que de trouver des commanditaires.

Je le savais de reste. Une dernière poignée de mains. Il monta, lourd, écroulé, dans ce fiacre baladeur. Je ne l'ai jamais revu depuis.

Rien n'est mystérieux comme ces sourdes préparations qui attendent l'homme au seuil de toute vie. Tout est joué avant que nous ayons douze ans.

Je croyais quand j'étais petit que les groupes travaillent. Aujourd'hui nous savons que les groupes ne font aucune œuvre. Ils font de l'agitation.

in short, there are a certain number of young men working for the "Cahiers" to whom you could give work. They are not famous. They do not chase after glory. But they are earnest. And they possess the virtue which has become the rarest of all in modern times: loyalty. Those who surround you are not conspicuous for their loyalty. And as for me, you know through what crises, through what straits the "Cahiers" have passed during the last five years: Not one of my collaborators has let me down. That in itself is more important than anything I have published. Doubtless this is the first time that this event has occurred since the foundation of the Third Republic." He was embarrassed. I insisted.—Whereupon he began to raise his arms to Heaven slightly, with an air of distress: "You know very well how it is. I had a full staff before beginning. It is easier to have contributors than to find financial backers."

That I already knew. A final handshake. Heavy, crumbling, he got into that loitering cab. I have never seen him since.

THERE IS NOTHING so mysterious as those secret preparations which await man at the threshold of all life. All is decided before we are twelve years old.

WHEN I WAS SMALL I believed that groups worked. Today we know that groups do not work. They create agitation.

PARIS

CAPITALE TEMPORELLE du monde, capitale intellectuelle —et capitale spirituelle, encore, toujours, quand même capitale spirituelle; *ville qui a le plus souffert pour le salut temporel de l'humanité.*

Ville odieuse de plus de pépiaillerie, et ville respectable, ville respectueuse, ville quand on veut du plus total silence, du plus infini, du plus éternel, du plus authentique silence.

Du plus grand des biens: le silence.—

La ville donc du jeu, du papotage et du *divertissement.* Ville du plus d'élévation, du plus de contemplation, du plus de méditation. Ville de la plus grande prière.

Ville où se fabrique, ville où se fomente et se cuit, comme on cuit le pain, ville où germe et se travaille le plus de cette matière de l'élévation dans cette forme de l'élévation, de la contemplation, de la méditation. De la prière.

Ville où se vend le plus de vice, où se donne le plus de prière.

P A R I S

TEMPORAL CAPITAL of the world, intellectual capital—and spiritual capital still, always, in spite of everything, spiritual capital. *The city which has suffered most for the temporal salvation of mankind.*

Odious city of the greatest chirruping, and respectable city, respectful city, when one wishes, city of the most total silence, of the most infinite, of the most eternal, of the most authentic silence.

Of the greatest of goods: silence.—

The city of gambling, of gossiping and of *entertainment.* City of the greatest elevation, of the greatest contemplation, of the greatest meditation. City of the greatest prayer.

City where they manufacture, city where they foment and where they bake, as bread is baked, city where germinates and rises the most of this substance of elevation, in that form of elevation, of contemplation, of meditation. Of prayer.

City where they sell the greatest amount of vice, where the greatest amount of prayer is given away.

Où vous avez ce Luxembourg ami pour ainsi dire à vous tout seul. Et vous êtes encore en très grand nombre qui l'avez ainsi à vous tout seuls. Et en septembre le soleil a un goût si fin, si ambré, si reposoir, d'une lumière si rare, après la légère, après la transparente buée de septembre du matin, si reposée,—d'une clarté si pure et si arrêtée, d'une admirable tiédeur d'adieu, calme, d'une odeur de fruit, d'une senteur de rose d'automne—et non pas encore de grande feuille sèche, passage de l'extérieur à l'intérieur, du plein air et du plein soleil aux intimités du foyer, approchement des veillées d'hiver, sentiment poignant doubleface, attente et crainte, espoir, calme, avec, peut-être, un soupçon de regret.—

Ville de la perdition. Ville du salut.—

Pour nous Français ville de France la plus française, la plus profondément, la plus essentiellement, la plus authentiquement, la plus traditionnellement française.—

Et pour tout le monde la ville du monde la plus insupportablement cosmopolite; une orgie des nations; un carrefour le plus banal du monde; un caravansérail des peuples; la plus antique des Babels modernes; la confusion des langues; la plus moderne des Babels antiques; un boulevard où on parle tout excepté français. Surtout quand on se met à y parler parisien.

Ville du monde la plus internationale, et la seule véritablement internationaliste, passage et séjour des peuples de la terre, de tous les peuples; et ville nationale, même étroitement, et nationaliste.

Ville du plus d'ordre et du plus de désordre; du plus grand ordre, du seul qui soit véritablement, réel; apparemment du plus grand désordre; réellement du plus grand désordre, du seul fécond.

Where you have that friendly Luxembourg garden practically to yourself. And yet there are a great number of you who have it thus entirely to yourselves. And in September the sun has such a delicate, such an ambered savor; a savor akin to the peace of a reposoir.* And the sunlight is of such a rare quality after the subtle, after the transparent haze of a September morning, and so tranquil. Of a clarity so pure and so motionless, of an admirable soft warmth like that of leave-taking, calm, having the odor of a fruit, the scent of an autumn rose,—and not yet that of the great dry leaf; the passage from outdoors to indoors, from open air and broad sunlight to the intimacies of the hearth, the approach of winter evenings,—poignant, double-faced sentiment, expectation and fear, hope, calm, with perhaps a dash of regret.—

City of perdition. City of salvation.—

For us French, the city of France the most French, the most profoundly, the most essentially, the most authentically, the most traditionally French.—

And for everybody, the city that is the most insupportably cosmopolitan in the world; an orgy of nations; the most common crossway in the world; the caravansary of peoples; the most ancient of modern Babels; the confusion of tongues; the most modern of ancient Babels; a boulevard where everything is spoken excepting French. Particularly when people set themselves to talking Parisian.

The most international city in the world and the only really internationalistic one, the thoroughfare and sojourn of the peoples of the earth, of all the peoples; and a national city, even narrowly so, and nationalistic.

* *A reposoir is an open-air altar erected in Catholic countries during the procession of Corpus Christi, on which to rest the Holy Sacrament.*

Ville de l'inquiétude, d'une inquiétude incurable, et des vicissitudes, des perpétuelles tribulations, des essentielles, de la tribulation essentielle.

Ville la plus païenne. La plus chrétienne. Certainement la plus catholique.

Ville apparemment la plus suiveuse, où toutes les folies, où toutes les facéties, où toutes les sottises, où toutes les insanités, où toutes les bêtises, où toutes les imbécillités du monde, où tous les orgueils, où toutes les futilités, où toutes les vanités de la terre trouvent immédiatement et automatiquement un asile. Plus qu'un asile, un temple. Une faveur, un crédit, un éclat incomparable. Unique. Ville de l'engouement. Et du plus sot. Et du plus inlassable. Imbécile pourtant le bénéficiaire qui s'y fierait. Aussi immédiatement ensuite, aussi automatiquement ville qui se débarrasse de la boue, de la gourme, de l'écume de tout engouement.

Ville la plus immobile. Et qui suit le moins. Qui ne suit jamais.—

Pour les fous, ville la plus folle, ville du plus de folie; pour les sages, ville la plus sage, ville du plus, de la plus grande sagesse. La seule ville sage. De la seule sagesse. La plus grande sagesse antique du monde, depuis la ruine du monde antique, depuis la mort d'Athènes (et de Rome). Et le plus de foi chrétienne. La foi chrétienne la plus fidèle.

Capitale de la luxure. Capitale de la prière. Capitale de la foi. Capitale de la charité. Capitale de tout.

Capitale aussi de la gloire (temporelle). Mais qu'est-ce que la gloire, après tout cela.

Capitale de la luxure (on le dit). Capitale du vice (on le prétend). Capitale de la vertu. Capitale, apparemment capi-

City of the most order and of the most disorder; of the greatest order, the only one which is truly real; apparently of the greatest disorder, really of the greatest disorder, the only fruitful one.

City of unrest, of incurable unrest and of vicissitudes, of perpetual tribulations, of essential tribulations, of the essential tribulation.

The most pagan of cities. The most Christian. Certainly the most catholic.

City apparently the most readily seduced, where all the follies, where all the jokes, where all the nonsense, where all the insanities, where all the foolishness, where all the stupidity in the world, where all the prides, where all the futilities, where all the vanities of the earth immediately and automatically find a haven. More than a haven, a temple. A gracious reception, a trustfulness, an incomparable splendor. Unique. City of infatuation, of the silliest, of the most indefatigable. But the man who benefits by this infatuation would be a fool to trust in it. For immediately after, it is a city which automatically rids itself of the mud, of the rash, of the scum of all infatuation.

The most motionless of cities. And the one that is least slavish. Which is never led.—

For madmen the maddest of cities, the city of most madness; for the wise the wisest of cities, the only city of the most, of the greatest wisdom. The only wise city. Of the only wisdom. The greatest antique wisdom in the world since the ruin of the ancient world, since the death of Athens (and Rome). And the one with the greatest amount of Christian faith. The most faithful Christian faith.

tale du péché. Ville de tant de grandeurs, de toute grandeur. Ville de tant de bassesses, de toute misère. Ville de toute charité, dans tous les sens de ce mot, excellemment, éminemment, infiniment dans ce sens technique qui l'emporte infiniment sur les autres. Ville d'orgueil et d'humilité, de modestie toujours. Capitale de la pensée. Capitale de la production et de la consommation de la pensée.

Ville du monde où les arrivistes temporels arrivent le plus, le plus vite, le plus infailliblement, le plus automatiquement. Et tous les snobs temporels. Ville aussi qui use le plus infailliblement, le plus accélérément les arrivistes temporels, et comme automatiquement, et qui presque tout de suite leur casse les reins, afin qu'on n'en parle plus.

Ville d'où rayonne, hélas, le plus d'intelligence dans le monde.—Cerveau où s'élabore le plus de pensée. Cœur d'où monte, dans toute cette buée que vous voyez de Montmartre, dans ce brouillard, dans toute cette buée de mer, dans cette buée industrielle, poussières de charbons, poussières de pavés de bois, poussières de pavés de pierre, poussières de résidus, de saletés de toute sorte, poussières de vapeur, vapeurs d'eau, vapeurs aujourd'hui d'essence et de pétrole et de tant d'huiles lourdes, vapeurs aussi de tant de respirations malsaines, cœur d'où monte, à travers toute cette buée temporelle, le plus de spécifiquement, le plus de techniquement véritable prière.

Capital of lust. Capital of prayer. Capital of faith. Capital of charity. Capital of everything.

Capital also of glory (temporal). But what is glory, after all that.

Capital of lust (so it is said). Capital of vice (so it is claimed). Capital of virtue. Capital, apparently capital of sin. City of so many grandeurs, of all grandeur. City of so much baseness, of all destitution. City of all charity, in all the meanings of this word, excellently, eminently, infinitely in this technical meaning which infinitely outweighs all the others. City of pride and humility, of modesty always. Capital of thought. Capital of the production and of the consumption of thought.

City in all the world where temporal "climbers" succeed the most, the quickest, the most infallibly, the most automatically. And all the temporal snobs. Also the city which wears out the temporal "climbers" the most infallibly and the most quickly and as it were automatically; and which, almost at once, breaks their backs, so that they need no more be mentioned.

City from which, alas, the greatest amount of intelligence radiates in the world.—Brain which elaborates the greatest amount of thought. Heart from which rises in all that mist visible from Montmartre, in that fog, in that marine vapor, in that industrial vapor, coal dust, dust from wooden pavings, dust from cobblestones, dust from leavings, filth of all kinds, dust of steam, water vapor, today's vapors of gasoline and petroleum and of so many heavy oils, vapors too of so many unhealthy exhalations . . . Heart from which rises past all this temporal mist, the greatest amount of specifically, the greatest amount of technically veritable prayer.

JEANNE D'ARC

ELLE ÉTAIT PEUPLE et chrétienne et sainte. Elle fut très certainement en un sens une femme d'armes; on pourrait presque dire une guerrière. Elle fut incontestablement un très grand chef militaire.—Elle fut une fleur de la race chrétienne et de la race française, une fleur de chrétienté, une fleur de toutes les vertus héroïques.—

Quelles que soient les forces des sources vives, quelles que soient les inventions et les perpétuels rejaillissements et jaillissements, quelles que soient les inépuisables nouveautés de la grâce il y a ensemble indéniablement une certaine technique, une certaine sainte hiérarchie comme professionnelle, une armature et une ossature presque de métier, une certaine sainte hiérarchie professionnelle de la Vertu héroïque et de la sainteté. Il y a des degrés qui sont les degrés même du Trône. Au premier degré Jeanne d'Arc eut dans leur plein les vertus de la guerre, qui ne sont pas petites. Je veux dire très expressément par là et très proprement qu'elle entra dans le

JOAN OF ARC

SHE WAS OF THE PEOPLE, and Christian, and saintly. She was most certainly in a sense a woman at arms. One might almost say a warrior. She was unquestionably a very great military leader.—She was a flower of the Christian race and of the French race, a flower of Christendom, a flower of all heroic virtues.—

Whatever may be the powers of the living springs, whatever may be the devices and the perpetual emission and effusion, whatever may be the inexhaustible innovations of grace, at the same time there indubitably exists a certain technique, a certain blessed hierarchic arrangement, as it were professional, a framework and a skeleton almost of the *métier*, a certain blessed professional hierarchy of heroic virtue and saintliness. There are degrees which are the very degrees of the Throne. To the first degree Joan of Arc possessed in their fullness the virtues of war, which are not small. I mean to say by that, very expressly and very properly, that she entered

jeu de la guerre et dans le risque de guerre à plein, sans aucune restriction, sans aucune intervention, sans aucune intercalation de protection divine propre. Elle obéissait, elle accomplissait une mission divine propre dans un monde humain sans avoir touché une protection divine propre correspondante. Elle avait reçu l'ordre; elle avait reçu la vocation; elle avait reçu la mission. Elle obéissait, elle exécutait l'ordre; elle répondait à la vocation; elle accomplissait sa mission. Elle procédait à l'exécution, à l'accomplissement de sa mission dans une humanité dure (et tendre), dans un monde, dans une chrétienté dure et tendre, elle-même douce et ferme, forte, douce, quelquefois apparemment dure. Apparemment rude. Pendant toute sa mission elle reçut assistance de conseil, nous le savons, par l'assistance et le conseil constamment renouvelé, constamment présent de ses voix. Par cette sorte d'assistance de conseil, presque féodale, perpétuellement renouvelée, perpétuellement présente. Pendant toute sa mission, et j'y compte sa captivité, quelques absences qu'elle ait eu à y souffrir, et sa mort. Pendant toute sa mission et dedans pendant sa captivité elle reçut constante assistance de conseil de ses voix et une abondance de grâces dont nous ne pouvons avoir aucune idée. Le jour de sa mort elle reçut une grâce qui ne fut jamais donnée peut-être, ainsi et à ce point, à aucune autre sainte, de sorte que le jour de sa mort ne fut déjà plus pour elle le dernier jour de la vie de cette terre mais littéralement réellement déjà le premier jour de sa vie éternelle. Mais enfin avec cette mission, avec cette vocation, avec toutes ces grâces, avec tous ces dons, avec cette présence constante de conseil elle ne reçut jamais ni la grâce, ni le don, ni le conseil, ni aucune faveur d'être invulnérable. Elle fit la guerre exposée à tous les accidents de la guerre. Elle fit

into the game of war and into the risk of war fully, without any restriction, without any intervention, without any interposition on the part of divine protection. She obeyed, she accomplished a divine mission proper in a human world without having felt a corresponding divine protection proper. She had received the commandment, she had received the vocation, she had received the mission. She obeyed, she carried out the commandment, she responded to the vocation, she accomplished her mission. She passed to the achievement, to the accomplishment of her mission in the midst of a hard (and tender) humanity, in a world, in a Christendom hard and tender, herself being gentle and firm, strong, gentle, sometimes apparently hard. Apparently harsh. During her whole mission she received assistance of counsel, this we know, through the constantly renewed, constantly present assistance and counsel of her voices. Through this sort of assistance of counsel, almost feudal, perpetually renewed, perpetually present. During her whole mission and in this I include her captivity, in spite of the few absences that she had to suffer in its course, and her death. During her whole mission which extended into her captivity she received constant assistance of counsel from her voices and an abundance of graces of which we can have no idea. The day of her death she received a grace which perhaps was never given similarly and to such an extent to any other saint, so that the day of her death already was no longer for her the last day of life on earth but literally, really, already the first day of her eternal life. But after all, with this mission, with this vocation, with all these graces, with all these gifts, with this constant presence of counsel, she never received either the grace, or the gift, or the counsel, or any privilege of being invulnerable. She waged

comme tout le monde une guerre comme tout le monde. Moins heureuse que tant de saintes, moins heureuse que tant de prophètes mêmes et que tant de chefs du peuple d'Israël, les anges qui l'assistaient de leurs conseil, ou les saints, ne combattaient point à ses côtés. Jamais la parole de Jésus: *Penses-tu que je ne puisse pas maintenant prier mon Père, qui me donnerait aussitôt plus de douze légions d'anges? Comment donc s'accompliraient les Ecritures qu'il faut que cela arrive ainsi?* ne s'accomplit aussi pleinement dans une sainte et nous rejoignons ici cette vocation, cette élection unique, cette imitation unique par laquelle on peut dire que de toutes les saintes elle fut celle à qui certainement il fut donné que sa vie et sa Passion et sa mort fut imitée au plus près de la vie et de la Passion et de la mort de Jésus.—

Douze légions d'anges. Elle ne les demanda pas non plus. Elle ne les demanda jamais. Ce conseil, qu'elle avait, qui était comme la conséquence, comme la suite naturelle de l'ordre, de la vocation, comme la suite naturelle, surnaturelle naturelle, venant des mêmes voix, porté par le même ministère, ce conseil qu'elle eut, qu'elle avait, presque familièrement pour ainsi dire, à son usage comme la prière quotidienne, ce conseil usager comme la prière du matin et du soir elle le (re)demanda souvent. Des secours surnaturels de guerre directs, physiques, une assistance de guerre, des troupes surnaturelles de guerre qu'elle n'avait pas, elle ne les demanda jamais.—

Il semble que jamais le roi du ciel n'ait voulu aussi expressément que dans la personne de cette grande sainte qu'une de ses filles gagnât elle-même les palmes du martyre.

Elle le savait. Non seulement elle n'était point garantie, elle n'était point assurée contre la maladie et contre la blessure et contre la défaite militaire mais elle savait qu'elle

war, exposed to all the accidents of war. She, like everybody else, waged a war like everybody else. Less fortunate than many saints, less fortunate than many prophets even, and than many rulers of the people of Israel, she did not find fighting beside her the angels who assisted her with their counsels, or the saints. Never have the words of Jesus: "*Thinkest thou that I cannot now pray to my Father and He shall presently give me more than twelve legions of angels? But how then shall the Scriptures be fulfilled, that thus it must be?*" never have they been so fully accomplished in a saint, and here we meet again with this vocation, this unique election, this unique imitation by which one can say that of all the saints, she it was to whom certainly it was given that her life and her Passion and her death should most closely imitate the life and the Passion and the death of Jesus.—

Twelve legions of angels. She did not ask for them any more than He did. She never asked for them. This counsel, which she had, which was like the consequence, like the natural sequence of the commandment, of the vocation, like the natural sequence, supernatural and natural, coming from the same voices, borne by the same agency, this counsel which she had and had still, almost familiarly, so to speak, for her use as daily prayer, this habitual counsel like morning and evening prayer, she asked for often and asked for it again. Supernatural, direct, physical help in war, assistance in war, supernatural troops of war which she did not have, she never asked for.—

It would seem that never had the King of Heaven wished so expressly as in the person of this great saint that one of His daughters should win of herself the palms of martyrdom.

She knew it. Not only was she not protected, she was not

n'était point assurée contre la maladie et contre la blessure et contre la défaite militaire.—

Elle accomplit une tâche divine par des moyens simplement humains. Elle exécuta un ordre divin par des moyens strictement humains. Elle répondit à une vocation divine par des moyens rigoureusement humains, par un travail, par une guerre militaire, par des opérations, par des efforts exactement humains. Elle accomplit une mission divine par des moyens simplement humains. C'est ce qui lui donne une place à part, une place toute éminente dans la hiérarchie des saintetés. Notons encore, notons en outre que la matière où devait s'exercer cette sainteté était la plus extraordinaire, la plus hors de l'ordre, habituel, on pourrait presque dire la plus étrangère aux matières habituelles de la sainteté. Et même la plus contraire et ennemie aux matières habituelles de la sainteté. Entre toutes elle fut véritablement envoyée en mission extraordinaire. Par ces deux commandements elle a une place unique dans la hiérarchie des saintetés, elle est sainte et bénie entre toutes les saintes et ensemble par le premier elle est femme entre toutes les saintes.

Que si d'autre part on veut la considérer non plus à son rang de sainteté mais à son rang d'humanité, qui ne voit aussitôt qu'elle est dans cet ordre une femme unique. Un être unique. Car si l'on veut elle est de la race des saints, et si l'on veut elle est de la race des héros. Venant de Dieu et retournant à Dieu et recevant constamment assistance de conseil de ses voix par tout son être elle est une sainte. Elle est de la race des saints. Mais dans cette dure humanité du quinzième siècle et de tous les siècles accomplissant par des moyens purement humains un tel ramassement d'exploits purement humains d'une guerre purement humaine, de toute une action

ensured against sickness and against wounds and against military defeat, but she knew that she was not ensured against sickness and against wounds and against military defeat.—

She accomplished a divine task through merely human means. She carried out a divine commandment through strictly human means. She responded to a divine vocation through exclusively human means, by a work, by a military war, by operations, by efforts strictly human. She accomplished a divine mission through simply human means. This is what gives her a place apart, a most eminent place in the hierarchy of sanctities. Let us also note, let us note further that the substance in which this sanctity had to be exerted was the most extraordinary, the farthest removed from the habitual order, one might almost say the most foreign to habitual substances of sanctity. And even that one most contrary and hostile to the habitual substances of sanctity. Among all saints she it was who was truly sent on a mission extraordinary. By these two commandments she has a unique place in the hierarchy of sanctities, she is holy and blessed among all saints while at the same time through the first commandment she is a woman among all the saints.

If on the other hand one wishes to consider her, no longer in her order of sanctity but in her order of humanity, who does not immediately perceive that in this order she is a unique woman. A unique being. For if one wishes, she is of the race of saints, and if one wishes, she is of the race of heroes. Coming from God and returning to God and constantly receiving assistance of counsel from her voices, in all her being she is a saint. She is of the race of saints. But in this hard humanity of the fifteenth century, and of all the centuries, accomplishing by purely human means such an array

purement humaine, par toute son action comme extérieure, par tout son engagement corps et âme dans l'action militaire, dans toute une action de guerre, par toute sa condition, par tout son être d'action elle est un héros, elle est de la race des héros.

Or non seulement la race des héros et la race des saints n'est pas la même. Mais ce sont deux races peu ou mal apparentées. On pourrait presque dire qui ne s'aiment pas, qui n'aiment pas frayer ensemble, qui sont gênées d'être ensemble. Il y a on ne sait quoi de profond et qu'il faudrait approfondir par quoi la race des héros et la race des saints ont on ne sait quelle contrariété profonde. Il n'y a peut-être point deux races d'hommes qui soient profondément aussi étrangères l'une à l'autre, aussi éloignées l'une de l'autre, aussi contraires l'une à l'autre que la race des héros et la race des saints. On découvrirait sans doute que cette contrariété profonde ne fait que traduire, mais sous une forme, sous sa forme peut-être la plus aiguë, sous sa forme éminente, cette profonde, cette éternelle contrariété du temporel et de l'éternel.

Or Jeanne d'Arc, précisément parce qu'elle exerçait sa sainteté dans des épreuves purement humaines par des moyens purement humains, précisément parce qu'elle était demeurée entièrement vulnérable militairement, vulnérable à la maladie, vulnérable à la blessure, vulnérable à la capture, vulnérable à la mort, vulnérable à la défaite et à toute défaite, exposée en son plein comme un héros antique à toute aventure de guerre elle est de la race des héros comme elle est de la race des saints. Et comme dans la race des saints elle est et une sainte entre toutes les saintes et une femme entre toutes les saintes, ainsi, parallèlement ainsi dans la race des héros

of purely human exploits in a purely human war, in all of this purely human action, through all her externally directed action, through her whole engagement of body and soul in military action, in an entire action of war, by her entire condition, by her entire active being she is a hero, she is of the race of heroes.

Now, not only are the race of heroes and the race of saints not identical, but they are two scarcely or ill-connected races. One might almost say that they do not care for each other, that they do not like to keep company together, that they are embarrassed to be in one another's company. There is something inexpressibly profound and which should be fathomed, through which the race of heroes and the race of saints stand in some inexpressibly deep contradiction. There are perhaps no two races of men that are so profoundly foreign one to the other, so far removed one from the other, so antithetical one to the other as are the race of heroes and the race of saints. Doubtless one would discover that this profound contradiction merely manifests, but under a form, perhaps under its sharpest form, under its eminent form, that eternal contradiction of the temporal and the eternal.

Now Joan of Arc, precisely because she exerted her saintliness in purely human trials, by purely human means, precisely because she had remained entirely vulnerable in battle, vulnerable to sickness, vulnerable to wounds, vulnerable to capture, vulnerable to death, vulnerable to defeat and to all defeat, fully exposed like an ancient hero to all warlike adventure, precisely for this reason she is of the race of heroes as she is of the race of saints. And as in the race of saints she is not only a saint among all saints and a woman among all saints, so in a parallel manner, so in the race of heroes, she is

elle est un héros entre tous et une femme. Elle n'est pas moins éminente dans la hiérarchie héroïque que dans la hiérarchie sacrée. Et ainsi elle est à un point d'intersection unique dans l'histoire de l'humanité. En elle se joignent deux races qui ne se joignent nulle part ailleurs. Par un recoupement unique de ces deux races, par une élection, par une vocation unique dans l'histoire du monde elle est à la fois sainte entre tous les héros, héroïque entre toutes les saintes.

JE NE CROIS PAS que j'aie jamais parlé du *monde catholique.* J'ai parlé souvent de l'Église, de la communion. Je ne me sens pleinement à moi, je ne touche vraiment le fond de ma pensée que quand j'écris la chrétienté. Alors je vois en plein ce que je dis.

a hero among all heroes and a woman. She is not less eminent in the heroic hierarchy than in the sacred hierarchy. And thus she is at a point of intersection unique in the history of humanity. In her two races meet that meet nowhere else. By a unique intersection of these two races, by an election, by a vocation unique in the history of the world she is at once saintly among all heroes, heroic among all the saints.

I DO NOT BELIEVE that I have ever spoken of the *Catholic world.* I have often spoken of the Church, of communion. I do not feel truly myself, I do not really touch the bottom of my thought save when I write Christendom. Only then I fully see what I say.

POETRY

MALÉDICTION SUR LA GUERRE

JEANNE D'ARC PARLE:

—Qu'importent nos efforts d'un jour? qu'importent nos charités? Je ne peux pourtant pas donner toujours. Je ne peux pas donner tout. Je ne peux pas donner à tout le monde. Je ne peux pourtant pas faire manger aux passants tout le pain de mon père. Et même alors, est-ce que ça paraîtrait? dans la masse des affamés. (Elle cesse insensiblement de filer.) Pour un blessé que nous soignons par hasard, pour un enfant à qui nous donnons à manger, la guerre infatigable en fait par centaines, elle, et tous les jours, des blessés, des malades et des abandonnés. Tous nos efforts sont vains; nos charités sont vaines. La guerre est la plus forte à faire la souffrance. Ah! maudite soit-elle! et maudits ceux qui l'ont apportée sur la terre de France.

Nous aurons beau faire, nous aurons beau faire, ils iront toujours plus vite que nous, ils en feront toujours plus que nous, davantage que nous. Il ne faut qu'un briquet pour brûler une ferme. Il faut, il a fallu des années pour la bâtir. Ça n'est pas difficile; ça n'est pas malin. Il faut des mois et des mois, il a fallu du travail et du travail pour pousser une

A CURSE ON WAR

JOAN OF ARC SPEAKS:

—What avail our efforts of a day? What avail our charities? I really can't give all the time. I can't give all. I can't give to every one. I really can't give the passers-by all my father's bread. And even if I did, would it make any difference? In the mass of the famished. (She stops spinning by imperceptible degrees.) For every wounded man we happen to look after, for every child we feed, indefatigable war makes hundreds of wounded, of sick and homeless people, every day. All our efforts are vain. War has more power than anything when it comes to making people suffer. Ah, a curse on war! And a curse on those who brought it to the land of France.

Try as we may, try as we may, they will always go faster than we, they will always do more than we, a deal more than we. All that is needed to set a farm ablaze is a flint. It takes, it took years to build it. It isn't difficult. One doesn't have to be so clever. It takes months and months, it took work and more work to make the crop grow. And all that is needed to set a crop ablaze is a flint. It takes years and years to make a man

moisson. Et il ne faut qu'un briquet pour flamber une moisson. Il faut des années et des années pour faire pousser un homme, il a fallu du pain et du pain pour le nourrir, et du travail et du travail et des travaux et des travaux de toutes sortes. Et il suffit d'un coup pour tuer un homme. Un coup de sabre, et ça y est. Pour faire un bon chrétien il faut que la charrue ait travaillé vingt ans. Pour défaire un chrétien il faut que le sabre travaille une minute. C'est toujours comme ça. C'est dans le genre de la charrue de travailler vingt ans. C'est dans le genre du sabre de travailler une minute; et d'en faire plus; d'être le plus fort. D'en finir. Alors nous autres nous serons toujours les moins forts. Nous irons toujours moins vite, nous en ferons toujours moins. Nous sommes le parti de ceux qui construisent. Ils sont le parti de ceux qui démolissent. Nous sommes le parti de la charrue. Ils sont le parti du sabre. Nous serons toujours battus. Ils auront toujours le dessus dessus nous, par dessus nous.

Nous aurons beau dire.

Pour un blessé qui se traîne au long des routes, pour un homme que nous ramassons au long des routes, pour un enfant qui traîne au bord des routes, combien la guerre n'en fait-elle pas, des blessés, des malades, et des abandonnés, de malheureuses femmes, et des enfants abandonnés; et des morts, et tant de malheureux qui perdent leur âme. Ceux qui tuent perdent leur âme parce qu'ils tuent. Et ceux qui sont tués perdent leur âme parce qu'ils sont tués. Ceux qui sont les plus forts, ceux qui tuent perdent leur âme par le meurtre qu'ils font. Et ceux qui sont tués, celui qui est le plus faible, perdent leur âme par le meurtre qu'ils subissent, car se voyant faibles et se voyant meurtris, toujours les mêmes fai-

grow, it took bread and more bread to feed him, and work and more work, and all kinds of work. And all that is needed to kill him is one blow. One swordthrust and it's done. To make a good Christian, the plough has to work twenty years. To kill a good Christian, the sword has to work one minute. It's always that way. It's like the plough to work twenty years and it's like the sword to work one minute. It's always that way. It's like the plough to work twenty years and it's like the sword to work one minute, and to do more, to be stronger, to make an end of things. So we people will always be the weaker ones. We will always go more slowly, we will always do less. We are the party of those who build up. They are the party of those who pull down. We are the party of the plough. They are the party of the sword. We will always be beaten. They will always get the better of us, on top of us.

No matter what we say.

For one wounded man dragging himself along the roads, for one man we pick up on the roads, for one child dragging himself along the roadsides, how many people are wounded, and sick, and forsaken, how many women are made unhappy and children forsaken because of the war, and how many are killed, and how many unfortunates lose their souls. Those who kill lose their souls because they kill. And those who are killed lose their souls because they are killed. Those who are strongest, those who kill lose their souls through the murder which they commit. And those who are killed, the man who is weaker, lose their souls through the murder which they suffer, for, seeing how weak they are and how bruised, always the same being weak, and the same unhappy, and the same beaten, and the same killed, then, unhappy ones, they despair of their sal-

bles, toujours les mêmes malheureux, toujours les mêmes battus, toujours les mêmes tués, alors les malheureux ils désespèrent de leur salut, car ils désespèrent de la bonté de Dieu. Et ainsi, de quelque côté qu'on se tourne, des deux côtés c'est un jeu où, comment qu'on joue, quoi qu'on joue, c'est toujours le salut qui perd, et c'est toujours la perdition qui gagne. Tout n'est qu'ingratitude, tout n'est que désespoir et que perdition.

Et le pain éternel. Celui qui manque trop du pain quotidien n'a plus aucun goût au pain éternel, au pain de Jésus-Christ.

Maudite soit-elle, maudite de Dieu.

vation, because they despair of the goodness of God. Thus, no matter where one may turn, on both sides, it is a game in which, no matter how one plays or what one plays for, salvation is always bound to lose and perdition always bound to win. There is nothing but ingratitude, nothing but despair and perdition.

And bread everlasting. He who is too much in lack of daily bread no longer has any desire for bread everlasting, the bread of Jesus Christ.

Cursed be war, cursed of God.

IL FAUT QUE FRANCE CONTINUE

Est-ce que le père aurait du cœur à travailler s'il n'y avait pas ses enfants.
Si ça n'était pas pour ses enfants.
Et l'hiver quand il travaille dur.
Dans la forêt.
Quand il travaille le plus dur.
De la serpe et de la scie et de la cognée et de la hache.
Dans la forêt glacée.
L'hiver quand les vipères dorment dans le bois parce qu'elles sont gelées.
Et quand il souffle une bise aigre.
Qui lui transperce les os.
Qui lui passe au travers de tous les membres.
Et il est tout transi et il claquerait des dents.
Et le givre lui fait des glaçons dans sa barbe.
Tout d'un coup il pense à sa femme qui est restée à la maison.
A sa femme qui est si bonne ménagère.
Dont il est l'homme devant Dieu.

FRANCE MUST GO ON

Would the father's heart be in his work if he did not have his children,
If it weren't for his children?
And in winter when he is hard at work
In the forest,
When he works hardest
With his pruning-hook and his saw and his axe and his hatchet,
In the icy forest,
In winter when the adders are asleep in the woods because they are frozen,
And when a bitter north wind blows,
Going through his bones,
Going clean through all his limbs,
And he is completely chilled and his teeth are likely to chatter,
And the frost puts icicles in his beard,
All of a sudden he thinks of his wife who has remained at home,
Of his wife who is such a good housekeeper,
Whose man he is before God,

Et à ses enfants qui sont bien tranquilles à la maison.
Qui jouent et qui s'amusent à c'te heure au coin du feu.
Et qui peut-être se battent.
Ensemble.
Pour s'amuser.
Ils passent devant ses yeux, dans un éclair devant les yeux de sa mémoire, devant les yeux de son âme.
Ils habitent sa mémoire et son cœur et son âme et les yeux de son âme.
Ils habitent son regard.
Dans un éclair il voit ses trois enfants qui jouent et qui rient au coin du feu.
Ses trois enfants, deux garçons et une fille.
Dont il est le père devant Dieu.
Son aîné, son garçon qui a eu douze ans au mois de septembre.
Sa fille qui a eu neuf ans au mois de septembre.
Et son cadet qui a eu sept ans au mois de juin.
Ainsi la fille est au milieu.
Comme il convient.
Afin qu'elle soit défendue par ses deux frères.
Dans l'existence.
Un avant et l'autre après.
Ses trois enfants qui lui succéderont et qui lui survivront.
Sur terre.
Qui auront sa maison et ses terres.
Et s'il n'a point de maison et de terres qui auront du moins ses outils.
(S'il n'a point de maison et de terres ils n'en auront point non plus.
Voilà tout.)

And of his children who are quite peacefully staying at home,
Playing, having fun right now by the fireside,
Fighting perhaps,
Together,
For fun;
They pass before his eyes, in a flash before his memory's eyes, before the eyes of his soul,
They dwell in his memory and in his heart and in his soul and in the eyes of his soul,
They dwell in his gaze,
In a flash he sees his three children playing and laughing by the fireside
His three children, two boys and a girl,
Whose father he is before God;
His eldest, his boy who was twelve in September,
His daughter who was nine in September,
And his youngest child who was seven in June,
Thus his daughter stands in the middle,
As it should be,
In order that she may be protected by her two brothers,
In this life,
One before and one after,
His three children who will succeed him and survive him
On earth,
Who will have his house and his land,
And should he own neither house nor land, will at least have his tools,
(Should he own neither house nor land, they won't own any either,
That is all),

(Il s'en est bien passé pour vivre.
Ils feront comme lui. Ils travailleront.)
Sa hache et sa cognée et sa serpe et sa scie.
Et son marteau et sa lime.
Et sa pelle et sa pioche.
Et sa bêche pour bêcher la terre.
Et s'il n'a pas de maison et de terre.
S'ils n'héritent pas sa maison et sa terre.
Au moins ils hériteront ses outils.
Ses bons outils.
Qui lui ont servi tant de fois.
Qui sont faits à sa main.
Qui ont tant de fois bêché la même terre.
Ses outils, à force de s'en servir, lui ont rendu la main toute calleuse et luisante.
Mais lui, à force aussi de s'en servir, il a rendu poli et luisant le manche de ses outils.
Et à force de travailler il a la peau aussi dure et aussi tannée que le manche de ses outils.
Au manche de ses outils ses fils retrouveront, ses fils hériteront la dureté de ses mains.
Mais aussi leur habileté, leur grande habileté.
Car il est un bon labourer et un bon bûcheron.
Et un bon vigneron.
Et avec ses outils ses fils hériteront, ses enfants hériteront.
Ce qu'il leur a donné, ce que nul ne pourrait leur ôter.
(Presque pas même Dieu.)
(Tant Dieu a donné à l'homme.)
La force de sa race, la force de son sang.

(He managed to live without house and land,
They will do as he did. They will work).
His hatchet and his axe, and his pruning-hook, and his saw,
And his hammer, and his file,
And his shovel, and his pickaxe,
And his spade to dig the soil;
And should he own neither house nor land,
Should they not inherit his house and his land,
At any rate, they will inherit his tools,
Good tools,
The tools that he has used so many times,
That were accustomed to his hand,
That so often digged the same soil;
His tools, from being used so often, have made his hand all callous and shiny,
But he, by using them so often, has made their handle smooth and shiny,
And by dint of hard work, he now has a skin as hard and as tanned as his tools' handles;
Through his tools' handles, his sons will find anew, his sons will inherit the hardness of his hands,
But also their skill, their great skill,
Because he is a good ploughman and a good woodcutter,
And a good winegrower;
And with his tools his sons will inherit, his children will inherit
What he has given them, what no one could take away from them,
(Not even God, almost)
(So much has God given to man),
The strength of his race, the strength of his blood;

Car ils sont sortis de lui,
Et ils sont Français et Lorrains.
Fils de bonne race et de bonne maison.
Or bonne race ne peut mentir.
Fils de bonne mère.
Et par dessus tout ce qui est par dessus tout avec ses outils et avec sa race et avec son sang ses enfants hériteront.
Ce qui vaut mieux qu'une maison et un morceau de terre à laisser à ses enfants.
Car la maison et la terre sont périssables et périront.
Et la maison et la terre sont exposées au vent de l'hiver.
A cette bise aigre qui souffle dans cette forêt.
Mais la bénédiction de Dieu n'est soufflée par aucun vent.
Ce qui vaut mieux que les outils, ce qui est plus laborieux, plus ouvrier que les outils.
Ce qui fait plus de travail que les outils.
Et les outils finissent tout de même par s'user.
Comme l'homme.
Ce qui vaut mieux, ce qui est plus durable que la race et le sang.
Même.
Car la race même et le sang ont périssables et périront.
Excepté le sang de Jésus.
Qui sera versé dans les siècles des siècles.
Et la race même et le sang sont exposés au vent de l'hiver.
Et il peut y avoir un hiver des races.
Avec sa maison peut-être s'il en a une et sa terre.
Avec ses outils sûrement et sa race et son sang ses enfants hériteront.
Ce qui est au dessus de tout.

For they came from him,
And they belong to France and to Lorraine,
Sons of a good race and of good stock.
Now good race does not belie itself,
Good mother's sons;
And above all that which is above all, with his tools and his race and his blood, his children will inherit
What is worth more than a house and a piece of land to leave to one's children,
For house and land are perishable and will perish,
And house and land are exposed to the winter wind,
To that bitter north wind that blows in that forest,
But God's blessing is blown by no wind;
What is worth more than tools, what is more hard-working, more workman-like than tools,
What accomplishes more work than tools,
And tools end up by wearing out,
Like man,
What is worth more, what lasts longer than race and blood,
Even,
For the race itself and the blood are perishable and will perish,
Except the blood of Jesus
Which shall be shed for centuries and centuries,
And the race itself and the blood are exposed to the winter wind,
And perchance there is a winter for races,
With his house perchance, if he has one, and his land,
Surely with his tools and his race and his blood, his children will inherit
That which is above everything:

La bénédiction de Dieu qui est sur sa maison et sur sa race.
La grâce de Dieu qui vaut plus que tout.
Il le sait bien.
Qui est sur le pauvre et sur celui qui travaille.
Et qui élève bien ses enfants.
Il le sait bien.
Parce qu'il l'a promis.
Et qu'il est souverainement fidèle dans ses promesses.

Ses trois enfants qui grandissent tellement.
Pourvu qu'ils ne soient pas malades.
Et qui seront certainement plus grands que lui.
(Comme il en est fier dans son cœur.)
Et ses deux gars seront rudement forts.
Ses deux gars le remplaceront, ses enfants tiendront sa place sur la terre.
Quand il n'y sera plus.
Sa place dans la paroisse et sa place dans la forêt.
Sa place dans l'église et sa place dans la maison.
Sa place dans le bourg, et sa place dans la vigne.
Et sur la plaine et sur le coteau et dans la vallée.
Sa place dans la chrétienté. Enfin. Quoi.
Sa place d'homme et sa place de chrétien.
Sa place de paroissien, sa place de laboureur.
Sa place de paysan.
Sa place de père.
Sa place de Lorrain et de Français.
Car c'est des places, grand Dieu, qu'il faut qui soient tenues.
Et il faut que tout cela continue.
Quand il n'y sera plus comme à présent.
Sinon mieux.

The blessing of God that is on his house and on his race,
The grace of God that is worth more than anything,
(He knows it well),
That is on the poor man and on him who works
And who brings up his children properly,
He knows it well,
Because he promised it
And because he is supremely faithful in his promises.

His three children who are growing so fast,
Let us hope they don't fall ill,
And who will certainly be taller than he,
(How proud he is of them in his heart),
And his two boys are going to be powerfully strong,
His two boys will replace him, his children will take his place
on earth,
When he is no longer there,
His place in the parish and his place in the forest,
His place in church and his place at home,
His place in the market-town and his place in the vineyard,
And in the plain, and on the hillside, and in the valley,
His place in christendom, don't you know,
His place as a man and his place as a christian,
His place as a parishioner, his place as a ploughman,
His place as a peasant,
His place as a father,
His place as a son of Lorraine and of France,
Because, good Lord, those are places which have to be kept,
And all that must go on,
When he is no longer there, just as it is going on now,
If not better;

Il faut que la paysannerie continue.
Et la vigne et le blé et la moisson et la vendange.
Et le labour de la terre.
Et le pâtour des bêtes.
Quand il n'y sera plus comme à présent.
Sinon mieux.
Il faut que la chrétienté continue.
L'Église militante.
Et pour cela il faut qu'il y ait des chrétiens.
Toujours.
Il faut que la paroisse continue.
Il faut que France et que Lorraine continue.
Longtemps après qu'il ne sera plus.
Aussi bien comme à présent.
Sinon mieux.
Il pense avec tendresse à ce temps où il ne sera plus et où ses enfants tiendront sa place.
Sur terre.
Devant Dieu.
A ce temps où il ne sera plus et où ses enfants seront.
Et quand on dira son nom dans le bourg, quand on parlera de lui, quand son nom sortira, au hasard des propos, ce ne sera plus de lui que l'on parlera mais de ses fils.
Ensemble ce sera de lui et ce ne sera pas de lui, puisque ce sera de ses fils.
Ce sera son nom et ce ne sera plus et ce ne sera pas son nom, puisque ce sera (devenu) le nom de ses fils.
Et il en est fier dans son cœur et comme il y pense avec tendresse.

Peasantry must go on,
And the wine and the wheat and the harvest and the vintage,
And the ploughing of the soil,
And the feeding of the animals,
When he is no longer there, just as now,
If not better,
Christendom must go on,
The Church militant,
And for that there must be christians,
Always;
The parish must go on,
France and Lorraine must go on
A long time after he is gone,
Just as well as at present,
If not better;
With tenderness he thinks of that time when he will no longer be there and when his children will have taken his place
On earth,
Before God,
Of that time when he will no longer be alive and when his children will live.
And when they mention his name in the market-town, when they talk about him, when his name is uttered, as conversation will have it, it won't be of him they will talk, but of his sons.
Altogether, it will be he and it won't be he, since it will be his sons;
It will be his name, and it will no longer be and it will not be his name since it will have become his sons' name;
And he is proud of that in his heart and how tenderly he thinks of it,

Que lui-même ne sera plus lui-même mais ses fils.
Et que son nom ne sera plus son nom mais le nom de ses fils.
Que son nom ne sera plus à son service mais au service de ses fils.
Qui porteront le nom honnêtement devant Dieu.
Hautement et fièrement.
Comme lui.
Mieux que lui.
Et quand on dira son nom, c'est son fils qu'on appellera, c'est de son fils qu'on parlera.
Lui il sera depuis longtemps au cimetière.
Entour de l'église.
Lui, c'est-à-dire son corps.
Côte à côte avec ses pères et les pères de ses pères.
Aligné avec eux.
Avec son père et son grandpère qu'il a connus.
Et avec tous les autres tous ceux qu'il n'a pas connus.
Tous les hommes et toutes les femmes de sa race.
Tous les anciens hommes et toutes les anciennes femmes.
Ses ancêtres et ses aïeux.
Et ses aïeules.
Tant qu'il y en a eu depuis que la paroisse a été fondée.
Par quelque saint fondateur.
Venu de Jésus.
Son corps, car pour son âme il y a longtemps.
Qu'il l'a recommandée à Dieu.
La mettant sous la protection de ses saints patrons.

Il dormira, son corps ainsi reposera.
Parmi les siens, (attendant les siens).

That he will no longer be himself but his two sons,
And that his name will no longer be his name but his sons' name;
That his name will no longer be at his service, but at his sons' service
Who will bear the name honestly before God,
Heads high, proudly,
Like him,
Better than he,
And when they say his name, it is his son they will be calling, it is his son they will mean.
As for him, he will long since have been in the graveyard
Around the church,
He, that is, his body,
Side by side with his fathers and the fathers of his fathers,
Aligned with them,
With his father and his grandfather whom he knew,
And with all the others, all those he never knew,
All the men and all the women of his race,
All the ancient men and all the ancient women,
His ancestors and grandsires
And grandams,
As many as there were since the parish was founded
By some holy founder
Who came from Jesus;
His body, for as regards his soul, it has been a long time
Since he commended it to God,
Placing it under the protection of his patron saints.

He will sleep, his body will thus be resting
Among his people, (awaiting his people),

Attendant la résurrection des corps.
Jusqu'à la résurrection des corps son corps ainsi reposera.

Il pense avec tendresse à ce temps où on n'aura pas besoin de lui.
Et où ça ira tout de même.
Parce qu'il y en aura d'autres.
Qui porteront la même charge.
Et qui peut-être, et qui sans doute la porteront mieux.

Il pense avec tendresse à ce temps où il ne sera plus.
Parce que n'est-ce pas on ne peut pas être toujours.
On ne peut pas être et avoir été.
Et où tout marchera tout de même.
Où tout n'en marchera pas plus mal.
Au contraire.
Où tout n'en marchera que mieux.
Au contraire.
Parce que ses enfants seront là, pour un coup.

Ses enfants feront mieux que lui, bien sûr.
Et le monde marchera mieux.
Plus tard.
Il n'en est pas jaloux.
Au contraire.
Ni d'être venu au monde, lui, dans un temps ingrat.
Et d'avoir préparé sans doute à ses fils peut-être un temps moins ingrat.
Quel insensé serait jaloux de ses fils et des fils de ses fils.

Est-ce qu'il ne travaille pas uniquement pour ses enfants.

Awaiting the resurrection of the bodies;
Until the resurrection of the bodies, thus will his body rest.

He thinks tenderly of the time when they will not need him
And when things will have to go on just the same,
Because there will be others
Who will bear the same load
And who, perhaps, and who, no doubt, will bear it better.

He thinks tenderly of the time when he will no longer be,
Because, you know, a man can't live forever,
A man can't be and at the same time have been,
And when everything will go on just the same,
When everything will go on no worse,
On the contrary,
When everything will go on better,
On the contrary,
Because his children will be there, all right!

His children will do better than he, to be sure,
And the world will fare better,
Later on.
He feels no jealousy on that score,
On the contrary,
Nor because he himself came into the world in sorry times
And doubtless prepared for his sons times perhaps less sorry.
What crazy fellow would be jealous of his sons and of his
son's sons?

He is working only for his children, is he not?

Il pense avec tendresse au temps où on ne pensera plus guère
à lui qu'à cause de ses enfants.
(Si seulement on y pense quelquefois. Rarement.)
Quand son nom retentira (cordialement) dans le bourg,
C'est que quelqu'un appellera son fils Marcel ou son fils
Pierre.
C'est que quelqu'un aura besoin de son fils Marcel ou de son
fils Pierre.
Et les appellera, heureux de les voir. Et les cherchera.
Car c'est eux qui régneront alors et qui porteront le nom.
C'est eux qui régneront avec les hommes de leur âge et de
leur temps.
C'est eux qui régneront sur la face de la terre.
Peut-être quelque temps encore un vieux qui se rappellera
Dira.
Les deux gars Sévin c'est des braves gars.
Ça n'est pas étonnant.
Ils ont de qui tenir.
Le père était un si brave homme.
Et quelque temps les jeunes rediront de confiance:
Le vieux était un si brave homme.
Mais déjà ils n'en sauront rien.
Puis ils ne sauront plus et cela même, ce propos même se
taira.
Il pense avec tendresse au temps où il ne sera plus même un
propos.
C'est à cela, c'est pour cela qu'il travaille, car n'est-ce pas
pour ses enfants que l'on travaille.

He thinks tenderly of the time when he will no longer be
much thought of, except because of his children,
(If only he is thought of sometimes; seldom);
When his name echoes (cordially) in the market-town,
It will be because someone calls his son Marcel or his son
Pierre,
It will be because someone needs his son Marcel or his son
Pierre,
And that man will call them, and will be happy to see them,
and will go look for them,
Because they will reign then and bear the name,
They will reign with the men of their age and of their time,
They will reign on the face of the earth;
Perhaps for some time still an old fellow will remember
And say:
'The two Sévin lads, they are good lads.
It's not surprizing.'
They have someone to take after.
'Their father was such a good man.'
And for some time, the young people will repeat confidently:
'The old man was such a good man.'
But already they won't know anything about it; even that
remark will cease to be heard
Then they won't know any more, and even that, even those
words will be silent
He thinks tenderly of the time when he won't even be a
remark;
That is what he is working at, that is what he is working for.
Indeed, isn't it for his children that a man works?

Il ne sera plus qu'un corps dans six pieds de terre sous six pieds de terre sous une croix.
Mais ses enfants seront.
Il salue avec tendresse le temps nouveau où il ne sera plus.
Où il ne sera pas.
Où ses enfants seront.
Le règne de ses enfants.

Il pense avec tendresse à ce temps qui ne sera plus son temps.
Mais le temps de ses enfants.
Le règne (de temps) de ses enfants sur la terre.
Dans ce temps-là quand on dira *les Sévin* ce ne sera pas lui mais eux.
Sans plus, sans explication.

Ses enfants porteront ce nom des Sévin.
(Ou ce nom des Chénin, ou ce nom des Jouffin, ou Damrémont ou tout autre nom de Lorraine.
Tout autre nom chrétien, français, lorrain.)

A la pensée de ses enfants qui seront devenus hommes et femme.
A la pensée du temps de ses enfants, du règne de ses enfants.
Sur la terre,
A leur tour,
Une tendresse, une chaleur, une fierté lui monte.
(Mon Dieu ne serait-ce pas un orgueil.
Mais Dieu lui pardonnera.)
Comme ses fils dans la forêt seront vaillants, juste Dieu.

He won't be any more than a body in six feet of earth, under six feet of earth, under a cross.
But his children will be living.
He greets with tenderness the new times when he will be no more,
When he will not be,
When his children will be,
His children's reign.

He thinks tenderly of that time which will no longer be his time,
But his children's time,
The reign (in time) of his children on earth.
At that time, when people say *the Sévins,* they will not mean him, but them,
No more, with no explanation.

His children will bear that name of Sévin,
(Or that name of Chénin, or that name of Jouffin, or Damrémont or any other name of Lorraine,
Any other name, christian, French or of Lorraine).

At the thought of his children who will have grown into men and women,
At the thought of his children's time, or his children's reign
On earth,
In their turn,
A tenderness, a warmth, a feeling of pride rise up within him.
(Lord, may not that be vainglory?
But God will forgive him).
God of justice, how valiant will his sons be in the forest,

Et des gars solides comme des chênes.
Dans la forêt quand soufflera la bise d'hiver.
La bise aigre.
Qui leur traversera les os.
Et fera des glaçons dans leur barbe.

Il rit en pensant à la tête qu'ils feront.
Il rit en lui-même et peut-être même en dessus.
En dehors.

Quand il pense à la tête qu'ils feront quand ils auront de la barbe.

Et il pense avec tendresse à sa fille qui sera une si bonne ménagère.
Parce que sûrement elle sera comme sa mère.
Il ne sera plus, lui c'est entendu, il ne sera plus.
Il aura perdu le goût du pain.
Mais il y en aura d'autres, Dieu juste il y en aura d'autres,
Il faut l'espérer,
Qui ont déjà le goût du pain et qui sauront mordre dans une bonne miche de pain.
Qui mangeront de bon appétit.
Leur pain de chaque jour.
Qui mangeront de bon appétit leur pain de chaque jour et leur pain éternel.
(On se passera très bien de lui, et il ne sera plus à (la) table, car il faut se pousser à table quand les nouveaux venus viennent et poussent.)

Lads as strong as oaks,
In the forest where the winter north wind blows,
The bitter north wind
That will go through their bones
And put icicles in their beards.

He laughs when he thinks how funny they will look,
He laughs within himself and perhaps even on the surface,
Outwardly.

When he thinks how they will look when they will have a beard.

And he thinks tenderly of his daughter who will be such a good housekeeper,
Because she will be like her mother.
As for him, he won't be living any more, that is understood,
He will have lost his taste for bread,*
But there will be others, just God, there will be others,
We must hope so,
Who already have a taste for bread and who will know how to bite into a fine loaf of bread,
Who will eat with a hearty appetite
Their daily bread,
Who will heartily eat their daily bread and their bread eternal,
(They will very easily do without him, and he will no longer be seated at the table, because you have to squeeze around the table when newcomers arrive and push),

* Perdre le goût du pain, *a French idiom meaning: to die.*

D'autres ses enfants qui vivront et qui mourront après lui si
tout se passe dans l'ordre.
Et qu'il retrouvera en paradis.

Il y en aura d'autres, Dieu merci:
Il faut que France continue.

Others, his children, who will live and die after him if all
turns out as it should,
And whom he will see again in heaven.

There will be others, thank God:
France must go on.

LE PÉCHÉ MORTEL ET LA LÈPRE

DIEU PARLE :

Quand une fois on a connu d'être aimé librement, les soumissions n'ont plus aucun goût.
Quand on a connu d'être aimé par des hommes libres, les prosternements d'esclaves ne vous disent plus rien.
Quand on a vu saint Louis à genoux, on n'a plus envie de voir
Ces esclaves d'Orient couchés par terre
Tout de leur long à plat ventre par terre. Être aimé librement,
Rien ne pèse ce poids, rien ne pèse ce prix.
C'est certainement ma plus grande invention.

This poem is based on a passage from Joinville's History of Saint Louis. *The king of France and his baron Joinville were talking one day of leprosy, not an uncommon subject in thirteenth century conversations, and Joinville declared that his horror of that disease was such that he would prefer committing thirty mortal sins rather than become a leper. Whereupon Saint Louis gently reproved him and said that it were better to be a leper than to commit one mortal sin. This is what God the Father has to say on the subject.*

MORTAL SIN AND LEPROSY

GOD SPEAKS:

Having once known what it is to be loved freely, one no longer finds any flavor in submissions.
When one has known what it means to be loved by free men, the prostrations of slaves no longer please.
When one has seen Saint Louis on his knees, one no longer wishes to see
Those Oriental slaves lying prone on the ground
At body's length, on their stomachs, on the ground. To be loved freely,
Nothing weighs as much as that weighty thing, nothing weighs as much as that thing of great price,
It is certainly my greatest invention.

Quand on a une fois goûté
D'être aimé librement
Tout le reste n'est plus que soumissions.
C'est pour cela, dit Dieu, que nous aimons tant ces Français,
Et que nous les aimons entre tous uniquement
Et qu'ils seront toujours mes fils aînés.
Ils ont la liberté dans le sang. Tout ce qu'ils font, ils le font librement.
Ils sont moins esclaves et plus libres dans le péché même
Que les autres ne le sont dans leurs exercises. Par eux nous avons goûté.
Par eux nous avons inventé. Par eux nous avons créé
D'être aimés par des hommes libres. Quand saint Louis m'aime, dit Dieu,
Je sais qu'il m'aime.
Au moins je sais qu'il m'aime, celui-là, parce que c'est un baron français. Par eux nous avons connu
D'être aimés par des hommes libres. Tous les prosternements du monde
Ne valent pas le bel agenouillement droit d'un homme libre. Toutes les soumissions, tous les accablements du monde
Ne valent pas une belle prière, bien droite agenouillée, de ces hommes libres-là. Toutes les soumissions du monde
Ne valent pas le point d'élancement
Le bel élancement droit d'une seule invocation
D'un libre amour. Quand saint Louis m'aime, dit Dieu, je suis sûr,
Je sais de quoi on parle. C'est un homme libre, c'est un libre baron de l'Ile de France. Quand saint Louis m'aime
Je sais, je connais ce que c'est que d'être aimé.

Once one has tasted
What it is to be loved freely
All the rest is no more than submissions.
That is why, says God, we are so fond of those Frenchmen,
And why, among all other people, we love them in an unparalleled way,
And why they will always be my eldest sons.
They have freedom in their blood. Everything they do, they do freely.
They are less slavish and freer in sin itself
Than the others in their exercises. Through them we have tasted,
Through them we have invented, through them we have created
This thing: to be loved by free men. When Saint Louis says that he loves me,
I know that he loves me,
At least I know that that one loves me, because he is a French baron. Through them we have known
What it is to be loved by free men. All the prostrations in the world
Are not worth the beautiful upright kneeling of a free man. All the submissions, all the self-abasements in the world
Are not worth a beautiful prayer, an upright, kneeling prayer of those free men. All the submissions in the world
Are not worth the soaring point
The beautiful straight soaring of a single invocation
Of a free love. When Saint Louis loves me, says God, I am sure,
I know what is meant. He is a free man, he is a free baron of the Ile de France. When Saint Louis loves me
I am aware, I know what it is to be loved.

(Or c'est tout.) Sans doute il craint Dieu.
Mais c'est d'une noble crainte, toute emplie, toute gonflée,
Toute pleine d'amour, comme un fruit gonflé de jus.
Nullement quelque lâche, quelque basse crainte, quelque sale peur
Qui prend dans le ventre. Mais une grande, mais une haute, mais une noble crainte,
La peur de me déplaire, parce qu'il m'aime, et de me désobéir, parce qu'il m'aime.
Et, parce qu'il m'aime, la peur
De ne pas être trouvé agréable
Et aimant et aimé sous mon regard. Nulle infiltration, dans cette noble crainte,
D'une mauvaise peur et d'une pernicieuse et vile lâcheté.
Et quand il m'aime, c'est vrai. Et quand il dit qu'il m'aime, c'est vrai. Et quand il dit qu'il aimerait mieux
Être lépreux que de tomber en péché mortel (tant il m'aime), c'est vrai.
Lui je sais que c'est vrai.
Ce n'est pas vrai seulement qu'il le dit. C'est vrai que c'est vrai. Il ne dit pas ça pour que ça fasse bien.
Il ne dit pas ça parce qu'il a vu ça dans les livres ni parce qu'on lui a dit de le dire. Il dit ça parce que ça est.
Il m'aime à ce point. Il m'aime ainsi. Librement. La preuve que j'en ai dans la même race
C'est que le sire de Joinville (que j'aime tant tout de même) qui est un autre baron français,
Qui aimerait mieux au contraire avoir commis trente péchés mortels que de devenir lépreux,
(Trente, le malheureux, comme il ne sait pas ce qu'il dit)

(Now that is everything). No doubt he fears God,
But with a noble fear, all filled, all swollen,
All replete with love, like a fruit swollen with juice.
In no wise a cowardly, a base fear, a nasty funk
Which claws at the stomach, but a great, but a lofty, but a noble fear,
The fear of displeasing me, because he loves me, and of disobeying me, because he loves me.
And because he loves me, the fear
Of not being found agreeable
And loving and loved under my gaze. No infiltration in that noble fear,
Of an evil funk and of a pernicious and vile cowardice.
And when he loves me, it is true. And when he says that he loves me, it is true. And when he says that he would prefer
To be a leper than to fall into mortal sin (so much does he love me), it is true.
When he says it, I know it is true.
It isn't only true that he says it. It is true because it is true. He doesn't say it because it sounds well.
He doesn't say that because he saw it in books nor because someone told him to say it. He says it because it is so.
He loves me to that extent. He loves me thus. Freely. A proof of it I have in the same race
And that is the Sire de Joinville (whom I love so very much, just the same), another French baron,
Who would on the contrary have committed thirty mortal sins rather than become a leper.
(Thirty, poor man, how little he knows what he is talking about)

Ne se gêne pas non plus pour dire ce qu'il pense
C'est-à-dire pour dire le contraire
En présence même d'un si grand roi
Et d'un si grand saint
Que pourtant il connaissait pour tel,
C'est-à-dire pour contrarier un si grand roi et un si grand saint. La liberté de parole
De celui qui ne veut pas risquer le coup
D'être lépreux plutôt que de tomber en péché mortel
Me garantit la liberté de parole de celui qui aime mieux être lépreux
Que de tomber en péché mortel.
Si l'un dit ce qu'il pense, l'autre aussi dit ce qu'il pense.
L'un prouve l'autre . . .
Dans leur histoire de la lèpre et du péché mortel voici comme je calcule, dit Dieu.
Quand Joinville aime mieux avoir commis trente péchés mortels que d'être lépreux
Et quand saint Louis aime mieux être lépreux que de tomber en un seul péché mortel,
Je n'en retiens pas, dit Dieu, que saint Louis m'aime ordinairement.
Et que Joinville m'aime trente fois moins qu'ordinairement.
Que saint Louis m'aime suivant la mesure, à la mesure,
Et que Joinville m'aime trente fois moins que la mesure.
Je compte au contraire, dit Dieu. Voici comme je calcule. Voici ce que je retiens.
J'en retiens au contraire que Joinville m'aime ordinairement

Doesn't mind saying what he thinks,
That is, saying the opposite
In the presence of even so great a king
And of so great a saint
Whom he nevertheless knew to be such,
That is, displeasing such a great king and such a great saint.
The freedom of speech
Of one who doesn't wish to run the risk
Of being a leper rather than falling into mortal sin,
Insures for me the freedom of speech of him who prefers being a leper
To falling into mortal sin.
If one says what he thinks, the other too says what he thinks.
One proves the other . . .
In their rigmarole about leprosy and mortal sin, this is how I figure, says God.
When Joinville had rather have committed thirty mortal sins than to be a leper,
And when Saint Louis had rather be a leper than to fall into one single mortal sin,
I do not conclude, says God, that Saint Louis loves me in an ordinary way
And that Joinville loves me thirty times less than the ordinary way.
That Saint Louis loves me according to measure, in just the wanted measure,
And that Joinville loves me thirty times less than the measure.
I reckon, on the contrary, says God, this is how I figure, this is how I conclude.
I conclude, on the contrary, that Joinville loves me in the ordinary way,

Honnêtement, comme un pauvre homme peut m'aimer,
Doit m'aimer.
Et que saint Louis au contraire m'aime trente fois plus qu'ordinairement,
Trente fois plus qu'honnêtement.
Que Joinville m'aime à la mesure,
Et que saint Louis m'aime trente fois plus qu'à la mesure.
(Et si je l'ai mis dans mon ciel, celui-là, au moins je sais pourquoi.)
Voilà comme je compte, dit Dieu. Et alors mon compte est bon. Car cette lèpre dont il s'agissait,
Cette lèpre dont ils parlaient et d'être lépreux
Ce n'était pas une lèpre d'imagination et une lèpre d'invention et une lèpre d'exercice.
Ce n'était pas une lèpre qu'ils avaient vue dans les livres ou dont ils avaient entendu parler
Plus ou moins vaguement
Ce n'était pas une lèpre pour en parler ni une lèpre pour faire peur en conversation et en figures,
Mais c'était la réelle lèpre et ils parlaient de l'avoir, eux-mêmes, réellement,
Qu'ils connaissaient bien, qu'ils avaient vue vingt fois
En France et en Terre-Sainte,
Cette dégoûtante maladie farineuse, cette sale gale, cette mauvaise teigne,
Cette répugnante maladie de croûtes qui fait d'un homme
L'horreur et la honte de l'homme,
Cet ulcère, cette pourriture sèche, enfin cette définitive lèpre
Qui ronge la peau et la face et le bras et la main,
Et la cuisse et la jambe et le pied

Honestly, just as a poor man is capable of loving me,
Must love me;
And that Saint Louis, on the contrary, loves me thirty times above the ordinary,
Thirty times more than honorably;
That Joinville loves me according to measure,
And that Saint Louis loves me thirty times more than according to measure.
(And if I put that one in my heaven, at least I know why).
That is how I reckon, says God. And so my reckoning is fair, because that leprosy which they had in mind,
That leprosy of which they talked, and about being a leper,
Was anything but an imaginary leprosy and a make believe leprosy and an exercise leprosy,
It wasn't a leprosy which they had seen in books and heard talked about
More or less vaguely,
It wasn't a leprosy to talk about, nor a leprosy to frighten people in conversation and in figures of speech,
But this was the real leprosy, and they talked about having it themselves, in very sooth,
They knew it well, they had seen it twenty times
In France and in Holy Land,
That disgusting mealy disease, that filthy itch, that evil mange,
That repellent scabby disease which makes man
The horror and shame of man,
That ulcer, that dry rot, in a word that definitive leprosy
Which eats into the skin and the face and the arm and the hand
And the thigh and the leg and the foot

Et le ventre et la peau et les os et les nerfs et les veines,
Cette sèche moisissure blanche qui gagne de proche en proche
Et qui mord comme avec des dents de souris,
Et qui fait d'un homme le rebut et la fuite de l'homme,
Et qui détruit un corps comme une granuleuse moisissure
Et qui pousse sur le corps ces affreuses blanches lèvres,
Ces affreuses lèvres sèches de plaies
Et qui avance toujours et jamais ne recule
Et qui gagne toujours et qui jamais ne perd
Et qui va jusqu'au bout,
Et qui fait d'un homme un cadavre qui marche,
C'est de cette lèpre-là qu'ils parlaient, de nulle autre.
C'est de cette lèpre-là qu'ils pensaient, de nulle autre.
D'une lèpre réelle, nullement d'une lèpre d'exercice.
C'est cette lèpre-là qu'il aimait mieux avoir, nulle autre.
Eh bien moi je trouve que c'est trente fois saisissant
Et que c'est m'aimer trente fois et que c'est trente fois de l'amour.

Ah sans doute si Joinville avec les yeux de l'âme avait vu
Ce que c'est que cette lèpre de l'âme
Que nous ne nommons pas en vain le péché *mortel,*
Si avec les yeux de l'âme il avait vu
Cette pourriture sèche de l'âme infiniment plus mauvaise,
Infiniment plus laide, infiniment plus pernicieuse,
Infiniment plus maligne, infiniment plus odieuse
Lui-même il eût tout de suite compris combien son propos était absurde.
Et que la question ne se pose même pas. Mais tous ne voient pas avec les yeux de l'âme.

And the stomach and the skin and the bones and the nerves
and the veins,
That dry white mold which spreads little by little
And bites as if with a mouse's teeth,
And makes a man the refuse and the flight of man,
And destroys a body like a granulous mold,
And grows on the body those awful white lips,
Those awful dry lips of wounds,
And which always advances and never draws back,
And always wins and never loses,
And goes to the end,
And makes of a man a walking corpse.
It was that leprosy they were talking about and of none other.
It was that leprosy they had in mind and none other,
A real leprosy, in no way a leprosy of exercise.
It was that leprosy which he preferred to have, none other.
Well, I think it is thirty times more startling
And that it means loving me thirty times and that it means
thirty times love.

Ah, to be sure, if Joinville with the eyes of the soul had seen
What manner of thing is that leprosy of the soul
Which we not in vain call mortal sin,
If with the eyes of the soul he had seen
That dry rot of the soul infinitely more evil,
Infinitely more ugly, infinitely more pernicious,
Infinitely more malignant, infinitely more odious,
He himself would immediately have understood how absurd
his remark was,
And that the question cannot be raised. But all do not see with
the eyes of the soul.

Je comprends cela, dit Dieu, tous ne sont pas des saints, ainsi est ma chrétienté.

Il y a aussi les pécheurs, il en faut, c'est ainsi.

C'était un bon chrétien, tout de même, ensemble, c'était un pécheur, il en faut dans la chrétienté.

C'était un bon Français, Jean, sire de Joinville, un baron de saint Louis. Au moins il disait ce qu'il pense.

Ces gens-là font le gros de l'armée. Il faut aussi des troupes. Il ne suffit pas d'avoir des chefs qui marchent en tête.

Ces gens-là partent fort honnêtement en croisade, au moins une fois sur les deux, et font très honnêtement la croisade.

Ils se battent très bien et se font tuer très proprement et gagnent le royaume du ciel

Tout comme un autre . . .

Mais voilà, ils se disent: Je n'ai qu'un corps (les sots, ils oublient le principal,

ils oublient non pas seulement l'âme, mais le corps de leur éternité,

le corps de la résurrection des corps),

Je n'ai qu'un corps, pensent-ils (ne pensant qu'à leur corps terrestre)

Si cette sale lèpre me prend, je suis perdu

(Ils veulent dire que leur corps temporel est temporellement perdu.)

Or ils y tiennent à leur corps. On dirait qu'ils croient qu'ils n'ont que ça.

Ils savent pourtant bien qu'ils ont une âme. La vie est l'union de l'âme et du corps,

La mort est leur séparation. Mais leur corps leur paraît

Solide et bon vivant.

I understand that, says God. All are not saints, such is my Christendom.
There are sinners too, there have to be some, it is thus.
He was a good christian, nevertheless, all in all, he was a sinner, there have to be some in Christendom.
He was a good Frenchman, Jean, sire de Joinville, a baron of Saint Louis! At least he spoke his mind.
Those people make up the bulk of the army. There have to be troops. It is not sufficient to have leaders who march ahead.
Those people start most honestly on a crusade, at least once every other time, and very honestly go on a crusade,
They fight very well and are very properly killed and win the kingdom of Heaven
Just like any other kingdom . . .
But there you are, they think: I have only one body (fools, they forget the principal thing,
They forget not only the soul but the body of their eternity,
The body of the resurrection of the bodies),
Only one body have I, they think (thinking only of their earthly body);
If that nasty leprosy takes hold of me, I am lost.
(They mean that their temporal body is temporally lost) . . .
Now they cling to their body. One would think that they believed it was the only thing they had.
Yet they know that they have a soul. Life is the union of soul and body.
Death lies in their sundering. But their body seems to them
A strong and jolly fellow.

Ils ont l'impression que la lèpre anéantira tout leur corps et qu'elle les tiendra jusqu'au bout (ils ne considèrent point qu'au bout de ce bout commence le véritable commencement)
Et alors ils aimeraient mieux avoir autre chose que la lèpre.
Je pense qu'ils aimeraient mieux attraper
Une maladie qui leur plairait. C'est toujours le même système.
Ils veulent bien affronter les plus terribles épreuves
Et m'offrir les plus redoutables exercices,
Pourvu que ce soient eux qui les aient préalablement
Choisis. Là-dessus les Pharisiens s'écrient et font des éclats
Et poussent des cris et font des mines, et ces exécrables Pharisiens
Surtout prient disant: Seigneur nous vous rendons grâces
De ce que vous ne nous avez point fait semblables à cet homme
Qui a peur d'attraper la lèpre. Or moi je dis au contraire, dit Dieu,
C'est moi qui dis: Ce n'est pas rien que d'attraper la lèpre.
Je sais ce que c'est que la lèpre. C'est moi qui l'ai faite.
Je la connais. Je dis: Ce n'est pas rien que d'attraper la lèpre.
Et je n'ai jamais dit que les épreuves et les exercices de leur vie,
Et les maladies et les misères de leur vie,
Et les détresses de leur vie ce n'était rien.
J'ai toujours dit au contraire et j'ai toujours pensé
Et j'ai toujours pesé que ce n'était pas rien.
Et il faut bien croire qu'en effet ce n'était pas rien
Puisque mon fils a fait tant de miracles sur les malades
Et puisque j'ai donné au roi de France.
De toucher les écrouelles.

They are under the impression that leprosy will annihilate
their whole body and that it will hold them unto the end
(they do not consider that at the end of that end begins the
real beginning)
And so they would prefer to have something else than leprosy.
I suppose they would prefer to catch
A disease of their liking. It is always the same business.
They don't mind facing the most terrible ordeals
And offering me the most awe-inspiring exercises,
So long as they themselves have beforehand
Chosen them. Thereupon the Pharisees cry out and exclaim
And shout and make faces, and those execrable Pharisees
Above all pray, saying: Lord, we thank Thee
That Thou hast not made us like unto that man
Who feareth to catch leprosy. Now I say, on the contrary, says
God,
I myself do say: it is something to catch leprosy.
I know what leprosy is. I made it.
I know it. I say: it is something to catch leprosy.
Nor did I ever say that the ordeals and the exercises of their
lives,
And the diseases and the miseries of their lives,
And the distresses of their lives were nothing.
I have always said, on the contrary, and I have always thought
And I have always weighed that it was something,
And indeed it must be believed that it was something
Since my Son performed so many miracles on the sick
And since I gave the king of France the power
To heal the king's evil.

Les Pharisiens poussent des cris sur celui qui ne veut pas attraper la lèpre.
Et ils sont scandalisés, ces vertueux.
Mais moi qui ne suis pas vertueux,
Dit Dieu,
Je ne pousse pas des cris et je ne suis pas scandalisé.

Je ne compte pas, je n'en retiens pas que ce Joinville est trente fois au dessous de l'ordinaire.
Mais j'en retiens, mais je compte au contraire
Que c'est ce saint Louis qui est peu ordinaire, trente fois peu ordinaire, trente fois extraordinaire, trente fois au dessus de l'ordinaire.

Je ne compte pas, je n'en retiens pas
Que Joinville est trente fois lâche.
Mais au contraire j'en retiens et je compte
Que c'est ce saint Louis qui est trente fois brave,
Trente fois brave au dessus de l'ordinaire et plus que la mesure.

Je ne compte pas, je n'en retiens pas
Que Joinville est trente fois plus bas.
Mais au contraire j'en retiens et je compte
Que c'est ce saint Louis qui est trente fois haut,
Trente fois haut au dessus de l'ordinaire et plus que la mesure.

Je ne compte pas, je n'en retiens pas
Que Joinville est trente fois petit.
Mais je sais seulement qu'il est homme.

The Pharisees raise a hue and cry over the one who doesn't want to catch leprosy,
And they are scandalized, those virtuous ones.
But I who am not virtuous,
Says God,
I do not shout neither am I scandalized.

I do not figure, I do not conclude that that Joinville is thirty times below the ordinary.
But I conclude, but I figure, on the contrary
That it is that Saint Louis who is out of the ordinary, thirty times out of the ordinary, thirty times extraordinary, thirty times above the ordinary.

I do not figure, I do not conclude
That Joinville is thirty times a coward.
But on the contrary, I conclude and I figure
That it is that Saint Louis who is brave thirty times,
Brave thirty times above the ordinary and more than the measure.

I do not figure, I do not conclude
That Joinville is thirty times lower,
But on the contrary I conclude and I figure
That it is that Saint Louis who is thirty times higher,
Thirty times high above the ordinary and more than the measure.

I do not figure, I do not conclude
That Joinville is thirty times small,
But I just know that he is a man.

Et au contraire j'en retiens et je compte,
Voici comme je compte,
Et c'est ainsi.
J'en retiens et je compte que c'est ce saint Louis, roi de France,
Qui est trente fois grand, trente fois au dessus de l'ordinaire et plus que la mesure

Et qui est trente fois près de mon cœur et trente fois le frère de mon fils.
Les Pharisiens crient le haro sur celui qui ne veut pas attraper la lèpre.
Mais le saint ne crie pas le haro et il n'est pas scandalisé.
Il connaît trop la nature de l'homme et l'infirmité de l'homme et il est seulement profondément peiné.

Les Pharisiens crient le haro sur cet homme qui ne veut pas attraper la lèpre.
Voyez au contraire comme le Saint lui parle doucement.
Fermement mais doucement.
Et cette fermeté est d'autant plus sûre et me donne d'autant plus de certitude et plus d'assurance et plus de garantie qu'elle est plus douce.
Les cœurs des pécheurs ne se prennent point par effraction.

Ils ne sont pas assez purs. Le seul royaume du ciel se prend par effraction.

And on the contrary I conclude and I figure,
This is how I figure,
And it is so.
I conclude and I figure that it is that Saint Louis, king of France,
Who is thirty times great, thirty times above the ordinary and more than the measure.

And who is thirty times close to my heart and thirty times my son's brother.
The Pharisees raise a hue and cry over the one who does not wish to catch leprosy,
But the saint does not raise a hue and cry and is not scandalized.
He knows human nature too well, and man's infirmity, and he is only profoundly grieved.

The Pharisees raise a hue and cry over that man who does not wish to catch leprosy.
See on the contrary how gently the Saint speaks to him,
Firmly but gently.
And that firmness is all the more sure and gives me all the more certainty, all the more assurance and all the more guaranty since it is gentle.
The hearts of sinners are not taken by violence.

They are not pure enough. Only the kingdom of heaven is taken by violence.

L'ESPÉRANCE

Je suis, dit Dieu, Maître des Trois Vertus.

La Foi est une épouse fidèle.
La Charité est une mère ardente.
Mais l'espérance est une toute petite fille.

Je suis, dit Dieu, le Maître des Vertus.

La Foi est celle qui tient bon dans les siècles des siècles.
La Charité est celle qui se donne dans les siècles des siècles.
Mais ma petite espérance est celle
qui se lève tous les matins.

Je suis, dit Dieu, le Seigneur des Vertus.

La Foi est celle qui est tendue dans les siècles des siècles.
La Charité est celle qui se détend dans les siècles des siècles.
Mais ma petite espérance
est celle qui tous les matins
nous donne le bonjour.

HOPE

I am, says God, Master of the Three Virtues.

Faith is a faithful wife.
Charity is an ardent mother.
But hope is a tiny girl.

I am, says God, the Master of Virtues.

Faith is she who remains steadfast during centuries and centuries.
Charity is she who gives herself during centuries and centuries.
But my little hope is she
Who rises every morning.

I am, says God, the Lord of Virtues.

Faith is she who remains tense during centuries and centuries.
Charity is she who unbends during centuries and centuries.
But my little hope
is she who every morning
wishes us good day.

Je suis, dit Dieu, le Seigneur des Vertus.

La Foi est un soldat, c'est un capitaine qui défend une forteresse,
Une ville du roi,
Aux marches de Gascogne, aux marches de Lorraine.
La Charité est un médecin, c'est une petite sœur des pauvres,
Qui soigne les malades, qui soigne les blessés,
Les pauvres du roi,
Aux marches de Gascogne, aux marches de Lorraine.
Mais ma petite espérance est celle
qui dit bonjour au pauvre et à l'orphelin.

Je suis, dit Dieu, le Seigneur des Vertus.

La Foi est une église, c'est une cathédrale enracinée au sol de France.
La Charité est un hôpital, un hôtel-Dieu qui ramasse toutes les misères du monde.
Mais sans l'espérance, tout ça ne serait qu'un cimetière.

Je suis, dit Dieu, le Seigneur des Vertus.

La Foi est celle qui veille dans les siècles des siècles.
La Charité est celle qui veille dans les siècles des siècles.
Mais ma petite espérance est celle
qui se couche tous les soirs
et se lève tous les matins
et fait vraiment de très bonnes nuits.

I am, says God, the Lord of Virtues.

Faith is a soldier, a captain holding a fort,
One of the king's cities,
In the borderland of Gascony, in the borderland of Lorraine.
Charity is a physician, a little sister of the poor,
Who nurses the sick, who nurses the wounded,
The king's poor,
In the borderland of Gascony, in the borderland of Lorraine.
But my little hope is she
Who says how do you do to the poor and to the orphan.

I am, says God, the Lord of Virtues.

Faith is a church, a cathedral rooted in the soil of France.
Charity is a hospital, an almshouse which gathers up all the miseries of the world.
But if it weren't for hope, all that would be nothing but a cemetery.

I am, says God, the Lord of Virtues.

Faith is she who watches during centuries and centuries.
Charity is she who watches during centuries and centuries.
But my little hope is she
who goes to bed every night
and gets up every morning
and really sleeps very well.

Je suis, dit Dieu, le Seigneur de cette vertu-là.

Ma petite espérance est celle
qui s'endort tous les soirs,
dans son lit d'enfant,
après avoir bien fait sa prière,
et qui tous les matins se réveille et se lève
et fait sa prière avec un regard nouveau.

Je suis, dit Dieu, Seigneur des Trois Vertus.

La Foi est un grand arbre, c'est un chêne enraciné au cœur de France.
Et sous les ailes de cet arbre la Charité, ma fille la Charité abrite toutes les détresses du monde.
Et ma petite espérance n'est rien que cette petite promesse de bourgeon qui s'annonce au fin commencement d'avril.

Et quand on voit l'arbre, quand vous regardez le chêne,
Cette rude écorce du chêne treize et quatorze fois et dix-huit fois centenaire,
Et qui sera centenaire et séculaire dans les siècles des siècles,
Cette dure écorce rugueuse et ces branches qui sont comme un fouillis de bras énormes,
(Un fouillis qui est un ordre),
Et ces racines qui s'enfoncent et qui empoignent la terre comme un fouillis de jambes énormes,
(Un fouillis qui est un ordre),
Quand vous voyez tant de force et tant de rudesse le petit bourgeon tendre ne paraît plus rien du tout.
C'est lui qui a l'air de parasiter l'arbre, de manger à la table de l'arbre.

I am, says God, the Lord of that virtue.

My little hope is she
who goes to sleep every night,
in that child's crib of hers,
after having said her prayers properly,
and who every morning wakes up and rises
and says her prayers with a new look in her eyes.

I am, says God, Lord of the Three Virtues.

Faith is a great tree, an oak rooted in the heart of France.
And under the wings of that tree, Charity, my daughter Charity shelters all the woes of the world.
And my little hope is nothing but that little earnest of a bud which shows itself at the beginning of April.

And when one sees the tree, when one looks at the oak,
That rough bark of the oak thirteen and fourteen hundred years old,
Which will be a centenarian and centuries old for centuries and centuries,
That hard, rough bark and those limbs which are like a confusion of huge arms,
(A confusion which is an order),
And those roots which thrust into the soil and lay hold of it like a confusion of huge legs,
(A confusion which is an order),
When one sees such strength and such roughness, the tender little bud no longer seems to be anything at all.
It is the bud that looks as if it were the tree's parasite, as if it ate at the tree's table,

Comme un gui, comme un champignon,

C'est lui qui a l'air de se nourrir de l'arbre (et le paysan les appelle des *gourmands*), c'est lui qui a l'air de s'appuyer sur l'arbre, de sortir de l'arbre, de ne rien pouvoir être, de ne pas pouvoir exister sans l'arbre. Et en effet aujourd'hui il sort de l'arbre, à l'aisselle des branches, à l'aisselle des feuilles et il ne peut plus exister sans l'arbre. Il a l'air de venir de l'arbre, de dérober la nourriture de l'arbre.

Et pourtant c'est de lui que tout vient au contraire. Sans un bourgeon qui est une fois venu, l'arbre ne serait pas. Sans ces milliers de bourgeons, qui viennent une fois au fin commencement d'avril et peut-être dans les derniers jours de mars, rien ne durerait, l'arbre ne durerait pas, et ne tiendrait pas sa place d'arbre, (il faut que cette place soit tenue), sans cette sève qui monte et pleure au mois de mai, sans ces milliers de bourgeons qui pointent tendrement à l'aisselle des dures branches.

Il faut que toute place soit tenue. Toute vie vient de tendresse. Toute vie vient de ce tendre, de ce fin bourgeon d'avril, et de cette sève qui pleure en mai, et de la ouate et du coton de ce fin bourgeon blanc qui est vêtu, qui est chaudement, qui est tendrement protégé d'un flocon d'une toison d'une laine végétale, d'une laine d'arbre. En ce flocon cotonneux est le secret de toute vie. La rude écorce a l'air d'une cuirasse, en comparaison de ce tendre bourgeon. Mais la rude écorce n'est rien, que du bourgeon durci, que du bourgeon vieilli. Et c'est pour cela que le tendre bourgeon perce toujours, jaillit toujours dessous la dure écorce.

Like mistletoe, like a mushroom.

It is the bud that looks as if it were getting nourishment from the tree (indeed the peasant calls them *greedies*), it is the bud that looks as if it were resting on the tree, coming out of the tree, as if it could not be, as if it could not exist without the tree. And today, in truth, it comes out of the tree, at the armpit of the limbs, at the armpit of the leaves, and it can no longer exist without the tree. It looks as if it came from the tree, as if it were robbing the tree of its sustenance.

And yet it is from that bud, on the contrary, that everything comes. Without a bud that once appeared, the tree would not exist. Without those thousands of buds that come out once at the beginning of April and sometimes in the last days of March, nothing would last, the tree would not last and would not keep its place as a tree (that place must be kept), without that sap which rises and weeps in the month of May, without those thousands of buds that begin to grow tenderly at the armpits of the hard limbs.

Every place must be kept. All life comes from tenderness. All life comes from that tender, delicate April bud and from that sap that weeps in May, and from the cotton-wool and the down of that delicate white bud that is clad, that is warmly, that is tenderly protected by the tuft of the fleece of a vegetable wool, the wool of a tree. In that cotton-like tuft lies the secret of all life. The rough bark looks like a cuirass in comparison with that tender bud. But the rough bark is nothing but a hardened bud, a bud grown old. And that is why the tender bud always pierces through, always springs up from under the rough bark.

L'homme de guerre le plus dur a été un tendre enfant nourri de lait; et le plus rude martyr, le martyr le plus dur sur le chevalet, le martyr à la plus rude écorce, à la plus rugueuse peau, le martyr le plus dur à la serre et à l'onglet a été un tendre enfant laiteux.

Sans ce bourgeon, qui n'a l'air de rien, qui ne semble rien, tout cela ne serait que du bois mort.

Et le bois mort sera jeté au feu.

Or je vous le dis, dit Dieu, sans ce bourgeonnement de fin avril, sans ces milliers, sans cet unique petit bourgeonnement de l'espérance, qu'évidemment tout le monde peut casser, sans ce tendre bourgeon cotonneux, que le premier venu peut faire sauter de l'ongle, toute ma création ne serait que du bois mort.

Et le bois mort sera jeté au feu.

Et toute ma création ne serait qu'un immense cimetière.

Or mon fils le leur a dit: *Il faut laisser les morts ensevelir leurs morts.*

Hélas mon fils, hélas mon fils, hélas mon fils;

Mon fils qui sur la croix avait une peau sèche comme une sèche écorce;

une peau flétrie, une peau ridée, une peau tannée;

une peau qui se fendait sous les clous;

mon fils avait été un tendre enfant laiteux;

une enfance, un bourgeonnement, une promesse, un engagement;

un essai; une origine; un commencement de redempteur;

une espérance de salut, une espérance de rédemption.

The toughest warrior was once upon a time a tender child, a child fed on milk; and the most rugged martyr, the toughest martyr on the wooden horse, the martyr with the most rugged bark, with the roughest skin, the hardest martyr clawed by talons and nails, was once upon a time a tender child, a child fed on milk.
Without that bud which does not look like anything, which seems as nothing, all that would be as dead wood.
And the dead wood will be cast into the fire.

Now I tell you, says God, that without that late April budding, without those thousands of buds, without that one little budding of hope, which obviously anyone can break off, without that tender, cotton-like bud, which the first man who comes along can snap off with his nail, the whole of my creation would be nothing but dead wood.
And the dead wood will be cast into the fire.

And my whole creation would be nothing than a huge cemetery.
Now my son has told them: *Let the dead bury their dead.*

Alas my son, alas my son, alas my son;
My son who, on the cross, had a skin as dry as dry bark;
A withered skin, a wrinkled skin, a tanned skin;
A skin that was split by the nails;
My son had been a tender child, a child fed on milk,
a childhood, a budding, a promise, a pledge;
an attempt, an origin; the beginning of a redeemer;
a hope of salvation, a hope of redemption.

O jour, ô soir, ô nuit de l'ensevelissement.

Tombée de cette nuit que je ne reverrai jamais.

O nuit si douce au cœur par ce que tu accomplis.

Et tu calmes comme un baume.

Nuit sur cette montagne et dans cette vallée.

O nuit j'avais tant dit que je ne te verrais plus.

O nuit je te verrai dans mon éternité.

Que ma volonté soit faite. O ce fut cette fois-là que ma volonté fut faite.

Nuit je te vois encore. Trois grands gibets montaient. Et mon fils au milieu.

Une colline, une vallée. Ils étaient partis de cette ville que j'avais donnée à mon peuple. Ils étaient montés.

Mon fils entre ces deux voleurs. Une plaie au flanc. Deux plaies aux mains. Deux plaies aux pieds. Des plaies au front.

Des femmes qui pleuraient tout debout. Et cette tête penchée qui retombait sur le haut de la poitrine.

Et cette pauvre barbe sale, toute souillée de poussière et de sang.

Cette barbe rousse à deux pointes.

Et ces cheveux souillés, en quel désordre, que j'eusse tant baisés.

Ces beaux cheveux roux, encore tout ensanglantés de la couronne d'épines.

Tout souillés, tout collés de caillots. Tout était accompli.

Il en avait trop supporté.

Cette tête qui penchait, que j'eusse appuyée sur mon sein.

Cette épaule que j'eusse appuyée à mon épaule.

Et ce cœur ne battait plus, qui avait tant battu d'amour.

O day, o evening, o night of the burial,
Fall of that night which I shall never see again,
O night so dear to the heart by what you accomplish
And because you are as soothing as balsam,
Night on that mountain and in that valley,
O night, I have so often said that I should not see you again,
O night, I shall see you in my eternity.
My will be done. O that time it was that my will was done.
Night, I see you still. Three great gallows went up, and my son in the middle.
A hill, a valley. They had gone up from that city which I had given to my people. They had gone up.
My son between those two thieves. One wound in his side. Two wounds in his hands. Two wounds in his feet. Wounds on his forehead.
Women who wept as they stood. And that leaning head, bowed upon his breast.
And that poor dirty beard, all sullied with dust and blood,
That red beard with two points,
And that sullied hair, all disordered, which I would have kissed so often,
That beautiful red hair, still wet with blood from the crown of thorns,
All sullied, all clotted with blood. All was fulfilled.
He had borne too much.
That head which leaned forward, which I should have placed on my breast,
That shoulder which I should have placed against my shoulder,
And that heart no longer beating which had so long beaten with love.

Trois ou quatre femmes qui pleuraient tout debout. Des hommes je ne me rappelle, je crois qu'il n'y en avait plus.

Ils avaient peut-être trouvé que ça montait trop. Tout était fini. Tout était consommé. C'était fini.

Et les soldats s'en retournaient, et dans leurs épaules rondes ils emportaient la force romaine.

C'est alors, ô Nuit, que tu vins. O nuit la même,

La même qui viens tous les soirs et qui étais venue tant de fois depuis les ténèbres premières.

La même qui étais venue sur l'autel fumant d'Abel et sur le cadavre d'Abel, sur ce corps déchiré, sur le premier assassinat du monde;

ô nuit la même tu vins sur le corps lacéré, sur le premier, sur le plus grand assassinat du monde. C'est alors, ô nuit, que tu vins.

La même qui étais venue sur tant de crimes depuis le commencement du monde;

Et sur tant de souillures et sur tant d'amertumes;

Et sur cette mer d'ingratitude, la même tu vins sur mon deuil;

Et sur cette colline et sur cette vallée de ma désolation c'est alors, ô nuit, que tu vins.

O nuit faudra-t-il donc, faudra-t-il que mon paradis

Ne soit qu'une grande nuit de clarté qui tombera sur les péchés du monde.

Sera-ce alors, ô nuit, que tu viendras.

C'est alors, ô nuit, que tu vins; et seule tu pus finir, seule tu pus accomplir ce jour entre les jours.

Three or four women who wept as they stood. As for the men,
I don't remember, I don't think there were any more.
Perhaps they had thought it was too much of a climb. All was
over. All was consummated. It was the end.
And the soldiers went away, and in their rounded shoulders
they carried away the Roman might.
It was then, o Night, that you came. O night, the same
The same that comes every evening and that had come so
many times since the primeval darkness,
The same that descended on Abel's smoking altar and on
Abel's dead body, on that mangled body, on the first murder committed in the world.
O selfsame night, you descended on the lacerated body, on
the first, on the greatest murder in the world. It was then,
o night, that you came.
The same that had descended on so many crimes since the
beginning of the world,
And on so many stains and on so much bitterness,
And on that sea of ingratitude, you were the same that descended on my grief.
And on that hill and in that valley of my desolation, it was
then, o night, that you came.
O night, will it then have to be, will it have to be that my
paradise
Be nought but a great transparent night falling on the sins of
the world?
Will it be thus, o night, that you will come?
It was then, o night, that you came, and you alone were able
to finish, you alone were able to fulfill that day among
days.

Comme tu accomplis ce jour, ô nuit accompliras-tu le monde.
Et mon paradis sera-t-il une grande nuit de lumière.
Et tout ce que je pourrai offrir
Dans mon offrande et moi aussi dans mon Offertoire
A tant de martyrs et à tant de bourreaux,
A tant d'âmes et à tant de corps,
A tant de purs et à tant d'impurs,
A tant de pécheurs et à tant de saints,
A tant de fidèles et à tant de pénitents,
Et à tant de peines, et à tant de deuils, et à tant de larmes et à tant de plaies,
Et à tant de sang,
Et à tant de cœurs qui auront tant battu,
D'amour, de haine,
Et à tant de cœurs qui auront tant saigné
D'amour, de haine,
Sera-t-il dit qu'il faut que ce soit
Qu'il faudra que je leur offre
Et qu'ils ne demanderont que cela,
Qu'ils ne voudront que de cela,
Qu'ils n'auront de goût que pour cela,
Sur ces souillures et sur tant d'amertumes,
Et sur cette mer immense d'ingratitude
La longue retombée d'une nuit éternelle.

O nuit tu n'avais pas eu besoin d'aller demander la permission à Pilate. C'est pourquoi je t'aime et je te salue.
Et entre toutes je te glorifie et entre toutes tu me glorifies
Et tu me fais honneur et gloire . . .

Just as you fulfilled that day, o night, you will fulfill the
world,
And my paradise will be a great luminous night,
And all I shall have to offer
In my offering, I too, in my offertory,
To so many martyrs and to so many tortioners,
To so many souls and to so many bodies,
To so many undefiled and to so many who are defiled,
To so many sinners and to so many saints,
To so many faithful and to so many penitents,
And to so many sorrows, and to so many bereavements, and
to so many tears, and to so many wounds,
And to so much blood,
And to so many hearts that have beaten so long
With love, with hatred,
And to so many hearts that have bled so long
With love, with hatred,
Shall it be said that it must be,
And that I shall perforce have to offer,
And that they will not ask any more than that,
That they will desire no more than that,
That they will not relish anything else but that,
On those stains and on so much bitterness,
And on that boundless sea of ingratitude
The slow descending of a night eternal.

O night, you did not have to go and ask Pilate's permission.
That is why I love and greet you,
And glorify you among all, and among all you glorify me,
And do me honor and glory . . .

Je suis, dit Dieu, le Seigneur des vertus.
La Foi est la lampe du sanctuaire
Qui brûle éternellement.
La Charité est ce grand beau feu de bois
Que vous allumez dans votre cheminée
Pour que mes enfants les pauvres viennent s'y chauffer dans les soirs d'hiver.
Et autour de la Foi je vois tous mes fidèles
Ensemble agenouillés dans le même geste et dans la même voix
De la même prière.
Et autour de la Charité je vois tous mes pauvres
Assis en rond autour de ce feu
Et tendant leurs paumes à la chaleur du foyer.
Mais mon espérance est la fleur et le fruit et la feuille et la branche
Et le rameau et le bourgeon et le germe et le bouton.
Et elle est le bourgeon et le bouton de la fleur
De l'éternité même.

I am, says God, the Lord of virtues.
Faith is the sanctuary lamp
That burns forever.
Charity is that big, beautiful log fire
That you light in your hearth
So that my children the poor may come and warm themselves
before it on winter evenings.
And all around Faith, I see all my faithful
Kneeling together in the same attitude, and with one voice
Uttering the same prayer.
And around Charity, I see all my poor
Sitting in a circle around that fire
And holding out their palms to the heat of the hearth.
But my hope is the bloom, and the fruit, and the leaf, and the
limb,
And the twig, and the shoot, and the seed, and the bud.
Hope is the shoot, and the bud of the bloom
Of eternity itself.

LES SAINTS INNOCENTS

Nemo poterat dicere canticum, nisi illa centum quadraginta quatuor millia, qui empti sunt de terra. (Apoc. XIV, 3).

Personne ne pouvait dire ce cantique, sinon ces cent quarante-quatre mille, qui furent enlevés de la terre. (Apoc. XIV, 3).

Qui empti sunt de terra. Tant d'autres sont morts au nom de mon Fils.
In nomine Patris, et Filii, et Spiritus Sancti.
Tant d'autres sont morts pour sauver l'honneur
Du Nom de mon fils. Et eux.
Qui seuls portent ce nom écrit sur le front
Et seuls peuvent chanter ce cantique nouveau,
Ils sont les seuls aussi assurément qui sur terre
Aient jamais ignoré totalement le nom de mon fils. Tel est mon décret.

The theme of this poem is that beautiful old hymn by Prudentius: Salvete Flores Martyrum, *or rather it is a commentary on a few lines from that hymn, the commentary being made with tenderness and humor by God the Father.*

THE HOLY INNOCENTS

Nemo poterat dicere canticum, nisi illa centum quadraginta quatuor millia, qui empti sunt de terra. (Apoc. XIV, 3).

No man could learn that song but the hundred and forty and four thousand, which were redeemed from the earth. (Apoc. XIV, 3).

Qui empti sunt de terra. So many others died in my Son's
  name,
In nomine Patris, et Filii, et Spiritus Sancti,
So many died to preserve the honor
Of my Son's name; and they
Who are alone to bear that name on their foreheads
And alone can sing that new song,
Are assuredly the only ones on earth
To whom my Son's name was totally unknown. Such is my
  decree.

Ce nom pour lequel ils sont morts, ils ne le connaissaient pas.
Ils ne l'ont jamais connu sur terre. Voilà ce que j'aime, dit Dieu.
A présent ils le connaissent peut-être. Éternellement on peut le lire écrit
Sur cent quarante-quatre mille fronts. Sur nul autre.
Sur pas un de plus. Mais vivants, mais sur terre
On peut dire qu'ils n'ont jamais su de quoi on parlait
Ni même que l'on parlait et que l'on pouvait parler
(De quelque chose). Voilà ce qui me plait, dit Dieu.
Or ils pleuraient, et ils riaient, et ils tétaient, et ils criaient, et ils dormaient.
C'était leur grande, c'était leur plus sérieuse occupation.
Et un jour vint.
Que.
Un jour (ils ne connaissaient pas plus le nom d'Hérode que le nom de Jésus)
(et ils ne connaissaient pas plus le nom de Jésus que le nom d'Hérode. J'ose dire.
Que ces deux noms leur étaient également indifférents). Or ces deux hommes,
Jésus, Hérode, Hérode, Jésus,
Antagonistes allaient tout simplement leur procurer
La gloire de mon paradis.
Le royaume des cieux et la gloire éternelle. Un jour vint
Qu'une horde de brutes soldats, qui faisaient leur métier,
(Mais qui le dépassaient peut-être un peu)
Une ruée de brutes passa, des espèces de gendarmes, des ogres comme dans les contes de fées, des Croquemitaines pour les enfants.
Portant des sabres qui étaient comme des grands coutelas.

That name for which they died, they did not know,
They never knew it on earth. That is what I like, says God.
Now, perhaps, they know it. For ever and ever, it can be read
On one hundred and forty-four thousand foreheads. On none
other.
On not one more. But when they were alive and on earth,
One can say that they never knew what people were talking
about,
Nor even that people were talking, nor that one could talk,
(about something). That is what pleases me, says God.
Now, they were crying, and laughing, and sucking, and
screaming, and sleeping.
It was their great, it was their most serious occupation.
And a day came
When,
A day (they did not know the name of Herod any more than
that of Jesus)
(and they did not know the name of Jesus any more than that
of Herod. I shall venture to say
That they were equally indifferent to both those names.) Now
both those men,
Jesus, Herod, Herod, Jesus,
Antagonists, were simply going to obtain for them
The glory of my paradise,
The kingdom of heaven and eternal glory. A day came
When a horde of soldier brutes, attending to their business
(But exceeding a little its limits, all the same),
An onrush of brutes went by, gendarmes of a kind, ogres as
in fairy tales, bogey men for children,
Carrying sabres that were like big cutlasses,

Et c'étaient les soldats d'Hérode.
Une ruée, un tumulte. Un fracas, des bras retroussés. Une clameur.
Des cris. Des dents. Des regards luisants.
Des femmes qui fuyaient, des femmes qui mordaient
Comme elles mordent toujours quand elles ne sont pas les plus fortes.
Et il n'y eut plus dans le sang et dans le lait
Qu'une grande jonchée de corps morts
Un cimetière de poupons et de jeunes femmes juives.
Vous savez, dit Dieu, ce que nous en avons fait.
Ces yeux qui s'étaient à peine ouverts à la lumière du soleil charnel
Pour éternellement furent clos à la lumière du soleil charnel.
Ces yeux qui s'étaient à peine ouverts à la lumière du soleil terrestre
Pour éternellement furent clos à la lumière du soleil terrestre.
Ces yeux qui s'étaient à peine ouverts à la lumière du soleil temporel
Pour éternellement furent clos à la lumière du soleil temporel.
Ces regards qui étaient à peine montés vers le jour et vers le soleil du temps
Pour éternellement furent clos à ces passagères,
A ces périssables lumières.
Ces voix, ces lèvres qui n'avaient jamais chanté les louanges de Dieu sur terre,
Qui ne s'étaient jamais ouvertes que pour demander à téter. (Mais il me plaît ainsi, dit Dieu).
Sont ainsi les seules, sont aujourd'hui les seules,
Sont aussi les seules qui puissent chanter ce cantique nouveau.

And they were Herod's soldiers.
An onrush, a tumult. An uproar; arms with sleeves rolled up, an outcry.
Shrieks. Teeth. Glistening looks.
Women fleeing, women biting,
Just as they always do when they are not the strongest;
And there was nothing in the blood and the milk
But a great strewing of dead bodies,
A cemetery of babes and of young Jewish women.
You know, says God, what we have done with them.
Those eyes that had hardly opened to the light of the carnal sun,
Forever and ever were shut to the light of the carnal sun;
Those eyes that had hardly opened to the light of the earthly sun
Forever and ever were closed to the light of the earthly sun;
Those eyes that had hardly opened to the light of the temporal sun
Forever and ever were closed to the light of the temporal sun;
Those gazes that had hardly ascended towards the day and the sun of time
Forever and ever were closed to those transient,
To those perishable lights.
Those voices, those lips that had never sung the praises of God on earth,
That had never opened but to ask to suck (But so does it suit me, says God),
Are thus the only ones, are today the only ones,
Are also the only ones that can sing that new song.

Qui empti sunt de terra. Vous voyez ce que nous en avons fait, dit Dieu.

Aux Innocents les mains pleines. C'est le cas de le dire. Ces Innocents avaient simplement ramassé dans la bagarre

Le royaume de Dieu et la vie éternelle. Qu'importent aujourd'hui

Leurs membres blancs rompus dans tous les bourgs de Judée.

Et leurs petits bras potelés coupés comme par des hommes qui émondent.

Et leurs petits doigts crispés qui se refermaient sur la paume de la main.

Et les cris renfoncés dans la gorge, les mains criminelles les renfonçant, s'enfonçant dans la gorge comme un bouchon. Comme un tampon.

Et le jeune sang jaillissant du cœur. Qu'importent les membres coupés.

Les cuisses blanches comme de la viande de chevreau et comme des cuisses tendres de petits cochons de lait.

Et leurs mères qui criaient comme des folles et qui mordaient les soldats au poignet. Comme dans une bataille, après la bataille

Les rôdeurs, les voleurs viennent dépouiller les blessés et les morts et les mourants et emporter et dérober tout ce qui compte.

Tout ce qui vaut quelque chose, nouveaux rôdeurs, nouveaux voleurs ces innocents

Dans cette bataille après cette bataille se sont dépouillés eux-mêmes

Et dans le fracas des armes, dans le tumulte et dans les cris.

Dans la galopade affolée, dans la poursuite effrénée, dans les femmes parterre ils ont ramassé tout ce qui compte.

Qui empti sunt de terra. You see what we have done with them, says God.

Let the Innocents' hands be filled. Here is a case in point. These Innocents had simply picked up in the scuffle

The kingdom of God and eternal life. What matter today

Their white limbs broken in the market-towns of Judea,

And their little dimpled arms cut off as by men pruning,

And their little fingers stiff and clenched in the palms of their hands,

And their cries thrust back into their throats, the criminal hands thrusting them back, hands crammed in their throats like a stopper, like a plug,

And the youthful blood gushing from the heart. What matter the severed limbs,

The white thighs like kid's flesh and like the tender thighs of little sucking pigs,

And their mothers shrieking like lunatics and biting the soldiers' wrists? As in a battle, after the battle

The prowlers, the robbers come and rifle the wounded and the dead and the dying to take away and steal all that is worthwhile.

All that is worth something, novel prowlers, novel thieves, those innocents

In that battle, after that battle, rifled themselves

And in the clangor of arms, in the tumult and among the shrieks,

In the maddened galloping, in the frenzied pursuit, among the women felled to the ground, they snatched up all that counts,

Ils ont dérobé tout ce qui vaut quelque chose car ils ont fait main basse
Comme des détrousseurs de cadavres et ils se sont détroussés eux-mêmes et ce qu'ils ont ramassé dans la bagarre ce n'est pas moins
Que le royaume des cieux et la vie éternelle. *Hi empti sunt ex hominibus*. Eux seuls,
Qui seuls peut-être sur terre non seulement n'avaient jamais chanté les louanges de Dieu,
Mais n'avaient jamais prononcé même mon nom ni le nom de mon fils,
Eux seuls aussi ne portent point aux commissures des lèvres l'ineffaçable pli,
Ce pli de l'infortune et de l'ingratitude
Et d'une amertume qui ne sera jamais rassasiée.

Immaculés dans la voie ainsi Jean les a vus
Sur la montagne de Sion
Autour de l'Agneau debout. Et il n'y en a que pour eux. *Ceux-ci suivent l'Agneau partout où il ira.*
(Les plus grands saints ne le suivent apparemment pas partout.)

Ceux-ci ont été enlevés des hommes:
(d'entre les hommes, de parmi les hommes, d'être des hommes)
Les plus grands saints ont été des hommes, n'ont point été enlevés d'être des hommes.

et dans leur bouche n'a pas été trouvé le mensonge:

ils sont en effet sans tache devant le trône de Dieu.

They stole all that was worth something, for they plundered
Like those who rob corpses and they robbed themselves, and what they snatched up in the scuffle was no less
Than the kingdom of heaven and eternal life. *Hi empti sunt ex hominibus.* They alone,
Who alone perhaps on earth not only had never sung the praises of God,
But had never pronounced even my name nor my son's name,
They too, only they do not have at the corners of their mouths that ineffaceable line,
That line of misfortune and ingratitude
And of a bitterness that can never be satiated . . .

Undefiled in the way, thus did John see them,
Upon Mount Sion
Around the standing Lamb. Everything seems to be for them.
They follow the Lamb whithersoever He goeth.
(The greatest saints, apparently, do not follow him everywhere).

These were redeemed from among men:
(from among men, from the midst of men, from being men)
The greatest saints have been men, have not been redeemed from being men.

and in their mouth was found no lie:

for they are spotless before the throne of God.

Et l'Apôtre les nomme *primitiae Deo, et Agno: prémices à Dieu, et à l'Agneau.* C'est-à-dire premiers fruits de la terre que l'on offre à Dieu et à l'Agneau. Les autres saints sont les fruits ordinaires, les fruits de la saison. Mais eux ils sont les fruits
De la promesse même de la saison.

Et suivant l'Apôtre l'Église répète: *Innocentes pro Christo infantes occisi sunt,*

les Innocents pour le Christ
enfants furent massacrés,

(*infantes,* tout jeunes enfants, tout petit enfant ne parlant pas encore);

ab iniquo rege
lactentes interfecti sunt:

par un inique Roi
laiteux ils furent assassinés:

(*lactentes,* pleins de lait, laiteux, à l'âge du lait, étant encore au régime du lait,
nourris de lait)

ipsum sequuntur Agnum sine macula
ils suivent l'Agneau lui-même sans tache

And the Apostle calls them *primitiae Deo, et Agno: firstfruits to God, and to the Lamb*. That is to say, the firstfruits of the earth that are offered to God and to the Lamb. The other saints are the ordinary fruits, the fruits of the season. But they are the fruits
Of the very promise of the season.

And following the Apostle, the Church repeats: *Innocentes pro Christo infantes occisi sunt,*

the Innocents for Christ
as children were massacred,

(*infantes*, very young children, very small children not yet able to speak);

ab iniquo rege
lactentes interfecti sunt:

by a wicked King
they, sucklings, were massacred:

(*lactentes*, full of milk, milky, at the age of milk, being yet on the milk diet,
fed on milk)

ipsum sequuntur Agnum sine macula
they follow the Lamb himself spotless

(et le texte est tel, mon enfant, que c'est ensemble l'Agneau qui est sans tache
et eux avec lui qui sont sans tache).

Mais l'Église va plus loin, l'Église passe outre, l'Église dépasse l'Apôtre.

L'Église ne dit plus seulement qu'ils sont des prémices à Dieu, et à l'Agneau.
L'Église les invoque et les nomme

fleurs des Martyrs.

Entendant littéralement par là que les *autres* martyrs sont les fruits mais que ceux-ci, parmi les martyrs, sont les fleurs mêmes.

Salvete FLORES *Martyrum:*

Salut FLEURS *des Martyrs.*

Couchés sur le chevalet, liés au chevalet comme des fruits liés à l'espalier
Les autres martyrs, vingt siècles de martyrs
Les siècles des siècles de martyrs
Sont littéralement les fruits de saison,
De chaque saison échelonnés sur l'espalier
Et notamment des fruits d'automne
Et mon fils même fut cueilli

(and such is the text, my child, that it is at the same time the
Lamb that is spotless
And they with him who are spotless).

But the Church goes further, the Church goes beyond, the
Church outstrips the Apostle.

No longer does the Church only say that they are the firstfruits
to God and to the Lamb,
But the Church invokes them and calls them

flowers of the Martyrs.

Literally meaning by those words that the *other* martyrs are
the fruits, whereas these, among martyrs, are the flowers
themselves.

Salvete FLORES *Martyrum:*

Hail, FLOWERS *of Martyrs.*

Laid out on the wooden horse, tied to the wooden horse like
fruit tied to an espalier,
The other martyrs, twenty centuries of martyrs,
Centuries of centuries of martyrs,
Are literally the fruits of the season,
Of each season arranged at intervals on the espalier,
And specially the autumn fruits;
And my son himself was gathered

Dans sa trente-troisième saison. Mais eux ces simples innocents,

Ils sont avant les fruits mêmes, ils sont la promesse du fruit.

Salvete flores Martyrum, ces enfants de moins de deux ans sont les fleurs de tous les autres Martyrs,

C'est-à-dire les fleurs qui donnent les autres martyrs.

Au fin commencement d'avril ils sont la rose fleur du pêcher.

Au plein avril, au fin commencement de mai ils sont la blanche fleur du poirier.

Au plein mai ils sont la rouge fleur du pommier.

Blanche et rouge.

Ils sont la fleur même et le bouton de la fleur et le coton du bouton.

Ils sont le bourgeon du rameau et le bourgeon de la fleur.

Ils sont l'honneur d'avril et la douce espérance.

Ils sont l'honneur et des bois et des mois.

Ils sont la jeune enfance.

Le dimanche de *Reminiscere* n'est que pour eux, parce qu'ils se rappellent.

Le dimanche d'*Oculi* n'est que pour eux, parce qu'ils voient.

Le dimanche de *Laetare* n'est que pour eux, parce qu'ils se réjouissent.

Le dimanche de la Passion n'est que pour eux, parce qu'ils furent la première Passion.

Le dimanche des Rameaux n'est que pour eux, parce qu'ils sont le rameau même qui a porté tant de fruits.

Et le dimanche du jour de Pâques n'est que pour eux, parce qu'ils sont ressuscités.

Ils sont la fleur de l'aubépine qui fleurit pendant la semaine sainte

In his three and thirtieth season. But they, those simple innocents,
They are before the fruits themselves, they are the promise of the fruit.
Salvete flores Martyrum, those children less than two years old are the flowers of all the other martyrs,
That is to say, the flowers that produce the other martyrs.
At the very beginning of April, they are the rosy blossom of the peach tree.
In mid-April, at the very beginning of May, they are the white blossom of the pear tree.
In mid-May, they are the red blossom of the apple tree,
White and red.
They are the blossom itself and the bud of the blossom and the down on the bud.
They are the bourgeon on the twig and the bud of the blossom.
They are the pride of April and its sweet hope,
They are the pride of the woods and of the months,
They are little childhood.
The *Reminiscere* Sunday is only for them, because they remember.
The *Oculi* Sunday is only for them, because they see.
The *Laetare* Sunday is only for them, because they rejoice.
Passion Sunday is only for them, because they were the first Passion.
Palm Sunday is only for them, because they are the palm itself that bore much fruit.
And Easter Sunday is only for them, because they are risen again.
They are the flower of the hawthorn that blooms during holy week.

Et la fleur de l'avant-courrière épine noire, qui fleurit cinq semaines plus tôt

Ils sont la fleur de toutes ces plantes et de tous ces arbres rosacés.

Promesse de tant de martyrs, ils sont les boutons de rose

De cette rosée de sang.

Salvete flores Martyrum,

Salut fleurs des Martyrs,

quos, lucis ipso in limine,

Christi insecutor sustulit,

ceu turbo nascentes rosas.

que, sur le seuil même de la lumière,

le persécuteur du Christ enleva,

(emporta)

ceu turbo nascentes rosas.

comme la tempête de naissantes roses.

(c'est-à-dire comme la tempête, comme une tempête enlève, emporte de naissantes roses).

Vos prima Christi victima,

Grex immolatorum tener,

Aram sub ipsam simplices

Palma et coronis luditis.

They are the flower of the blackthorn that blooms five weeks earlier.
They are the flower of all those plants and of all those rosaceous trees.
Promise of so many martyrs, they are rosebuds in a dew of blood.*
Salvete flores Martyrum,
Hail, flowers of Martyrs.

quos, lucis ipso in limine,
Christi insecutor sustulit,

ceu turbo nascentes rosas.

whom, on the very threshold of light,
Christ's persecutor took away
(carried away)

ceu turbo nascentes rosas.

as a tempest with budding roses.
(that is, as the tempest, as a tempest takes away, carries away budding roses)

Vos prima Christi victima,
Grex immolatorum tener,
Aram sub ipsam simplices
Palma et coronis luditis.

* *An untranslatable pun on* rose *and* rosée *(dew). There are numerous puns in Péguy's poems; they have well nigh driven this translator to despair.*

Vous première victime du Christ,
Troupeau tendre des immolés,
Au pied de l'autel même simples,
Simplices, âmes simples, simples enfants,
Palma et coronis luditis. Vous jouez avec la palme et les couronnes. Avec votre palme et vos couronnes.

Tel est mon paradis, dit Dieu. Mon paradis est tout ce qu'il y a de plus simple.
Rien n'est aussi dépouillé que mon paradis.
Aram sub ipsam au pied de l'autel même
Ces simples enfants *jouent* avec leur palme et avec leurs couronnes de martyrs.
Voilà ce qui se passe dans mon paradis. A quoi peut-on bien jouer
Avec une palme et des couronnes de martyrs
Je pense qu'ils jouent au cerceau, dit Dieu, et peut-être aux grâces
(du moins je le pense, car ne croyez point
qu'on me demande jamais la permission)
Et la palme toujours verte leur sert apparemment de bâtonnet.

Ye, first victim of Christ,
Tender flock of innocents slain
At the foot of the altar itself, simple
Simplices, simple souls, simple children,
Palma et coronis luditis. You play with the palm and the crowns. With your palm and your crowns.

Such is my paradise, says God. My paradise is just as simple as possible.
Nothing is so bare as my paradise.
Aram sub ipsam at the foot of the altar itself
These simple children *play* with their palms and with their martyrs' crowns.
That is what goes on in my paradise. What game can one play
With a palm and with martyrs' crowns?
I suppose they roll hoops, says God, and perhaps they play at 'graces,' *
(that is, I think so, for you must not believe
that they ever ask me for my permission),
And the evergreen palm apparently serves as a stick.

* *It is very characteristic of Péguy to end the third of his* Mysteries *with a pun; he could never resist a play on words. Here the reference is to a game played in France forty or fifty years ago. It was called* jeu de grâces *and required two sticks about the length of drumsticks, one small hoop and the ability to throw the hoop towards the sky with the help of the sticks and catch it again. Ladies excelled at this and their attitudes, when correct, were deemed worthy of the Graces. Hence the name, I suppose.*

LA NUIT

NIGHT

This poem might be described as one of the greatest moments of contemporary French poetry, and indeed of all French poetry. Péguy is here at his best. He is now a complete master of the language, that is, not content with obeying its laws, he compels it to follow him in all the intricacies of his thought and to express what, I believe, had never been said before him. He has subdued it as the magician in the Arabian Nights subdues a genie. Péguy's French is so intensely his own that no one can use it after him without openly declaring himself a thief. There is much to be said about Péguy's grammar. At times, it is peculiar. I do not mean that it is uncertain. Péguy knew all the vast resources of grammar. He knew his grammar as only a Frenchman knows it who has studied Latin, French being little else than Latin continued, as Remy de Gourmont called it, Latin brought into Gaul by soldiers and merchants and thriving there until it became not another tongue, but Latin of another time. Quite often, however, Péguy's grammar goes wild, just as Blake's went wild, under the pressure of inspiration, and his syntax seems simply to burst asunder. He insists on the language saying things it has never said, and the language obeys, not without some awful stutterings. An example of this is the expression pour toujours, *which means, simply: forever. But forever, in the mouth of God the Father, does not seem adequate to Péguy. He wants more eternity in that phrase, so, instead of saying forever, God the Father says, in spite of grammar, in spite of usage, in spite of generations of professors: for eternally.*

Another of Péguy's characteristics is his inordinate love of puns. Not puns as jokes, not puns in the child-like manner of Charles Lamb, but serious puns, almost sacred puns. There are many such puns in the poem on night. Some have almost disappeared in the translation, but they never mar the beauty of the poem. Péguy who did everything in all seriousness, Péguy who proudly asserted that there was not one mortal sin in any of his books, Péguy raised the pun to a level which it had almost never known, I say almost because there is in the Gospels a most solemn and fundamental play on words.

LA NUIT

DIEU PARLE :

Les nuits se suivent et se tiennent et pour l'enfant les nuits sont continues et elles sont le fond de son être même.
C'est là qu'il retombe. Elles sont le fond même de sa vie.
Elles sont son être même. La nuit est l'endroit, la nuit est l'être où il se baigne, où il se nourrit, où il se crée, où il se fait.
Où il fait son être.
Où il se refait.
La nuit est l'endroit, la nuit est l'être où il se repose, où il se retire, où il se recueille.
Où il rentre. Et il en sort frais. La nuit est ma plus belle création.
Or pourquoi l'homme n'en use-t-il pas. On me dit qu'il y a des hommes qui ne dorment pas la nuit.
La nuit est pour les enfants et pour ma jeune
Espérance ce qu'elle est réellement. Ce sont les enfants qui voient et qui savent. C'est ma jeune espérance
Qui voit et qui sait. Ce que c'est que l'être.

NIGHT

GOD SPEAKS:

Nights follow each other and are linked, and for the child nights are continuous and are the innermost part of his very being.
Therein does he fall back. They are the innermost part of his life,
They are his very being. Night is the place, night is the being wherein he bathes, and is nourished, and is created, and is made,
Wherein he accomplishes his being,
Wherein he recovers his strength.
Night is the place, night is the being wherein he rests, wherein he retires, wherein he collects himself,
Wherein he enters again. And he comes out refreshed. Night is my most beautiful creation.
Now why doesn't man make use of it. I am told that there are men who don't sleep at night.
Night, for my children and for my young
Hope, is what it really is. It is the children who see and who know. It is my young hope
Who sees and who knows. Who knows what being means,

Ce que c'est que cet être la nuit. C'est la nuit qui est continue.
Les enfants savent très bien. Les enfants voient très bien.
Et ce sont les jours qui sont discontinus. Ce sont les jours qui percent, qui rompent la nuit
Et nullement les nuits qui interrompent le jour.
C'est le jour qui fait du bruit à la nuit.
Autrement elle dormirait.
Et la solitude, et le silence de la nuit est si beau et si grand
Qu'il entoure, qu'il cerne, qu'il ensevelit les jours mêmes.
Qu'il fait une bordure auguste aux agitations des jours.
Les enfants ont raison, ma petite Espérance a raison. Toutes les nuits ensemble
Se rejoignent, se joignent comme une belle ronde, comme une belle danse
De nuits qui se tiennent par la main et les maigres jours
Ne font qu'une procession qui ne se tient pas par la main.
Les enfants ont raison, ma petite Espérance a raison. Les nuits toutes ensemble
Se rejoignent, se joignent par dessus les bords des jours, se tendent la main
Par dessus les jours, font une chaîne et plus qu'une chaîne,
Une ronde, une danse, les nuits se prennent la main
Par dessus le jour, du matin au soir
Du bord du matin à celui du soir, se penchant l'une vers l'autre.
Celle qui descend du jour précédent se penche en arrière
Celle qui monte
Du jour suivant
Se penche en avant

What the being called night is. Night it is that continues.
Children know very well. Children see very well.
And it is the days that are discontinuous. It is the days that pierce, that disrupt night,
And in no wise the nights that interrupt day.
It is day that troubles night with its noise,
Otherwise night would sleep.
And the solitude, and the silence of night is so beautiful and so great
That it surrounds and corners and buries the days themselves,
That it makes an august enclosure around the restlessness of days.
Children are right, my little hope is right. All nights together
Meet and join as in a beautiful roundelay, as in a beautiful dance,
A dance of nights holding each other by the hand, whereas lean days
Make nothing more than a procession in which hands are not joined.
Children are right, my little Hope is right. Nights all together
Meet and join above the borders of days, hold out their hands to each other
Above the days, form a chain and more than a chain,
A roundelay, a dance, nights grasp each other's hands
Above the day, from morn till eve,
From the border of morn to the border of eve, leaning one towards the other,
The one coming down from the preceding day, leans back;
The one going up
To the next day,
Leans forward,

Et les deux se joignent, joignent leurs mains,
Joignent leur silence et leur ombre
Et leur piété et leur auguste solitude
Par dessus les bords difficiles
Par dessus les bords du laborieux jour.
Et toutes ensemble, ainsi se tenant la main,
Débordant par dessus les bords, les poignets liés
Aux poignets toutes les nuits l'une après l'autre
Ensemble forment la nuit et les jours l'un après l'autre
Ensemble ne forment pas le jour. Car ils ne sont jamais que des maigres jours
Qui ne se donnent pas la main. Or de même que la vie
Terrestre
En grand (si je puis dire) n'est qu'un passage entre deux bords
Une ouverture entre la nuit d'avant et la nuit d'après
Un jour
Entre la nuit de ténèbres et la nuit de lumière
Ainsi en petit chaque jour n'est qu'une ouverture.
Un jour.
Non pas seulement entre la nuit d'avant et la nuit d'après.
Entre les deux bords.
Mais comme les enfants le voient, comme les enfants le sentent, et ma jeune Espérance, comme les enfants le savent,
Dans la nuit, dans une seule et même,
Dans la seule et même nuit
Où se retrempe l'être.
En plein dans la nuit.
C'est la nuit qui est continue, où se retrempe l'être, c'est la nuit qui fait un long tissu continu,

And both join, join hands,
Join their silence and their shadow,
And their piety and their august solitude,
Above the difficult borders,
Above the borders of hard working day.
And all together, thus holding hands,
Overlapping the borders, wrists tied
To wrists, all the nights, one after another,
Together constitute night, and the days, one after another,
Together do not constitute day. For they are nought but lean
days
That do not join hands. Now, just as life,
Earthly life,
In a big, general way (if I may say), is only a passage between two borders,
An opening between the night before and the night after,
A day,
An opening between the night of darkness and the night of
light,
So, in a small way, each day is only an opening.
A day.
Not only between the night before and the night after,
Between the borders,
But as children see it, as children sense it, and my young
Hope too, just as children know it,
In the night, in one and the same,
In one and the same night,
Where being recruits itself,
Deep in the night,
It is night that is continuous, wherein being recruits itself, it
is night that forms one long, continuous texture,

Un tissu continu sans fin où les jours ne sont que des jours.
Ne s'ouvrent que comme des jours.
C'est-à-dire comme des trous, dans une étoffe où il y a des jours.
Dans une étoffe, dans un tissu ajouré.
C'est la nuit qui est ma grande muraille noire
Où les jours ne s'ouvrent que comme des fenêtres
D'une inquiète et d'une vacillante
Et peut-être d'une fausse lumière.
Où les jours ne s'ouvrent que comme des jours.
Où les jours ne s'ouvrent que comme des lucarnes.
Car il ne faut point dire que la chaîne des temps
Serait une chaîne sans fin
Où la maille suit la maille, où le chaînon suit le chaînon,
Où les jours et les nuits se suivraient égaux dans une même chaîne.
Un chaînon blanc, un chaînon noir, la nuit accrochant le jour, le jour accrochant la nuit.
Mais ils ne sont point égaux, ils n'ont point la même dignité dans cette chaîne.
C'est la nuit qui est continue. C'est la nuit qui est le tissu
Du temps, la réserve d'être
Et le jour n'ouvre là-dessus que par de méchantes fenêtres et des poternes.
C'est le jour qui rompt et le jour n'ouvre là-dessus
Que par de pauvres jours
De souffrance. C'est le jour qui crève et les jours sont comme des îles dans la mer.

An endless continuous texture wherein days are nothing but days,*
Opening only like days,
That is, like holes, in a stuff where there is open work,
In a stuff, in an open-work texture.
It is night that is my great black wall,
Where days open only like windows
With a restless and flickering
And perhaps a false light,
Where days open only like days,
Where days open only like attic windows;
For it must not be said that the chain of times
Is comparable to an endless chain
In which link follows link, in which ring follows ring,
And days and nights are equal and follow each other in the same chain,
One white ring, one black ring, night hooking on to day, day hooking on to night,
For they are not equal, they do not share the same dignity in that chain.
It is night that is continuous. It is night that forms the texture
Of time, the store of being,
And day looks out on that only through wretched windows and posterns.
It is day that disrupts, and day looks out on that
Only through sorry
Borrowed lights.† It is day that rends, and days are like isles in the sea,

* *A play on* jour *meaning an aperture in an open-work stuff and* jour *meaning day.*

† *One of Péguy's numerous plays on words. The French* jour de souffrance *may mean* borrowed light *as well as* day of suffering.

Comme des îles interrompues qui interrompent la mer.
Mais la mer est continue et ce sont les îles qui ont tort.
Ainsi ce sont les jours qui ont tort et interrompus ils interrompent la nuit.
Mais ils ont beau faire et eux-mêmes
Ils baignent dans la nuit.
Comme la mer est la réserve d'eau ainsi la nuit est la réserve d'être.
C'est le temps que je me suis réservé. Tous ces jours fiévreux ont beau faire.
Comme en pleine mer, en plein dans la nuit ils baignent en pleine nuit.
Ce sont eux qui sont dispersés, ce sont eux qui sont brisés.
Les jours sont des Sporades et la nuit est la pleine mer
Où naviguait saint Paul
Et le bord qui descend de la nuit vers le jour
Est toujours un bord qui monte
Un bord abrupt et le bord qui remonte du jour vers la nuit
Est toujours un bord qui descend. Dans la pleine nuit.
O nuit, ma plus belle invention, ma création auguste entre toutes.
Ma plus belle créature. Créature de la plus grande Espérance.
Qui donnes le plus de matière à l'Espérance.
Qui es l'instrument, qui es la matière même et la résidence de l'Espérance.
Et aussi, (et ainsi), au fond créature de la plus grande Charité.
Car c'est toi qui berces toute la Création
Dans un Sommeil réparateur.
Comme on couche un enfant dans son petit lit,

Like interrupted isles that interrupt the sea,
But the sea continues and it is the isles that are wrong.
In the same way, the days are wrong, and interrupted they interrupt night.
But no matter what they do, they themselves
Are immersed in the night.
Just as the sea is the water supply, so is night the reserve of being.
It is time which I have reserved for myself. All those feverish days try in vain:
As on the high seas, right in the middle of night, they are immersed in the depth of night.
It is they that are dispersed, they that are broken up.
Days are scattered bodies, night is the open sea
In which Saint Paul sailed,
And the border that comes down from night towards day
Is always an ascending border,
An abrupt border, and the border that re-ascends from day towards night
Is always a descending border, in the depth of night.
O night, my most beautiful invention, my creation august among all,
My most beautiful creature, creature of the greatest Hope,
Giving most substance to Hope,
You who are the instrument, who are the very substance and abode of Hope,
And also, (and thus), are really the creature of greatest Charity,
For it is you who rock all Creation to sleep,
A refreshing sleep,
Just as one puts a child in his little bed,

Comme sa mère le couche et comme sa mère le borde
Et l'embrasse (Elle n'a pas peur de le réveiller.
Il dort tellement bien.)
Comme sa mère le borde et rit et le baise au front
En s'amusant.
Et lui aussi rit, lui rit en réponse en dormant.
Ainsi, ô nuit, mère aux yeux noirs, mère universelle,
Non plus seulement mère des enfants (c'est si facile)
Mais mère des hommes mêmes et des femmes, ce qui est si difficile,
C'est toi, nuit, qui couches et fais coucher toute la Création
Dans un lit de quelques heures.
(En attendant.) Dans un lit de quelques heures
Image, faible image, et promesse et avant réalisation du lit de toutes les heures.
Réalisation anticipée. Promesse tenue d'avance
En attendant le lit de toutes les heures.
Où moi, le Père, je coucherai ma création.
O Nuit tu es la nuit. Et tous ces jours ensemble
Ne sont jamais le jour, ils ne sont jamais que des jours.
Semés. Ces jours ne sont jamais que des clartés.
Douteuses, et toi, la nuit, tu es ma grande lumière sombre.
Je m'applaudis d'avoir fait la nuit. Les jours sont des îlots et des îles
Qui percent et qui crèvent la mer.
Mais il faut bien qu'ils reposent dans la mer profonde.
Ils sont bien forcés.

Just as his mother puts him to bed, just as his mother tucks him in
And kisses him (She is not afraid of waking him.
He sleeps so soundly),
Just as his mother tucks him in and laughs and kisses him on the brow,
Enjoying it,
And he too laughs, he laughs in response as he sleeps;
Thus, o night, black-eyed mother, universal mother,
Not only mother of children (that is so easy),
But mother of men themselves and of women, which is so difficult,
It is you, night, who put to bed and make all Creation lie down
In a bed of a few hours
(in the mean time), in a bed of a few hours,
An image, a feeble image, and a promise and a realisation beforehand of the bed of all the hours,
An anticipated realisation, a promise held in advance,
While waiting for the bed of all hours,
In which I, the Father, will put my creation.
O Night, you are the night. And all those days together
Are never the day, they are never anything but days,
Sown. Those days are never anything but lights,
Uncertain lights, and you, night, you are my great dark light.
I congratulate myself on having made night. Days are islets and isles
That pierce and rend the sea,
But they have to rest in the deep sea,
They are compelled to do so.

Ainsi vous autres jours vous êtes bien forcés.
Il faut bien que vous reposiez dans la profonde nuit.
Et toi nuit tu es la mer profonde
Où naviguait saint Paul, non plus ce petit lac de Tibériade.
Tous ces jours ne sont jamais que des membres
Démembrés. Ce sont les jours qui émergent, mais il faut bien qu'ils soient assis dans la pleine eau.
Dans la nuit pleine. Nuit ma plus belle invention c'est toi qui calmes, c'est toi qui apaises, c'est toi qui fais reposer
Les membres endoloris
Tout démanchés du travail du jour.
C'est toi qui calmes, c'est toi qui apaises, c'est toi qui fais reposer
Les cœurs endoloris
Les corps meurtris, les membres meurtris du labeur, les cœurs meurtris du labeur
Et de la peine et du souci quotidien.
O Nuit, ô ma fille la Nuit, la plus religieuse de mes filles
La plus pieuse.
De mes filles, de mes créatures la plus dans mes mains, la plus abandonnée.
Tu me glorifies dans le Sommeil encore plus que ton Frère le Jour ne me glorifie dans le Travail.
Car l'homme dans le travail ne me glorifie que par son travail.
Et dans le sommeil c'est moi qui me glorifie moi-même par l'abandonnement de l'homme.
Et c'est plus sûr, je sais mieux m'y prendre.
Nuit tu es pour l'homme une nourriture plus nourrissante que le pain et le vin.

Thus, you, days, are compelled,
You have to rest in the deep night,
And you, night, are the deep sea
In which Saint Paul sailed, no longer that little lake of Tiberias.
All those days are never anything but limbs
Dismembered. It is the days that emerge, but they have to be fixed in deep water,
In deep night. Night, my most beautiful invention, it is you who calm, it is you who soothe, it is you who put to rest
The aching limbs
All disjointed by the day's work.
It is you who calm, it is you who soothe, it is you who put to rest
The aching hearts,
The bruised bodies, the limbs bruised by toil, the hearts bruised by toil
And by trouble and daily care.
O Night, o my daughter Night, the most religious of my daughters,
The most pious;
Of all my daughters, of all my creatures, you are the one who is most in my hands, the one who most completely yields;
You glorify me in Sleep even more than your Brother Day glorifies me in Work,
For in work, man glorifies me only by his work,
And in sleep, it is I who glorify myself by the yielding of man,
And it is safer, I know better how to manage that.
Night, you are for man a food more nourishing than bread and wine,

Car celui qui mange et boit, s'il ne dort pas, sa nourriture ne lui profite pas.
Et lui aigrit, et lui tourne sur le cœur.
Mais s'il dort le pain et le vin deviennent sa chair et son sang.
Pour travailler. Pour prier. Pour dormir.
Nuit tu es la seule qui panses les blessures.
Les cœurs endoloris. Tout démanchés. Tout démembrés.
O ma fille aux yeux noirs, la seule de mes filles qui sois, qui puisses te dire ma complice.
Qui sois complice avec moi, car toi et moi, moi par toi
Ensemble nous faisons tomber l'homme dans le piège de mes bras
Et nous le prenons un peu par une surprise.
Mais on le prend comme on peut. Si quelqu'un le sait, c'est moi.
Nuit tu es une belle invention
De ma sagesse.
Nuit ô ma fille la Nuit ô ma fille silencieuse
Au puits de Rébecca, au puits de la Samaritaine
C'est toi qui puises l'eau la plus profonde
Dans le puits le plus profond
O nuit qui berces toutes les créatures
Dans un sommeil réparateur.
O nuit qui laves toutes les blessures
Dans la seule eau fraîche et dans la seule eau profonde
Au puits de Rébecca tirée du puits le plus profond.
Amie des enfants, amie et sœur de la jeune Espérance
O nuit qui panses toutes les blessures
Au puits de la Samaritaine toi qui tires du puits le plus profond
La prière la plus profonde.

For if he who eats and drinks does not sleep, he will derive
no benefit from his food,
It will turn to sourness and make him sick;
But if he sleeps, bread and wine will become his flesh and
blood,
To work, to pray, to sleep.
Night, you are the only one who dress wounds,
Aching hearts, all disjointed, all dismembered.
O my black-eyed daughter, you alone among my daughters
who are, who can call yourself my accomplice,
Who acts in complicity with me, for you and I, I through you,
Together we cause man to fall in the snare of my arms
And take him somewhat by surprise,
But one takes him as best one can. If someone knows that,
it is I.
Night, you are a beautiful invention
Of my wisdom.
Night, o my daughter Night, o my silent daughter,
At Rebecca's well, at the Samaritan woman's well,
It is you who draw the deepest water
From the deepest well;
O night, you who put all creatures to sleep,
A refreshing sleep,
O night, you who wash all wounds
In the only fresh water, in the only deep water,
At Rebecca's well, drawn from the deepest well;
Friend of children, friend and sister of young Hope,
O night, you who dress all wounds,
You who, at the Samaritan woman's well, draw from the
deepest well
The deepest prayer,

O nuit, ô ma fille la Nuit, toi qui sais te taire, ô ma fille au beau manteau.
Toi qui verses le repos et l'oubli. Toi qui verses le baume, et le silence, et l'ombre
O ma Nuit étoilée je t'ai créée la première.
Toi qui endors, toi qui ensevelis déjà dans une Ombre éternelle
Toutes mes créatures
Les plus inquiètes, le cheval fougueux, la fourmi laborieuse,
Et l'homme ce monstre d'inquiétude.
Nuit qui réussis à endormir l'homme
Ce puits d'inquiétude.
A lui seul plus inquiet que toute la création ensemble.
L'homme, ce puits d'inquiétude.
Comme tu endors l'eau du puits.
O ma nuit à la grande robe
Qui prends les enfants et la jeune Espérance
Dans le pli de ta robe
Mais les hommes ne se laissent pas faire.
O ma belle nuit je t'ai créée la première.
Et presque avant la première
Silencieuse aux longs voiles
Toi par qui descend sur terre un avant goût
Toi qui répands de tes mains, toi qui verses sur terre
Une première paix
 Avant-coureur de la paix éternelle.
Un premier repos
 Avant-coureur du repos éternel.
Un premier baume, si frais, une première béatitude
 Avant-coureur de la béatitude éternelle.
Toi qui apaises, toi qui embaumes, toi qui consoles.

O night, o my daughter Night, you who know how to hold
your peace, o my daughter of the beautiful mantle,
You who shed rest and oblivion, you who shed balm, and
silence, and darkness,
O my starry Night, I created you first.
You who put to sleep, you who, already, in an eternal Dark-
ness bury
All my creatures,
The most restless, the spirited horse, the hard-working ant,
And man, that monster of restlessness,
Night, you who succeed in putting to sleep man,
That well of restlessness,
More restless in himself than all creation put together,
Man, that well of restlessness,
Just as you put to sleep the water in the well.
O my night of the long robe,
You who gather children and young Hope
In the folds of your robe,
But men won't allow themselves to be treated thus,
O my beautiful night, I created you first,
And almost before that,
Silent one of the long veils,
You by whom there comes down on earth a foretaste,
You who spread with your hands, you who shed on earth
A first peace,
Fore-runner of eternal peace,
A first rest,
Fore-runner of eternal rest,
A first balm, so cool, a first beatitude,
Fore-runner of eternal beatitude,
You who soothe, you who smell sweet, you who comfort,

Toi qui bandes les blessures et les membres meurtris.
Toi qui endors les cœurs, toi qui endors les corps
Les cœurs endoloris, les corps endoloris,
Courbaturés,
Les membres rompus, les reins brisés
De fatigue, de soucis, des inquiétudes
Mortelles,
Des peines,
Toi qui verses le baume aux gorges déchirées d'amertume
Si frais
O ma fille au grand cœur je t'ai créée la première
Presque avant la première, ma fille au sein immense
Et je savais bien ce que je faisais.
Je savais peut-être ce que je faisais.
Toi qui couches l'enfant au bras de sa mère
L'enfant tout éclairé d'une ombre de sommeil
Tout riant en dedans, tout riant secret d'une confiance en sa mère.
Et en moi,
Tout riant secret d'un pli des lèvres sérieux
Toi qui couches l'enfant tout en dedans gonflé, débordant d'innocence
Et de confiance
Au bras de sa mère.
Toi qui couchais l'enfant Jésus tous les soirs
Au bras de la Très Sainte et de l'Immaculée.
Toi qui es la sœur tourière de l'espérance.
O ma fille entre toutes première. Toi qui réussis même,
Toi qui réussis quelquefois
Toi qui couches l'homme au bras de ma Providence

You who dress wounds and bruised limbs,
You who put hearts to sleep, you who put bodies to sleep,
Aching hearts, aching bodies,
Bodies all stiff,
Limbs overwhelmed with fatigue, backs broken with weariness,
With tiredness, with cares, with restlessness,
Mortal restlessness,
With troubles,
You who shed balm on throats rent by bitterness,
Such a cool balm,
O my daughter of the great heart, I created you first,
Almost before the first, my daughter of the limitless bosom,
And well I knew what I was doing,
Perchance I knew what I was about;
You who lay the child in his mother's arms,
The child suffused with light by a shadow of sleep,
All laughter within himself, secretly laughing because of his confidence in his mother
And in me,
Secretly laughing with a serious pucker of his lips,
You who lay the child that is replete and overflowing with innocence
And confidence,
In his mother's arms.
You who lay the child Jesus every evening
In the arms of the Very Holy and Immaculate one,
You who are the portress of Hope,
O my daughter, first among all, you who succeed even, in this,
You who sometimes succeed, in this,
You who lay man in the arms of my Providence,

Maternelle
O ma fille *étincelante et sombre* je te salue
Toi qui répares, toi qui nourris, toi qui reposes
O silence de l'ombre
Un tel silence régnait avant la création de l'inquiétude.
Avant le commencement du règne de l'inquiétude.
Un tel silence régnera, mais un silence de lumière
Quand toute cette inquiétude sera consommée,
Quand toute cette inquiétude sera épuisée.
Quand ils auront tiré toute l'eau du puits.
Après la consommation, après l'épuisement de toute cette inquiétude
D'homme.
Ainsi ma fille tu es ancienne et tu es en retard
Car dans ce règne d'inquiétude tu rappelles, tu commémores, tu rétablis presque,
Tu fais presque recommencer la Quiétude antérieure
Quand mon esprit planait sur les eaux.
Mais aussi ma fille étoilée, ma fille au manteau sombre, tu es très en avance, tu es très précoce.
Car tu annonces, car tu représentes, car tu fais presque commencer d'avance tous les soirs
Ma grande Quiétude de lumière
Éternelle.
Nuit tu es sainte, Nuit tu es grande, Nuit tu es belle.
Nuit au grand manteau.
Nuit je t'aime et je te salue et je te glorifie et tu es ma grande fille et ma créature.
O belle nuit, nuit au grand manteau, ma fille au manteau étoilé

My maternal Providence,
O my *dark and gleaming* daughter, I greet you,
You who restore, you who nourish, you who rest,
O silence of darkness,
Such a silence reigned before the creation of unrest,
Before the beginning of the reign of unrest,
Such a silence will reign, but it will be a silence of light,
When all that unrest is brought to an end,
When all that unrest is exhausted,
When they have drawn all the water from the well,
After the end, after the exhaustion of all that unrest
Of man.
Thus, daughter, you are ancient and you are late,
For in this reign of unrest, you call to mind, you commemorate, you almost establish anew,
You almost cause to begin again the former Quietude
When my spirit moved upon the face of the waters.
But also, my starry daughter, daughter of the dark mantle, you are very much ahead of time, you are very precocious,
For you announce, for you represent, you almost cause to begin, ahead of time, every evening,
My great Quietude of light,
Of eternal light.
Night, you are holy, Night, you are great, Night, you are beautiful,
Night of the great mantle.
Night, I love you and greet you, and I glorify you, and you are my big daughter and my creature.
O beautiful night, night of the great mantle, daughter of the starry mantle,

Tu me rappelles, à moi-même tu me rappelles ce grand silence qu'il y avait
Avant que j'eusse ouvert les écluses d'ingratitude.
Et tu m'annonces, à moi-même tu m'annonces ce grand silence qu'il y aura
Quand je les aurai fermées.
O douce, ô grande, ô sainte, ô belle nuit, peut-être la plus sainte de mes filles, nuit à la grande robe, à la robe étoilée
Tu me rappelles ce grand silence qu'il y avait dans le monde
Avant le commencement du règne de l'homme.
Tu m'annonces ce grand silence qu'il y aura
Après la fin du règne de l'homme, quand j'aurai repris mon sceptre.
Et j'y pense quelquefois d'avance, car cet homme fait vraiment beaucoup de bruit.
Mais surtout, Nuit, tu me rappelles cette nuit.
Et je me la rappellerai éternellement.
La neuvième heure avait sonné. C'était dans le pays de mon peuple d'Israël.
Tout était consommé. Cette énorme aventure.
Depuis la sixième heure il y avait eu des ténèbres sur tout le pays, jusqu'à la neuvième heure.
Tout était consommé. Ne parlons plus de cela. Ça me fait mal.
Cette incroyable descente de mon fils parmi les hommes.
Chez les hommes.
Pour ce qu'ils en ont fait.
Ces trente ans qu'il fut charpentier chez les hommes.
Ces trois ans qu'il fut une sorte de prédicateur chez les hommes.
Un prêtre.

You remind me, even me, you remind me of that great silence there was
Before I had opened up the floodgates of ingratitude,
And you announce to me, even me, you announce the great silence there will be
When I will have closed them.
O sweet, o great, o holy, o beautiful night, perhaps the holiest of my daughters, night of the long robe, of the starry robe,
You remind me of that great silence there was in the world
Before the beginning of the reign of man.
You announce to me that great silence there will be
After the end of the reign of man, when I will have resumed my scepter.
And at times I think of it beforehand, for that man really makes a lot of noise.
But specially, Night, you remind me of that night,
And I shall remember it eternally:
The ninth hour had struck. It was in the land of my people Israel.
All was over. That enormous adventure.
From the sixth hour, there had been darkness over all the land until the ninth hour.
All was over. Let us not mention it any more. It hurts me.
That unbelievable coming down of my son among men,
In the midst of men,
When you think what they made of it,
Those thirty years during which he was a carpenter among men,
Those three years during which he was a kind of preacher among men,
A priest,

Ces trois jours où il fut une victime chez les hommes.
Parmi les hommes.
Ces trois nuits où il fut un mort chez les hommes.
Parmi les hommes morts.
Ces siècles et ces siècles où il est une hostie chez les hommes.
Tout était consommé, cette incroyable aventure
Par laquelle, moi, Dieu, j'ai les bras liés pour mon éternité.
Cette aventure par laquelle mon Fils m'a lié les bras.
Pour éternellement liant les bras de ma justice, pour éternellement déliant les bras de ma miséricorde.
Et contre ma justice inventant une justice même.
Une justice d'amour. Une justice d'Espérance. Tout était consommé.
Ce qu'il fallait. Comme il avait fallu. Comme mes prophètes l'avaient annoncé. Le voile du temple s'était déchiré en deux, depuis le haut jusqu'en bas.
La terre avait tremblé; des rochers s'étaient fendus.
Des sépulcres s'étaient ouverts, et plusieurs corps des saints qui étaient morts étaient ressuscités.
Et environ la neuvième heure mon Fils avait poussé
Le cri qui ne s'effacera point. Tout était consommé. Les soldats s'en étaient retournés dans leurs casernes.
Riant et plaisantant parce que c'était un service de fini.
Un tour de garde qu'ils ne prendraient plus.
Seul un centenier demeurait, et quelques hommes.
Un tout petit poste pour garder ce gibet sans importance.
La potence où mon Fils pendait.
Seules quelques femmes étaient demeurées.
La Mère était là.
Et peut-être aussi quelques disciples, et encore on n'en est pas bien sûr.

Those three days during which he was a victim among men,
In the midst of men,
Those three nights during which he was a dead man among men,
In the midst of dead men,
Those centuries and centuries when he is a host among men.
All was over, that unbelievable adventure
By which I, God, have tied my arms for my eternity,
That adventure by which my Son tied my arms,
For eternally tying the arms of my justice, for eternally untying the arms of my mercy,
And against my justice inventing a new justice,
A justice of love, a justice of Hope. All was over.
That which was necessary. In the way that was necessary. In the way my prophets had announced it. The veil of the temple was rent in twain from top to bottom;
The earth did quake; the rocks rent;
The graves were opened; and many of the bodies of the saints which slept arose.
And about the ninth hour, my Son uttered
The cry that will never be still. All was over. The soldiers returned to their barracks,
Laughing and joking because that duty was over,
One more guard duty they would not have to stand.
Only one centurion remained, with a few men,
A very small post to guard that unimportant gallows,
The gallows on which my Son was hanged.
A few women only had remained.
The Mother was there.
And perhaps a few disciples too, and even so, one is not sure of that.

Or tout homme a le droit d'ensevelir son fils.
Tout homme sur terre, s'il a ce grand malheur
De ne pas être mort avant son fils. Et moi seul, moi Dieu,
Les bras liés par cette aventure,
Moi seul à cette minute père après tant de pères,
Moi seul je ne pouvais pas ensevelir mon fils.
C'est alors, ô nuit, que tu vins.
O ma fille chère entre toutes et je le vois encore et je verrai cela dans mon éternité
C'est alors ô Nuit que tu vins et dans un grand linceul tu ensevelis
Le Centenier et ses hommes romains,
La Vierge et les saintes femmes,
Et cette montagne, et cette vallée, sur qui le soir descendait,
Et mon peuple d'Israël et les pécheurs et ensemble celui qui mourait, qui était mort pour eux

Et les hommes de Joseph d'Arimathée qui déjà s'approchaient

Portant le linceul blanc.

Now every man has the right to bury his son,
Every man on earth, if he has had that great misfortune
Not to have died before his son. And I alone, I, God,
Arms tied by that adventure,
I alone, at that moment, father after so many fathers,
I alone could not bury my son.
It was then, o night, that you came,
O my daughter, beloved among all, and I still see it, and I shall see that in my eternity.
It was then, o Night, that you came, and in a great shroud you buried
The centurion and his Romans,
The Virgin and the holy women,
And that mountain, and that valley on which evening was descending,
And my people Israel and the sinners, and together him who was dying, who had died for them,

And the men of Joseph of Arimathea who already were approaching,

Bearing the white shroud.

EDITOR'S NOTE

The title and subtitles are not Péguy's. Omissions in the text are indicated by dashes. The whole text is quoted from Charles Péguy's 'Cahiers de la Quinzaine', Paris 1900–1914. Therefore the dates of quotations refer to their first publication. The roman numerals indicate the Series numbers of the 'Cahiers', the arabic numerals indicate the number of the issue. Spelling and punctuation correspond to the text of the 'Cahiers'.

LES HUMANITÉS

				PAGE
Souhaitons-nous...	*Louis de Gonzague*	VII, 8	1905	22
C'est une angoisse...	*Toujours de la grippe*	I, 7	1900	30
Les crises...	*Pour la rentrée*	VI, 2	1904	30
L'héroisme...	*De la situation*	IX, 1	1907	32
L'homme...	*Les suppliants*	VII, 2	1905	34
Chez les modernes...	*Les suppliants*	VII, 2	1905	40
Nous ne courons pas...	*De la grippe*	I, 6	1900	50
Nous sommes aussi...	*Nouveau théologien*	XIII, 2	1911	50

L'ANCIENNE FRANCE

C'était en 1880...	*L'argent*	XIV, 6	1913	52
Retrancher...	*Nouveau théologien*	XIII, 2	1911	70
Notre socialisme...	*Nouveau théologien*	XIII, 2	1911	70

LE MONDE MODERNE

Nous vivons...	*A nos amis*	X, 13	1909	72
Sur les arrivismes...	*De la situation*	VIII, 3	1906	78
Un philosophe...	*De la situation*	VIII, 3	1906	82
Le génie exige...	*Toujours de la grippe*	I, 7	1900	84
Je suis épouvanté...	*Notre jeunesse*	XI, 12	1910	86
On nous parle...	*Notre jeunesse*	XI, 12	1910	92
Les fondateurs...	*Notre jeunesse*	XI, 12	1910	92
Nous sommes des vaincus...	*A nos amis*	X, 13	1909	94
Tout n'est point...	*Nouveau théologien*	XIII, 2	1911	96
Le monde moderne...	*De la situation*	IX, 1	1907	98

L'AFFAIRE DREYFUS

J'essaierai...	*Notre jeunesse*	XI, 12	1910	100
C'est pas facile...	*Notre jeunesse*	XI, 12	1910	114
Ils (les Juifs)...	*Notre jeunesse*	XI, 12	1910	116

PORTRAITS

				PAGE
Le prophète...	*Notre jeunesse*	XI, 12	1910	118
Je n'éprouve...	*Casse-cou*	II, 7	1901	132
Il n'est pas mort...	*Notre jeunesse*	XI, 12	1910	134
La méconnaissance...	*Notre jeunesse*	XI, 12	1910	140
La dernière fois...	*Courrier de Russie*	VII, 5	1905	142
Rien n'est...	*L'argent*	XIV, 6	1913	158
Je croyais...	*Personnalités*	III, 12	1902	158
Capitale temporelle...	*De la situation*	IX, 1	1907	160
Elle était peuple...	*Nouveau théologien*	XIII, 2	1911	168
Je ne crois pas...	*Nouveau théologien*	XIII, 2	1911	178

POESIE

Qu'importent...	*Jeanne d'Arc*	XI, 6	1910	182
Est-ce que...	*La deuxième vertu*	XIII, 4	1911	188
Quand une fois...	*Saints Innocents*	XIII, 12	1912	212
Je suis, dit Dieu...	*Saints Innocents*	XIII, 12	1912	232
Qui empti sunt...	*Saints Innocents*	XIII, 12	1912	250
Les nuits se suivent...	*La deuxième vertu*	XIII, 4	1911	272